TRANSFORMING
McLUHAN

PETER LANG

New York • Washington, D.C./Baltimore • Bern
Frankfurt • Berlin • Brussels • Vienna • Oxford

TRANSFORMING McLUHAN

CULTURAL, CRITICAL,
AND POSTMODERN PERSPECTIVES

EDITED BY Paul Grosswiler

PETER LANG
New York • Washington, D.C./Baltimore • Bern
Frankfurt • Berlin • Brussels • Vienna • Oxford

Library of Congress Cataloging-in-Publication Data

Transforming McLuhan: cultural, critical,
and postmodern perspectives / edited by Paul Grosswiler.
p. cm.
Includes bibliographical references and index.
1. McLuhan, Marshall, 1911–1980. 2. Mass media and culture.
3. Mass media—Philosophy. 4. Critical theory.
5. Mass media criticism. I. Grosswiler, Paul.
P92.5.M3.T73   302.23092—dc22   2010021537
ISBN 978-1-4331-1066-5 (hardcover)
ISBN 978-1-4331-1067-2 (paperback)

Bibliographic information published by **Die Deutsche Nationalbibliothek.**
Die Deutsche Nationalbibliothek lists this publication in the "Deutsche
Nationalbibliografie"; detailed bibliographic data is available
on the Internet at http://dnb.d-nb.de/.

∞

© 2010 Peter Lang Publishing, Inc., New York
29 Broadway, 18th floor, New York, NY 10006
www.peterlang.com

Printed in the United States of America

In memory of

James W. Carey

and

Liss Jeffrey

TABLE OF CONTENTS

Section One: McLuhan and Cultural Studies

Section Two: McLuhan and Critical Theory

Section Three: McLuhan and Postmodernism

Transforming McLuhan

PAUL GROSSWILER

This book has been a decade in the making. The decade before that was a contin-uing process of creating imagined dialogues among writers whose work on McLuhan I admired. The idea of bringing some of these voices together was planted when my wife, Marie Tessier, suggested in 1999 that I invite a group of McLuhan scholars to contribute their work to an edited book.

The list of scholars itself was transformed over the years, with some names added as time passed, and others who were ultimately unable to contribute. The pro-ject took time to shape, time to find a publisher, and more time to work with those whose chapters I anticipated. To all of those whose essays follow, I am indebted for their perseverance, patience and good humor, as work on the book ebbed and flowed, disappeared and resurfaced.

To those I have known since the beginning of the project, Lance Strate, Donna Flayhan, and Bob Hanke, I am grateful for their constant reminders that time was passing. I have always felt a special affinity for their work, and am proud to be able to include it here. All of the contributors provide a full mosaic of voic-es which gives the book its spectrum of perspectives. Patrick Brantlinger's juxta-position of McLuhan and the Frankfurt school, and Douglas Kellner's bringing together of McLuhan and Baudrillard, were both early beacons that showed the way more than twenty years ago toward some measure of compatibility between McLuhan and critical media studies. Glenn Willmott, Nick Stevenson, Gary

Genosko, and Richard Cavell, offer inspiration as McLuhan adaptations by a newer generation of scholars.

Lance Strate also provided the first publication opportunity as editor of the Media Ecology Series at Hampton Press. The final manuscript was transferred to Peter Lang last year when Hampton began winding down its publications. I appreciate both publishers for their work on the book. At Peter Lang, the quickened pace of publication this year has been supported by acquisitions editor Mary Savigar and production manager Bernadette Shade. Their e-mail presence has helped keep me productively on task—even offering me the unexpected opportunity to select the cover image. McLuhan's foremost example that the medium is the message, the electric lightbulb, provided the inspiration for the cover image that I suggested. These works do indeed transform McLuhan's signature metaphor into a kaleidoscope of intellectual light.

Along the way, however, the work of several McLuhan scholars I invited to participate is not to be found within these covers. I was especially grieved, not at the loss of their envisioned essays, but of the loss of two great voices in McLuhan scholarship. James Carey almost single-handedly focused a critical but appreciative eye on McLuhan for almost half a century in the United States. His tremendous reach and depth in communication and media studies helped bridge McLuhan's work with mainstream American media and culture studies. Without him, McLuhan's controversial work most certainly would have fared far worse in the United States. Liss Jeffrey brought energy and insight to a new generation of Canadian McLuhan scholarship, creating a connection between McLuhan's thought and a plethora of public policy initiatives centering on new technologies and the democracy in Canada. Their deaths have been inexpressibly felt in measure with the depth of their warmth, humor and humanity. To their memories, I wish to dedicate this book.

Transforming McLuhan

PAUL GROSSWILER

This collection of essays arises from the argument that Marshall McLuhan's place in communication and cultural theory is best suited to critical, cultural and post-modern interpretations of his work. Debates about modernity, postmodernism, new technologies and media have reverberated with themes that found a unique con-fluence in McLuhan's thought. Steven Best and Douglas Kellner (1997) rehearsed the widespread historical shift from modernity to postmodernity across an array of disciplines and experiences in ways that are manifestly similar to McLuhan's work—although McLuhan is only a footnote in their analysis. Several years later, however, McLuhan was included with Roland Barthes, Guy Debord, Raymond Williams, Stuart Hall and Ien Ang as foundational thinkers in critical approach-es to the study of communication and culture (Durham and Kellner, 2001). Most recently, Routledge has published a multiple-volume tome of more than 70 criti-cal interpretations of McLuhan (Genosko, 2005). That is itself a transformation of scholarly reception of McLuhan since Roger Friedland and Deirdre Boden (1994) traced the convergence of interest in space and time, and in communication media across many disciplines in their work on contemporary society, which they main-tained is still one of modernity—although they too relegate McLuhan to footnotes.

Despite the tendency to relegate him to footnotes in contemporary media and culture theory, McLuhan has resurfaced in both popular and scholarly forums since the beginning of the 1990s. McLuhan's rapid rise as a communication scholar and popular media pundit in the 1960s and his equally rapid fall in the 1970s left his work in limbo during the 1980s. During the 1980s, his ideas reappeared tentatively, including the writings of former student Walter Ong (1982) and, media ecologists Neil Postman (1985) and Joshua Meyrowitz (1985). Beginning with two posthumous McLuhan books co-authored with Eric McLuhan (1988) and Bruce Powers (1989) and a collection of his letters (1987), along with journalist Philip Marchand's biography (1989), more scholars began returning to McLuhan's work and ideas. If it cannot be called a renaissance or a revival or a resurrection, the 1990s still yielded a renewed scholarly interest in reappraising McLuhan. At the same time, wide-ranging changes in a host of computer technologies and the growth of the Internet and World Wide Web have helped to reboot popular media interest in some of McLuhan's aphorisms and concepts.

McLuhan's re-emergence as a popular culture figure may be mercurial, but his retrieval is more substantial in a broad range of fields in academic scholarship, including mass communication, sociological, cultural, political and literary theory. Most American communication and media scholars dismissed McLuhan well before his death, reflected in damning analyses such as Daniel Czitrom's (1982). Perhaps only James Carey maintained a constant scholarly interest—although an ambivalent one—in McLuhan for almost forty years (Carey, 1968, 1981, 1983, 1987, 1989, 1998; Grosswiler, 2006). In his most positive reading, Carey (1998) alluded to McLuhan, along with Harold Innis, asking the right questions using the only language available to them, and that discussions of the extent of their technological determinism were misplaced. Despite this lack of a place in communication scholarship, some recent empirical research based on McLuhan's concepts has found its way into communication journals (Bross, 1992; Brummett and Duncan, 1992; Miles, 1996). McLuhan also remained a source of intrigue and criticism (Ferguson, 1991).

This sporadic response to McLuhan has become steadier as scholarly books about McLuhan began to appear out of the ranks of doctoral theses and beyond. Canadian political theorist Judith Stamps' dissertation (1991) on Innis, McLuhan and the early Frankfurt School led to a book (1995). English scholar and Canadian Glenn Willmott's dissertation under postmodernist cultural theorist Fredric Jameson (1992) also was published (1996). Based at the McLuhan Program in Culture and Technology at the University of Toronto, which is the institutional home of McLuhan in Canada, Liss Jeffrey's work (1989, 1997) reappraised and repositioned McLuhan as a member of the Toronto School of Communication. In the United States, my journalism dissertation research (Grosswiler, 1990) led to a conference paper (1991), a journal article (1996), and eventually resulted in a book interpreting McLuhan's theories in the context of critical theory (1998). A communication dissertation drawing together medium theorists, including

McLuhan, with activist rather than academic Marxism has been written by Donna Flayhan (1997). Reflecting this renewed interest was the appearance of McLuhan-centered academic conferences in both the United States and Canada. "The McLuhan Legacy: A Symposium" was organized at Fordham University in New York City in 1998, which has led to a book (2005) containing essays from among the fifty scholars and media critics who presented research papers and essays. The McLuhan Program at the University of Toronto also held a celebration and scholarly conference in 1998 to mark the 30th anniversary of the new home for McLuhan's Center for Culture and Technology.

As Canadian authors with Canadian publishers, Stamps and Willmott are examples of the greater acceptance of McLuhan in his native country, where several media texts offer McLuhan a central role (Crowley and Mitchell, 1994; Crowley and Heyer, 1995). McLuhan has been the basis of a consistent tradition of media scholarship in Canada, figuring prominently in the works of Arthur Kroker (1984), for example. McLuhan's former student Donald Theall and John Fekete, who both became senior scholars in cultural studies at Trent University, represent a thread leading from early critiques of McLuhan to more recent commentaries (Theall, 1971 1989; 2001; Fekete, 1973, 1977, 1994).

Newer readings of McLuhan continued to emerge in Canada in addition to Stamps's and Willmott's. Jody Berland's work (1992, 1998) has applied McLuhan's concepts in her analysis of cultural technologies. Gary Genosko has drawn on the historical connection between McLuhan and postmodernist Jean Baudrillard (1999), in addition to his exhaustive, three-volume anthology of critical appraisals of McLuhan (2005). Another current sign of McLuhan's continued centrality is an online Canadian journal that made its debut in 2008. MediaTropes, whose 'inspiration' came from the legacy of McLuhan, asserts that McLuhan's famous phrase, 'the medium is the message,' suggests that media studies should focus on 'the medium itself as a kind of language with its own conventions for generating meaning.'(MediaTropes, 2008).

Feminist reappraisals of McLuhan have been initiated by Janine Marchessault (1998, 2005a) and Nancy Shaw (1998). Marchessault's study of McLuhan has led to a new critical and intellectual biography from Sage (2005b). Further, an authorized biography by W. Terrence Gordon (1997b), which,unfortunately, omits mention of Marchand's ground-breaking biography, has followed Gordon's earlier introduction to McLuhan in comic-book form (1997). University of Ottawa's Robert Babe has devoted a section of his book (2000) on Canadian communication theory to McLuhan. Humanities scholar Donald Theall weighed in on McLuhan in his second book on McLuhan in 30 years, *Virtual McLuhan* (2001), and literary scholar Richard Cavell probed McLuhan's concepts of visual and acoustic space (2002).

The *Canadian Journal of Communication* dedicated a double issue to McLuhan's legacy 25 years after publication of *Understanding Media* ("The Medium's Messenger: Understanding McLuhan," 1989), but in this regard, U.S. communication scholars had already taken the lead, paying tribute to McLuhan in an issue planned before his death but appearing shortly afterward ("The Living McLuhan," *Journal of Communication*, 1981). U.S. scholars also pursued the link between McLuhan and postmodernism in the work of Baudrilllard biographer Douglas Kellner (1989a, 1989b), and historians Donald Lowe (1982) and Mark Poster (1990, 1994), as well as by Baudrillard himself (1981, 1983.) The 1990s resurgence brought other books than mine focused on McLuhan, notably Paul Levinson's *Digital McLuhan* (1999).

Beyond North America, renewed interest in McLuhan also has been found in a most unlikely, yet logical location: the new generation of British cultural studies scholars. Having been founded in part by McLuhan's fellow Cambridge University and New Criticism student Raymond Williams, British cultural studies had expressed a growing disdain for McLuhan over the years (Williams, 1967, 1977, 1983, 1992; Hall, 1996; Hartley, 1992; Spigel, 1992; Turner, 1990). But works by British sociologist Nick Stevenson (2002) and John B. Thompson (1990, 1994, 1995) revisited McLuhan's mass communication and social theories and provided him central roles in their own theoretical frameworks. Cultural studies scholars in addition to Carey in the United States and Berland in Canada also are revisiting McLuhan, such as American James Lull (1990, 2000) and Danish scholar Klaus Bruhn Jensen (1995).

These scholarly responses to McLuhan have been accompanied by reissues of McLuhan's books, as well as edited collections of his writings with various academic and popular commentaries. *Undertstanding Media* (1964), which one national study of communication educators found to be among the core literature for mass media (Lombard et al. 1996), was reissued in 1994 by MIT Press, following *Gutenberg Galaxy* (1962), which was reissued in 1990. Hardwired Books reprinted *The Medium Is the Massage* (1967) in 1996 and *War and Peace in the Global Village* (1968) in 1997. In addition to new editions of McLuhan's collaborations with Eric McLuhan and Bruce Powers, Eric McLuhan published a book based on his father's theories (1998) that followed the pictorial-literary collage of many of McLuhan's most popular books. Works containing McLuhan's writings and commentaries also have helped refocus attention on his ideas (Sanderson and MacDonald, 1989; Eric McLuhan and Zingrone, 1996; Benedetti and Dehart, 1997; McLuhan and Moos, 1997).

Throughout this crescendo in McLuhan criticism, two distinct strains of McLuhan studies can be identified that reflect McLuhan's "heterogeneity," as Marchessault pointed out (1998). At least two McLuhans—the conservative and the radical—have survived since his initial popularity, his eclipse and his revival. Genosko drew two contradictory lines of descent for McLuhan: the corporate interpretation and the oppositional one (1999, 5–6). On one hand, McLuhan can be viewed as an uncritical herald of technological utopia and as an accomplice of corporate capitalism. On the other, he may be seen as a radical critic of modernity resisting uncontrolled technological change, who seeks ways to construct new social and media systems with a human face. There also is McLuhan the social scientist and McLuhan the humanist. Trained in the qualitative methods of New Criticism and literary analysis, McLuhan moved later in his lifetime towards the aspiration of being a scientist who promulgated "laws" of the media. As far as the generally conservative, or administrative, approach of social scientific mass communication research was concerned, though, his scientific credentials were inadequate. Having adopted the neutral stance of the social scientist, his positivism and perceived technological determinism were criticized by the generally more radical cultural, critical and postmodern approaches to media and social theory.

This book is dedicated to the proposition that the radical, critical, oppositional, humanistic line of descent in McLuhan interpretations is worthy of preservation and application to communication and media research. The book presents an effort to continue to retrieve and reposition McLuhan as a uniquely important thinker in critical, cultural and postmodern media and social theories. Contributions to the book come from an international group of authors representing the United States, Canada and the United Kingdom who have written significantly about McLuhan from this broad perspective. Each contributor has been invited to reflect anew on McLuhan's historical and theoretical importance in the study of media and culture. These authors range from neo-Marxists to cultural studies scholars to postmodernists from diverse disciplines of sociology, English, communication, cultural studies, humanities and journalism.

These authors, whose work has constituted part of what has been identified as a McLuhan revival, have been interpreting McLuhan afresh from critical, cultural and postmodern perspectives from the 1980s to the 2000s. This volume reflects the Canadian focus of much of this work, with four Canadian contributors. Reflecting McLuhan's influence in the United States, four of the contributors and I are Americans. McLuhan's trans-Atlantic reach in cultural and media theory is represented by the work of a British sociologist.

Several authors contributing to this volume first wrote about McLuhan in the1980s, helping to put him in context then as a critical theory, cultural studies or postmodern thinker. American literary scholar Patrick Brantlinger, who is an English professor, ventured into new territory, juxtaposing McLuhan and the early Frankfurt School critical theorists (1983). Philosopher Douglas Kellner compared the media and culture theories of McLuhan with those of French postmodernist

Jean Baudrillard (1989b). Cultural theory has been the focus of several other authors, including Canadians Gary Genosko (1994, 1996, 1999), Richard Cavell (2002), Glenn Willmott (1992, 1996), and Bob Hanke, and British sociologist Nick Stevenson (1995).

Communication scholar Donna Flayhan's Ph.D. dissertation (1997) brings together marxisms, the medium theory of McLuhan and others, and American cultural studies, giving cultural theory an activist base. My book (Grosswiler, 1998) similarly seeks to link McLuhan with critical theory, as well as cultural studies and postmodernism through the application of dialectical method in understanding media and social change. From the discipline of media ecology, Lance Strate's work has given McLuhan and media ecology much higher visibility in media and communication studies (2005, 2006).

These essays have been grouped into three sections: McLuhan and Cultural Studies; McLuhan and Critical Theory; and McLuhan and Postmodernism.

In Section One, McLuhan and Cultural Studies, Gary Genosko reaches back in time to compare the passive audience in the "transmission" communication theory that McLuhan rejected and the active audience found in the "transformative" or "ritual" communication theory that McLuhan—and cultural studies—espoused. In "Coping with the McLuhans: The Passively Active Receiver in Communication Theory and Cultural Studies," Genosko bridges communication theory and cultural studies by positioning McLuhan's work in the cultural studies tradition, which emphasizes modeling communication. McLuhan's theory of communication was developed in opposition to the dominant cybernetic model of the time, which conceptualized the receiver as passively reproducing encoded and transmitted messages. In the essay, Genosko brings McLuhan into cultural studies by focusing on how communication is modeled.

Nick Stevenson's chapter, based on a section of his book *Understanding Media Cultures* (2002), brings McLuhan into cultural studies through his work on the impact of new forms of communication on the dimensions of space, time, and human perception. Stevenson decries the chronically under-researched problem of the media's impact on spatial and temporal dimensions of social life—and demands further investigation of this problem. In "Marshall McLuhan and Media and Cultural Studies," Stevenson argues against McLuhan's most audible critics to urge that his work be re-evaluated by cultural media theorists. Although Stevenson addresses problems in McLuhan's work raised by cultural studies, he defends McLuhan's emphasis on technical media as significant for understanding different modes of cultural communication—oral, literate, typographic and electronic—and argues that these media deeply affect social relations.

McLuhan's cultural theory is the subject of Glenn Willmott, who revisits and builds on arguments he developed in *McLuhan, or Modernism in Reverse* (1996) in "Waking Up to the Call Girl." Finding McLuhan's cultural theory coherent, although not marked or explicitly stated as a theory, Willmott locates that theory in the social and material life meant for the discourse itself—such as in the media themselves as central to the invisible modes of production appropriate to various historical eras. McLuhan creates an anti-environment through probes that retain the mark of "McLuhan" even as it transcends his intended or moral interpretation. Evoking McLuhan's private title for *Understanding Media—The Electronic Call Girl*—Willmott summarizes the development of "McLuhan" as a popular celebrity and a cultural product in the 1960s, then argues that this mediated commodity, "McLuhan," assumes greater edification and significance in light of his understanding of modernity as a fantasy world—a social system permeated by unconscious processes that form the limits of individual experience in psychological, political and social arenas.

In his essay "Studying Media *as* Media: McLuhan and the Media Ecology Approach," which was originally published in the online journal *MediaTropes* (2008), Lance Strate argues that we must use our capacity for observation to become aware of hidden media environments—and develop our understanding in order to make sense of media environments and their effects. McLuhan's famous aphorism, "the medium is the message" (1964, p. 7) is his wake-up call to everyone who neglects the medium itself and thinks only the content is important. McLuhan's intention was to help free humans from our subordination to media technologies and symbolic codes. This first requires a wake-up call to take the medium itself into account, because the medium is what exerts the greatest influence on society, not the content that the media provide. Strate contextualizes McLuhan's work within the broader field of media ecology, which examines media forms and media environments in relationship to culture.

In Section Two, McLuhan and Critical Theory, Donna Flayhan argues for the compatibility between dialectical materialism and media ecology. Building on work that links critical theory, western Marxism and media ecology, Flayhan contrasts these traditions while drawing similarities in activist Marxist scholarship and media ecology. While critical theory and western Marxism may be radical in criticism, they are not radical as tools for action, but activist Marxism and media ecology, by contrast are.

My essay moves McLuhan both backward and forward in time to connect McLuhan with Marxisms from Marx's *Communist Manifesto* to Jurgen Habermas's *Structural Transformation of the Public Sphere*, Immanuel Wallerstein's world system theory and Jacques Ellul's writings on anarchy in technological society. I suggest that these connections help reclaim McLuhan for contemporary critical communication theory as a dialectical theorist in the mold of Marx and the late Frankfurt School.

In Section Three, McLuhan and Postmodernism, Richard Cavell writes in "Specters of McLuhan: Derrida, Media, and Materiality" that as Jacques Derrida increasingly considered the role of media, or "teletechnologies," within philosophical discourse, he continued to come up against the specter of McLuhan, whose ghost he had attempted to leave behind as early as 1971. This chapter opens with a critique of McLuhanism before exploring McLuhan's media theories as they continue to influence Derrida, a haunting that presents challenges to McLuhan while becoming especially intrusive for Derrida, as his writing focused on the media and the philosophical issues raised by "virtuality" and related issues of materiality.

Patrick Brantlinger's "McLuhan, Crash Theory, and the Invasion of the Nanobots" argues that McLuhan remains relevant to a radical offshoot of postmodernist, posthumanist cultural theory in France, Canada and elsewhere. This side theory is aptly called "crash theory," a term that originated with Arthur Kroker and Michael Weinstein's *Data Trash*. A catastrophic variant of postmodernism, crash theory warns that technology is an unstoppable force moving humanity toward annihilation, or at least "imploding" reality toward its opposite. Brantlinger considers the main crash theorists, Kroker and Weinstein, as well as Paul Virilio and Jean Baudrillard, who both recognize that McLuhan influenced their work somewhat. Brantlinger also draws on several computer scientists and robotics experts who refer minimally or not at all to either McLuhan or to the crash theorists, but whose thoughts about the impact of technological change are undoubtedly related to crash theory. The crash theorists constitute one approach to the "the postmodern condition," a phrase deriving from both McLuhan and poststructuralism.

Douglas Kellner juxtaposes Baudrillard and McLuhan in "Reflections on Modernity and Postmodernity in McLuhan and Baudrillard," a study drawing on Kellner's earlier article (1989a) and book (1989b). During the 1980s, Baudrillard was put forth as the new McLuhan, as the most radical media and society theorist of postmodernity. Baudrillard's theory is based on the premise that the media, simulations and "cyberblitz" establish an unprecedented world of experience, period of history and kind of society. Kellner explores how McLuhan's media theory influenced Baudrillard, their shared positions and significant differences. Kellner also examines the ways that McLuhan presaged a postmodern turn in history and the global implosion of the Internet and a networked society. The emergence of personal computers and the Internet legitimates the provocative claims McLuhan made concerning a new stage of culture and society. McLuhan's work is read in the narrative of postmodern theory that posits a rupture between modern and postmodern societies. While showing the links between Baudrillard and McLuhan helps explain the genesis of postmodern society, re-reading McLuhan in the light of Baudrillard and postmodern theory also sheds new light on McLuhan. In submitting this essay, Kellner acknowledged the critical responses of Arthur Kroker, Steve Best, Peter Bruck and Rhonda Hammer to earlier versions.

Paul Virilio and McLuhan are compared in Bob Hanke's "McLuhan, Virilio and Speed." In a version of his essay "McLuhan, Virilio and Electric Speed in the Age of Digital Reproduction" (2005), Hanke argues that McLuhan's media critique explored, among other psychological and cultural effects, the switch from the experience of temporality to that of increasing speed. Living in the global media culture that is simultaneous, immediate, uncertain and unpredictable was a theme in McLuhan's early work. Increasing speed was a minor, yet significant focus in his later work. These are among the many ways that McLuhan foreshadows Virilio's themes, and Virilio may have incorporated more of McLuhan than he acknowledges. The destruction of space and the intensifying effort to control the real-time environment of human experiences place us on the verge of a temporal accident, in Virilio's term—a transformation of the idea of time itself. Virilio's writings about old and emerging media extend and deviate from McLuhan's thesis on speed. McLuhan employed the concept of visual and acoustic space, while Virilio pursued the concept of territorial and vectorial space, yet both theorists addressed the accelerating speed of modernity and its effects, especially as Western media culture's effort to increase speed at last is able to annihilate space for good.

Taken as a whole, these essays from different disciplines within similar traditions of critical, cultural and postmodern perspectives agree that McLuhan holds an important if contentious place in the history of communication, as well as its future.

References

Babe, Robert. *Canadian Communication Thought: Foundational Writers,* Toronto: University of Toronto Press, 2000.

Baudrillard, Jean. "Requiem for the Media" In *For a Critique of the Political Economy of the Sign* . St. Louis MO.: Telos, 1981.

Baudrillard, Jean. *Simulations.* New York: Semiotext(e), 1983.

Baudrillard, Jean. *The Illusion of the End.* Stanford, Calif.: Stanford University Press, 1994.

Benedetti, Paul, and Nancy Dehart. *Forward through the Rearview Mirror: Reflections on and by Marshall McLuhan.* Cambridge, MA.: MIT Press, 1997.

Berland, Jodi. "Angels Dancing: Cultural Technologies and the Production of Space." In *Cultural Studies.* Edited by Lawrence Grossberg, Cary Nelson, and Paula Treichler, 38–51. New York: Routledge, 1992.

Berland, Jodi, "Cultural Technologies and the 'Evolution' of Technological Cultures." In Andrew Herman and Thomas Swiss (Eds.) The World Wide Web and Contemporary Cultural Theory, pp. 235- 257. New York: Routledge, 2000.

Best, Steven, and Douglas Kellner. Postmodern Turn. New York: Guilford Press, 1997.

Brantlinger, Patrick. Crusoe's Footprints: Cultural Studies in Britain and America. New York: Routledge, 1990.

Bross, Michael. "McLuhan's Theory of Sensory Functions: A Critique and Analysis." Journal of Communication Inquiry 16, no. 1 (1992): 91–107.

Brummett, Barry, and Margaret Carlisle Duncan. "Toward a Discursive Ontology of the Media." Critical Studies in Mass Communication 9, no. 3 (1992): 229–249.

Carey, James. "Harold Adams Innis and Marshall McLuhan." In McLuhan: Pro and Con. Edited by Raymond Rosenthal, 270–308. Baltimore, MD.: Penguin, 1968.

Carey, James. "McLuhan and Mumford: The Roots of Modern Media Analysis." Journal of Communication 31 (summer 1981): 162–178.

Carey, James. "The Origins of Radical Discourse on Cultural Studies in the United States." Journal of Communication 33, no. 3 (summer 1983): 311–313.

Carey, James. "Walter Benjamin, Marshall McLuhan, and the Emergence of Visual Society." Prospects: An Annual of American Cultural Studies 12 (1987): 29–38.

Carey, James. "Mass Communication and Cultural Studies." Communication as Culture: Essays on Media and Society, 37–68. Boston: Unwin Hyman, 1989.

Carey, James. "Space, Time, and Communication: A Tribute to Harold Innis." In Communication as Culture: Essays on Media and Society, 142–172. Boston: Unwin Hyman, 1989.

Carey, James, with John J. Quirk, "The Mythos of the Electronic Revolution." In Communication as Culture: Essays on Media and Society, 113–141. Boston: Unwin Hyman, 1989.

Carey, James, and Jonathan Game. "Communication, Culture and Technology: An Internet Interview with James Carey." Journal of Communication Inquiry 22, no. 2 (1998): 117–130.

Crowley, David, and David Mitchell (Eds.) Communication Theory Today. Stanford, CA.: Stanford University Press, 1994.

Crowley, David, and Paul Heyer, (Eds.) Communication in History. 2nd ed. White Plains, NY: Longman, 1995.

Czitrom, Daniel J. Media and the American Mind: From Morse to McLuhan . Chapel Hill, NC: University of North Carolina Press, 1982.

Durham, Meenakshi Gigi, and Douglas M. Kellner (Eds.) Media and Cultural Studies: KeyWorks. Malden, MA: Blackwell, 2001.

Fekete, John. "McLuhanacy: Counterrevolution in Cultural Theory." Telos 15 (spring 1973): 75–123.

Fekete, John. The Critical Twilight: Explorations in the Ideology of Anglo-American Literary Theory from Eliot to McLuhan. London: Routledge and Kegan Paul, 1977.

Fekete, John. Moral Panic: Biopolitics Rising. Montréal-Toronto: Robert Davies, 1994.

Ferguson, Marjorie. "Marshall McLuhan Revisited: 1960s Zeitgeist Victim or Pioneer Postmodernist?" Media, Culture and Society 13, no. 1 (1991): 71–90.

Flayhan, Donna. "Marxism, Medium Theory, and American Cultural Studies: The Question of Determination." Ph.D. diss., University of Iowa, 1997.

Friedland, Roger, and Deirdre Boden (Eds.) *NowHere: Space, Time and Modernity*. Berkeley, CA.: University of California Press, 1994.

Genosko, Gary. *Baudrillard and Signs*. London: Routledge, 1994.

Genosko, Gary. (Ed.) *The Guattari Reader*. London: Blackwell, 1996.

Genosko, Gary (Ed.) *Marshall McLuhan: Critical Evaluations in Cultural Theory*. New York: Routledge, 2005.

Genosko, Gary. *McLuhan and Baudrillard: The Masters of Implosion*. London: Routledge, 1999.

Gordon, W. Terrence. *McLuhan for Beginners*. London: Writers and Readers, 1997.

Gordon, W. Terrence. *Marshall McLuhan: Escape into Understanding: A Biography*. Toronto: Stoddart, 1997b.

Grosswiler, Paul. "The Shifting Sensorium: A Q-Methodology and Critical Theory Exploration of Marshall McLuhan's Visual and Acoustic Typologies in Media, Aesthetics and Ideology." Ph.D. diss., University of Missouri, 1990.

Grosswiler, Paul. "A Dialectical Synthesis of Marshall McLuhan and Critical Theory." Paper presented at the annual meeting of the International Communication Association, Chicago, IL, May 1991.

Grosswiler, Paul. "The Dialectical Methods of Marshall McLuhan, Marxism, and Critical Theory." *Canadian Journal of Communication* 21 (winter 1996): 95–124.

Grosswiler, Paul. *The Method Is the Message: Rethinking McLuhan Through Critical Theory*. Montréal: Black Rose, 1998.

Grosswiler, Paul. "The Transformation of Carey On McLuhan: Admiration, Rejection, and Redemption." *Explorations in Media Ecology* 5(2) (2006): 137–148.

Hall, Stuart. "On Postmodernism and Articulation: An Interview with Stuart Hall." Edited by Lawrence Grossberg. In *Stuart Hall: Critical Dialogues in Cultural Studies*. Edited by David Morley and Kuan-Hsing Chen, 131–150. London: Routledge, 1996.

Hanke, Bob. "McLuhan, Virilio and Electric Speed in the Age of Digital Reproduction." In *Marshall McLuhan: Critical Evaluations in Cultural Theory. Volume III—Renaissance for a Wired World*. Edited by Gary Genosko, 121-156. New York: Routledge, 2005.

Hartley, John. *The Politics of Pictures: The Creation of the Public in the Age of Popular Media*. London: Routledge, 1992.

Jeffrey, Liss. "The Heat and the Light: Towards a Reassessment of the Contribution of H. Marshall McLuhan." *Canadian Journal of Communication* 14 (winter 1989): 1–29.

Jeffrey, Liss., "The Heat and the Light of Marshall McLuhan: A 1990s Reappraisal," Ph.D. diss., McGill University, Montréal, 1997.

Jensen, Klaus Bruhn. *The Social Semiotics of Mass Communication*. London: Sage, 1995.

Kellner, Douglas. "Resurrecting McLuhan? Jean Baudrillard and the Academy of Postmodernism." In *Communication: For or Against Democracy*. Edited by Marc Raboy and Peter A. Bruck, 131–146. Montréal: Black Rose, 1989a.

Kellner, Douglas. *Jean Baudrillard: From Marxism to Postmodernism and Beyond*. Stanford, CA: Stanford University Press, 1989b.

Kroker, Arthur. *Technology and the Canadian Mind: Innis/McLuhan/Grant*. Montréal: New World Perspectives, 1984.

Kroker, Arthur, and Michael Weinstein. *Data Trash: The Theory of the Virtual Class*. New York: St. Martin's, 1994.

Levinson, Paul. *The Digital McLuhan: A Guide to the Information Millennium*. London: Routledge, 1999.

"The Living McLuhan." *Journal of Communication* 31, no. 3 (summer 1981): 116–199.

Lombard, Matthew, Selcan Kaynak, Jodi Linder, Sherrie Madia, Alexis Pasqua, and Donnalyn Pompper. "Toward a Mass Communication Core Literature." Paper presented to the annual meeting of the International Communication Association, Chicago, IL, 1996.

Lowe, Donald M. *History of Bourgeois Perception*. Chicago: University of Chicago Press, 1982.

Lull, James. *Inside Family Viewing: Ethnographic Research on Television Audiences*. London: Routledge, 1990.

Marchand, Philip. *Marshall McLuhan: The Medium and the Messenger*. New York: Ticknor and Fields, 1989.

Marchessault, Janine. "Mama's Boys or the Mechanical Bride: Gender and Technology in Early McLuhan." Paper presented at the annual meeting of the Canadian Communication Association, Ottawa, Ontario, June 1998.

Marchessault, Janine. "Mechanical Brides and Mama's Boys: Gender and Technology in Early McLuhan." In *Marshall McLuhan: Critical Evaluations in Cultural Theory. Volume III— Renaissance for a Wired World*. Edited by Gary Genosko, 161–180. New York: Routledge, 2005a.

Marchessault, Janine. *Marshall McLuhan: Cosmic Media*. London: Sage, 2005b.

McLuhan, Eric. *Electric Language: Understanding the Message*. New York: St. Martin's, 1998.

McLuhan, Marshall. *The Mechanical Bride: The Folklore of Industrial Man*. New York: Vanguard, 1951.

McLuhan, Marshall. *The Gutenberg Galaxy: The Making of Typographic Man*. Toronto: University of Toronto Press, 1962.

McLuhan, Marshall. *Understanding Media: The Extensions of Man*. New York: Mentor, 1964.

McLuhan, Marshall. With Quentin Fiore and Jerome Agel. *The Medium Is the Massage: An Inventory of Effects*. New York: Bantam, 1967.

McLuhan, Marshall. With Quentin Fiore and Jerome Agel. *War and Peace in the Global Village*. New York: Bantam, 1968.

McLuhan, Marshall. *Letters of Marshall McLuhan*. Edited by Matie Molinaro, Corinne McLuhan, and William Toye. Toronto: Oxford University Press, 1987.

McLuhan, Marshall. With Eric McLuhan. *Laws of Media: The New Science*. Toronto: University of Toronto Press, 1988.

McLuhan, Marshall, with Bruce Powers. *The Global Village: Transformations in World Life and Media in the Twenty-first Century*. New York: Oxford University Press, 1989.

McLuhan, Marshall, and Michael Moos (Eds.) *Media Research: Technology, Art, Communications*. Newark, NJ: Gordon and Breach, 1997.

McLuhan, Marshall, Eric McLuhan, and Frank Zingrone. *The Essential McLuhan*. New York: Basic, 1996.

MediaTropes. University of Toronto (2008). http://www.mediatropes.com/index.php/Mediatropes/about/editorialPolicies#focusAndScope

"The Medium's Messenger: Understanding McLuhan." *Canadian Journal of Communication* 14, nos. 4 and 5 (winter 1989): 1–160.

Meyrowitz, Joshua. *No Sense of Place: The Impact of Electronic Media on Social Behavior.* New York: Oxford University Press, 1985.

Miles, David. "The CD-ROM Novel *Myst* and McLuhan's Fourth Law of Media: *Myst* and Its 'Retrievals.'" *Journal of Communication* 46, no. 2 (spring 1996): 4–18.

Ong, Walter. *Orality and Literacy: The Technologizing of the Word.* New York: Methuen, 1982.

Poster, Mark. *The Mode of Information: Post-Structuralism and Social Context.* Chicago: University of Chicago Press, 1990.

Poster, Mark. "The Mode of Information and Postmodernity." In *Communication Theory Today.* Edited by David Crowley and David Mitchell, 173–192. Stanford, CA: Stanford University Press, 1994.

Postman, Neil. *Amusing Ourselves to Death: Public Discourse in the Age of Show Business.* New York: Penguin, 1985.

Sanderson, George, and Frank McDonald (Eds.). *Marshall McLuhan: The Man and His Message.* Golden, CO: Fulcrum, 1989.

Shaw, Nancy. "Raymond Williams and Marshall McLuhan: New Criticism, Media Studies and the Critique of Modernity at Cambridge in the 1930s." Paper presented at the annual meeting of the Canadian Communication Association, Ottawa, Ontario, June 1998.

Spigel, Lynn. Introduction to *Television: Technology and Cultural Form,* by Raymond Williams. Hanover, NH, and London: Wesleyan University Press, 1992.

Stamps, Judith. "Negative Dialogues: A Study of Harold Innis and Marshall McLuhan in the Light of the Negative Dialectics of Theodor Adorno and Walter Benjamin." Ph.D. diss., University of Toronto, 1991.

Stamps, Judith. "The Bias of Theory: A Critique of Pamela McCallum's 'Walter Benjamin and Marshall McLuhan: Theories of History.'" *Signature: A Journal of Theory and Canadian Literature* 1, no. 3 (1990): 44–62.

Stamps, Judith. *Unthinking Modernity: Innis, McLuhan and the Frankfurt School.* Montréal: McGill-Queen's University Press, 1995.

Stevenson, Nick. *Understanding Media Cultures: Social Theory and Mass Communication.* London: Sage, 1995.

Strate, Lance, and Edward Wachtel (Eds.). *The Legacy of McLuhan.* Cresskill, NJ: Hampton, 2005.

Strate, Lance. *Echoes and Reflections: On Media Ecology as a Field of Study.* Cresskill, NJ: Hampton, 2006.

Strate, Lance. "Studying Media *as* Media: McLuhan and the Media Ecology Approach." In Twyla Gibson (Ed.), Marshall McLuhan's "Medium is the Message": Information Literacy in a Multimedia Age [Special Issue]. vol. 1 (2008): 127–142, http://www.mediatropes.com

Theall, Donald F. *Understanding McLuhan: The Medium is the Rear View Mirror.* Montréal: McGill-Queen's University Press, 1971.

Theall, Donald F. Guest editor's introductory remarks. *Canadian Journal of Communication* 14, (winter 1989): vii-ix.

Thompson, John B. *Ideology and Modern Culture.* Stanford, CA: Stanford University Press, 1990.

Thompson, John B. "Social Theory and the Media." In *Communication Theory Today*. Edited by David Crowley and David Mitchell, 27–49. Stanford, CA: Stanford University Press, 1994.

Thompson, John B. *The Media and Modernity: A Social Theory of the Media*. Stanford, CA: Stanford University Press, 1995.

Turner, Graeme. *British Cultural Studies: An Introduction*. Boston: Unwin Hyman , 1990.

Virilio, Paul. "The Third Interval: A Critical Transition." In *Rethinking Technologies*. Edited by Verena Andermatt Conley, 5. Minneapolis, MN: University of Minnesota Press, 1993.

Williams, Raymond. "Paradoxically, If the Book Works It to Some Extent Annihilates Itself." In *McLuhan Hot and Cool*. Edited by Gerald E. Stearn, 188–191. New York: Dial, 1967.

Williams, Raymond. *Marxism and Literature*. Oxford: Oxford University Press, 1977.

Williams, Raymond. *The Year 2000*. New York: Pantheon, 1983.

Williams, Raymond. *Television: Technology and Cultural Form*. Hanover, NH, and London: Wesleyan University Press, 1992.

Willmott, Glenn. "Marshall McLuhan: From Modernism to Minimalism." Ph.D. diss., Duke University, 1992.

Willmott, Glenn. *McLuhan, or Modernism in Reverse* Toronto: University of Toronto Press, 1996.

Section One: McLuhan and Cultural Studies

CHAPTER ONE

Coping with the McLuhans:
The Passively Active Receiver in Communication Theory and Cultural Studies

GARY GENOSKO

Introduction

One of the great insights of cultural studies is that the receiver-reader-audience is active and productive of meaning. If we look at statements of this insight by John Fiske as prime examples, it is for the sake of an appreciation of his refinement of earlier work in different cultural studies traditions and the terms with which he constructed the receiver's *activeness*. The construction of such *activeness* is the subject of this paper, and my claim is that this activeness is presented as passive. I am not simply stating a paradox. Attention to this modification of activity will permit me to build a bridge between communication theory and cultural studies by situating the work of Marshall McLuhan, singly and with his son Eric, in the cultural studies tradition in which modeling communication played a central role. McLuhan's own theory of communication was articulated against the reigning cybernetic model of the time in which the receiver was thought to merely (re)produce and "match" what was encoded and sent, often having to turn to a supervisor to deliver the goods to their final destination. McLuhan, as Donald Theall has recently pointed out (*Virtual McLuhan* 56, 60), did not appreciate the rationality of the linear mathematical model of communication developed in the Bell Labs by Claude Shannon and William Weaver. However, the point about passive activity is that it is an idea shared by the McLuhans and many theorists aligned with the cultural studies and popular culture studies traditions—notably Fiske, but also Michel de Certeau. The receiver is one who copes, makes do, gets on with it, sucks it up, as it were. The distinction that was often made by McLuhan between "matching" and "making" marks out two apparently different conceptions of communication.

While this insight into the receiver's character has changed the face of communication modeling since the time when the mathematical model held sway, before being displaced in content but not form by the remarkable accomplishments in poetics by Roman Jakobson, then in cultural studies by Stuart Hall, in semiotics by Umberto Eco, in the criticism of Jakobson by Jean Baudrillard, etc., it still raises questions about the implication of its qualification of active by passive. I want to find the positive and affirmative features of the insight and its qualification. To what extent is this an advance on the mathematical model?

Elsewhere I developed a strategy for thinking McLuhan's work together with cultural studies by focusing on foundational books on popular culture by Richard Hoggart, Roland Barthes and McLuhan, written in quite different places during the 1950s—Birmingham, Paris, St. Louis (*McLuhan and Baudrillard*, 27ff). Here I want to bring McLuhan into cultural studies by focusing on how communication is modeled. The backdrop against which communication has been remade and remodeled is undoubtedly the celebrated Shannon and Weaver model of communication which was described in two essays dating from 1948 and 1949: Warren Weaver's "Recent Contributions to the Mathematical Theory of Communication" and Claude E. Shannon's "The Mathematical Theory of Communication." This mathematical rendering of communication has come to be known as the "transportation" or "transmission" or "transfer" model and it is represented in its bare bones in a wide variety of communication and culture texts.

Despite its notoriety, and wide deployment as a foil, many may not be familiar with its details. Briefly, let's review some of the key terms as they were described by Weaver and augmented by Shannon. The point of this exercise is to recover from the original statements of Shannon and Weaver a sense of the receiving of messages. This review is also necessary because of the many caricatures of this model that we find throughout the literature; these cannot help us appreciate the precise character of the contrast between modeling communication in cybernetics and cultural studies. Still, there is something important in the mathematical model and it directly concerns the stratified—or to use a less sociological term, staggered—character of the receiving process. And the discovery of this feature will not, I believe, erase or weaken the contrast between the mathematical and cultural models of communication but, rather, provide a hitherto not obvious relationship of interests. For if the trope of "coping" is fully elaborated by theorists of communication in cultural studies, then the situation, perhaps "condition," of the social mediations of communication buried and trapped within the technical terms of the mathematical model, may be seen as a resource which may be utilized to heighten and elaborate an over-simplistic and underproductive contrast. To put it bluntly, "matchers" too have a need to cope.

Background: The Construction of the Receiver in the Transportation Model

In the terms of the mathematical model, communication poses problems at three levels: technical—concerning the accuracy of transmitting a finite set of symbols conceived as an engineering problem (accuracy); semantic—a concern with the precise conveyance of meaning, posing the problem of identity between intended and received meaning (philosophical problem); and effectiveness—does the received meaning have the desired effect on the decoder, influencing his or her conduct (again, another philosophical issue)?

At the level of technical communication, the two terminal models present an information source from which issues a message to a transmitter that sends a signal through a channel subject to a certain amount of noise; the signal is received by a "receiver" who delivers the message to its final destination. Weaver's model presents a host of problems because it doubles the efforts of communication at both terminals of the model. The information source, to begin with, involves the selection of a message out of a set of possible messages (the message may consist of words, pictures, music, etc.). The transmitter changes or translates the message into a signal; the signal is sent through a communication channel from the transmitter to the receiver. On the encoding side, messages are selected, translated, and then transmitted.

The process is threefold. The model seems to be telegraphy, involving the selection of a message consisting of written words and their translation into a series of dots, dashes and spaces; the receiver on the decoding side must share this code and functions, as Weaver puts it, as an *inverse transmitter* ("Recent Contribution," 7). Sometimes, noise gets into the transmission. It is unwanted and distorting, adding or subtracting from the signal, thereby creating uncertainty about the message. As for the message, the transmitter encodes it from an information source. Despite the technical nature of the representation, the interpersonal drama of the situation is fairly obvious: a message is delivered to an operator who then translates it into code for mechanical transmission, but what comes out the other end is telegraphese, a broken English, if you will, pared down to its essentials. This is a subcode within the encoding operation that Weaver neglects to mention, upon which may be grafted other subcodes.

The other two levels raise semantic issues and call for the invention, in Weaver's estimation, of a semantic receiver that is interposed between the engineering receiver (changing signals back into messages) and the destination ("Recent Contribution," 26). There is implicit in this communication a chain of command that will become clear in a moment. The addition of a second decoding has the goal of "match[ing] the statistical semantic characteristics of the message to the statistical semantic capacities of the totality of receivers, or of that subset of receivers which constitute the audience one wishes to affect" (26). Implied here is the need for audience research or at least sensitivity to small groups of receivers, but in the language of matching statistically the characteristics of messages with the capacities of audiences. The idea of the capacity of the audience is particularly rich and it works on the analogy of crowding too much information over a channel since, no matter how efficient and clean the encoding, it is still possible to overwhelm the audience's capacity to receive the message. The audience may be filled up and then spill the remainder of the message; overwhelming the audience will also produce error and confusion. Of course, this is conceived of statistically. Information theoretical models of communication were little concerned with meaning and not at all with individual messages, but with the statistical characteristics of messages. To put it briefly, information is not meaning: engineering triumphs over semantics.

It is not my intent to follow Weaver as he clears the ground for the statistical study of language. It turns out upon closer examination that the social scene of the engineering problem of communication is stratified in various ways, the most obvious of which is gender in a service environment. Weaver writes: "An engineering communication theory is just like a very proper and discreet girl accepting your telegram. She pays no attention to the meaning, whether it be sad, or joyous, or embarrassing. But she must be prepared to deal with all that comes to her desk. This idea that a communication system ought to try to deal with all possible messages, and that the intelligent way is to base design on the statistical character of the source, is surely not without significance for communication in general" ("Recent Contribution," 27). Indeed, Shannon remarked at the outset of his paper that semantics are irrelevant to engineering; the focus is on the selection of a message from a set of possible messages. In terms of Weaver's analogy, the telegraph girl should be discreet and show no interest in meaning; her task is to translate English or whatever language into telegraphese. The social scene here is a service environment, the telegraph office; but in the chain of command, orders are issued by superiors and delivered for execution by inferiors at the telegraph desk. Translation of the message is a gendered activity of prurient interest and moral imperatives. It is almost as if the engineering theory is bogged down in censorship issues that restrict its proper testing, and this makes the training of a disciplined secretary of vital concern. The secretary is, however, separated from meaning, which she neither pursues nor peruses; one is reminded here of Antonio Gramsci's compositor who is separated from meaning—"intellectual content"—by the forces of Taylorist production to the extent that any "noise" introduced into the system in the form of typesetting errors would be considered a sign of intellectual interest in the message and thus a failing ("Americanism and Fordism," 308–9). The shift from telegraph to telephone saw the feminization and progressive machinization of the switchboard operator (*Hello Central?*, 50ff) "mediating" the messages of subscribers on her circuit, in adherence to the specific "tones" of voice cultivated and inculcated by Bell trainers.

Shannon figures the receiver as the one who reconstructs backwards the messages from the signal, but the destination is the person (or thing) for whom the message is intended. The receiver is not the destination. The receiver is another telegraph girl or an operator-technician low in the hierarchy who then gives the message to her superiors or customers. The model of communication is subject, then, to metamodeling operations around gender and chain of command or at least an oppressive service environment.

Let's return to the technical problem of noise, which would be analogous to indiscretion. What is to be done about noise in the channel? How does one combat this chance variable? The issue is formulated this way: the received signal E is a function of the transmitted signal S and the variable N, so that $E = f(S, N)$. The Shannon and Weaver solution is to situate an auxiliary observer (let's call it a surveillor) in the communication model. This observation-device surveys what is sent and received, noting the errors, and transmitting data about them over a correction channel so that the receiver can make the corrections; correction is a clean up operation, a surveillance function. In-between the information source and the transmitter, the original message branches off and upward toward an observation device, back to which flows corrections concerning the received message from the receiver; but from the observation device flows forward correction data past the receiver and the received message to a correcting device that sends the repaired message to its destination. This is a cumbersome solution. Not only is another channel required, but it doesn't eliminate noise, even though it reduces it considerably, still leaving an arbitrarily small fraction of errors.

Many analyses of the Shannon and Weaver model underrepresent it to the point of creating a straw model that is easily subject to criticism. The point of my somewhat lengthy but by no means exhaustive treatment was to bring out several factors (the "telegraph girl" and the "auxiliary observer") that are normally neglected, even by insightful critics. Take as an example Ian Angus's remarks on the ideological effects of the model. Angus rightly suggests that the transportation model figures communication as the "transfer of content" from one place to another in which "the origin and destination of the transfer pre-exist the transference itself and are not altered by it." ("From Competitive Capitalism," 85) Angus duly notes the separation of channel from content, but without the specific gender and class dynamics at stake. The identity, he adds, of the sender and receiver is erased— "another question entirely." This is not so, as we have discovered, for what is pre-supposed is a particular subject of the communicative process. And it is from this that we want to learn something about what transpires at the receiving end of the model. This much is certain: receiving is deeply stratified, but the engineers had nothing to tell us about these crucial factors, despite flagging analogically at least one of them. The activeness of the transference of the message in reverse to the final destination raises, within this tradition of modeling, interesting questions about the culture of the communication situation.

Fiskean Ethnosemiotics

It seems far, very far, from Shannon and Weaver to Fiske. But keep in mind our quarry: the modeling of the receiver and the contrast at issue. In *Television Culture*, Fiske distinguishes between two kinds of subjects: a textual, inactive and passive subject as opposed to an active, socially formed subject (the so-called "actual TV viewer" with a history). The former is passive because the text subjects, that is, subjugates, the reader to its ideological power (*Television Culture*, 66). The latter emerges, however, as productive of meaning through, for example, existing subject positions negotiating and grappling with those that the text prefers (*Television Culture*, 65). Fiske's point is that ethnographic methods applied to receivers temper semiotic tendencies to move directly from text to social structure, thus neglecting the contact points between a text's dominant meaning and a receiver's social situation. Hence, Fiske considered that method should be ethnosemiotic. In *Introduction to Communication Studies*, Fiske described his method: "Ethno-semiotics links the reading of texts with the everyday lives of their readers" (*Introduction*, 162).

Ethnosemiotics is also political as senders and receivers are in Fiske's analysis in a relation of economic and social subordination and antagonistic resistance (the latter "under" the former) by the subordinated (the latter releasing a text's progressive potentiality, but there is no guarantee of this oppositionality). Fiske wrote about the political vicissitudes of ethnosemiotics in *Understanding Popular Culture*: "There is no guarantee that the politics of any cultural form or practice will be mobilized in any particular reading, any oppositionality may remain 'sleeping' potential; and, if mobilized, there is equally no guarantee as to whether its direction will be progressive or conservative" (*Understanding*, 167).

Like Stuart Hall before him, Fiske contemplates "structures of preference" (cf. "structures of discourse in dominance") that open certain meanings while simultaneously closing off others (which in Hall is the work of preferring dominant meanings). Preference is a modality of encoding; it is neither deterministic nor prescriptive. It is a question of constructing some of the limits and parameters within which decodings will operate ("Encoding and Decoding," 135). Formal semiology cannot ignore the work of decoding, the management of the semiotic scaffolding it receives. Encoding prefers; decoding is constrained by the parameters of encoding. Some degree of correspondence exists between encoding and decoding, but it is constructed and not guaranteed. But it is not totally open, either. Viewers-readers-receivers are active in the sense of "*making* [my emphasis] their own socially pertinent meanings out of the semiotic resources provided by television" (*Television Culture*, 65). This making is, as it was in the case of Hall's work, carried forward with reference to a dialogical process. The text's message is "worked on" by a subject already full of contradictory and partial discourses and their ideological traces. Such making is sometimes a matter of shifting or bending meanings so that they connect with one's social experience and situation in a way that helps to initiate personal and social changes. The making of meaning may be socially transformative by providing a piece of hitherto missing cultural capital (*Television Culture*, 75) by enabling one to participate in an exchange from/in which one was otherwise marginalized or excluded; indeed, ways of watching television—listening without viewing, sitting glued to the screen, occasionally glancing up from some other project—are "regimes of watching" with social determinations that for Fiske contribute to this process of meaning construction.

Meaning is, then, constructed from the "conjuncture of the text with the socially situated reader" (*Television Culture*, 80). The text is a "resource," to use one of Fiske's cherished expressions, with which a receiver works (extracting, refining, turning, etc.). Working with semiotic resources is a participatory practice: productivity shaped by actuality. Resources are typically cultural commodities like TV shows, CDs, clothes, tourist sights, etc. Such resources carry dominant meanings and interests to receivers but, importantly, they "must also carry contradictory lines of force" (*Reading the Popular*, 2).

What is it to be a non-resource? In Fiske's work on popular culture, the implication is that a non-resource is a failed cultural commodity—failure meaning that it has not become or been made popular. Another way to understand this failure is that a resource's potential is nil if it lacks characteristics that would allow for its actualization by receivers (i.e., it is too inflexible, closed, "nonproducerly"; an artifact's popular potential may remain "asleep" for some time because the conditions for its productive reception do not yet exist).

Generally, Fiske thinks from within Hall's first position of decoding that operates with the preferred code, augmented by subtle professional codes, of the dominant-hegemonic position. In this sense, Fiske's active receivers are all subordinate to capitalist exchange relations. If one of the defining characteristics of the dominant position examined by Hall was the globality, and totality, of its interpretive horizon, his second position of negotiated code may be defined in contrast by its reserving of the right to refocus the global in terms of local conditions. The negotiated code operates by the exceptions of situated logics, its work involves making its own ground rules. Hall uses this position to rethink the meaning of what counts as a misunderstanding of the contradictions that arise from the adaptive and oppositional elements put to work on negotiating dominant encodings (i.e., one may acknowledge, in the politics of neo-liberal deficit management, the dominant-hegemonic economic message at the level of a nation's accounts, trade balances, etc., as long as this does not entail closing one's local hospital).

It is in the midst of the second position that Hall defines the hegemonic viewpoint: it defines within its terms the "mental horizon, the universe, of possible meanings . . . it carries with it the stamp of legitimacy it appears coterminous with what is natural, inevitable, taken for granted about the social order" ("Encoding and Decoding," 137). A mental horizon like consumer culture, stamped with legitimacy and naturalness, is essentially what is meant by consent in discussions of hegemonic dominance, and is the space in which acceptance and contestation take place. This horizon is a container, a frame that doesn't appear to have any particular interests. Hall's second position nicely clarifies a significant feature of dominant-hegemonic meaning: it is actually won and requires care, cultivation and defense (technically, it is temporary and conjunctural) since the consensus it has achieved threatens to shift and slide apart in the moving social, political and moral field of relations. In this way Hall's positions progressively trace a vector of dissent as consent fractures into dissensus, the first glimmer of which is exposed in the disjuncture of translating the global into the local and, finally, with an explicit decoding against the global.

For Fiske, receivers are, however, said to "make do" in two ways: through tactical evasions (pleasure over meaning) or resistances (meaning over pleasure). Despite such subordination, active receivers engage in the "activation" (release and distribution) of a resource's "potentialities" according to their relevance for everyday life (where text meets the social and the making becomes a "vital base" for redeployments of pleasure and power). The potential of a resource is very much a matter of "excess semiosis" that escapes hegemonic discipline. Fiske writes of a "producerly popular text" that "exposes, however reluctantly, the vulnerabilities, limitations, and weaknesses of its preferred meanings . . . its meanings exceed its own power to discipline them. . . ." (*Understanding Popular Culture*, 104). The producerly popular text is undisciplined at the contact points between lines of social force and the texts in question: the producerly text is a resource for the producerly receiver in the process making popular culture.

Such activity needs to be accessed for study in some manner, and here we see a truly heterogeneous array of methods at play in cultural studies. Even here, though, the terms are far from straightforward. Take Ien Ang's work on *Dallas*. *(Watching Dallas)* Ang takes the step of placing an advertisement asking for responses in writing. She acknowledges the gender bias of the selected channel, and situates herself among the *Dallas* viewers from whom she wants responses (which she reads symptomatically). Ang's own ambivalence (as an intellectual and feminist) about the show is also at issue. What she wants to understand is how the show gives viewers pleasure (the question of the receiver's pleasure—and pain—is an underappreciated organizing principle in its own right in cultural studies all the way from Barthes to Fiske and beyond).

Consider a further example. Henry Jenkins searches, in "*Star Trek* Rerun, Reread, Rewritten: Fan Writing as Textual Poaching," for the constraints of fan rewriting and reproducing of television shows and films such as *Star Trek*. He finds, then, in a vast terrain of fanzines, conventions, and Web rings, that the activity of fan writing as reworking itself has debts to specific genres (this is most evident in women's creative recastings). Jenkins uncovers the semiotic constraints of rewriting practices (the borrowings—romantic, utopian, erotic—that themselves shape textual poaching operations or reaping what one has not sown). Activity is socio-semiotically constrained, and it is the task of the ethnosemiotician to creatively uncover and analyze the complex factors that limit resignification.

Participatory Communication Beyond Shannon and Weaver

Counterposing cultural studies with a more rigid communication model in which the receiving process involves "inverse transmission" has been a matter of concern for a wide variety of thinkers of communication working in quite different traditions. In the language of Shannon and Weaver, "inverse transmission" of a signal reconstitutes the message and then gives it to the destination–given the technological determinations, gender, and power relations at play.

Marshall and Eric McLuhan, for instance, devoted a few pages in *The Laws of Media* to a critique of the Shannon and Weaver model on precisely the terms made famous by Hall and then Fiske: the assumption is that "communication is a kind of literal *matching* rather than resonant *making*" (*Laws of Media*, 86ff). Hall underlined repeatedly that dominant didn't mean determined, pointing to the non-identity of encoding and decoding. To borrow the terms used by the McLuhans, the Shannon and Weaver model is figure without ground; left hemisphere (quantity, precision) over right hemisphere (holistic, simultaneous); matching over making. The model embodies efficient causality–a force that is testable and controllable, without paying proper attention to the "side-effects" of communication, which it excludes, and in so doing misses the new ground or "environment" that emerges and shapes the experience of users; indeed, it transforms their worlds. For the McLuhans, communication is about making and interaction ("participation"), about freedom from fixity and rigidity. And the study of the "total situation" in which communication takes place, including residues of rational models, involves something quite in keeping with the investigation of sociosemiotic constraints—suggested in Eco's expression of the receiver's rediscovery of the *freedom of decoding*— in cultural studies (*A Theory of Semiotics*, 150).

Consider a further example. What did McLuhan and Wilfred Watson write of Mrs. Leavis's book *Fiction and the Reading Public* in their assessment of its outdated presumptions in *From Cliché to Archetype?* She was stuck in matching or "checking" communication between artist and public on the basis of the former's ability at "managing a symbolisation of something which was previously the property" of the latter. For McLuhan and Watson, "Mrs. Leavis is making the familiar literary assumption that matching, rather than making, is the function of literary training" (*From Cliché*, 174).

Making Do

Like Fiske, the McLuhans consider almost any artifact to be amenable to the study of its transformative effects on users and grounds. But their construction of the receiver liberated from the "hardware model of information theory—transportation of data from point to point" (*Laws*, 111)—is in the service of a description of the sensory surround of the new electric environment of "tactile acoustic space." In other words the McLuhans announced a theory of perception that took making to mean that receivers were creative artists. Theirs was a poetics of adaptation by degrees. I want to put this in somewhat negative terms. If for Fiske oppositionality was not guaranteed, then for McLuhan the failure to create an anti-environment "leaves us in the role of automata merely" ("Relation of Environment to Anti-Environment," 124). To claim this, McLuhan adds, is not even to give a name to it:

> That basic aspect of the human condition by which we are rendered incapable of perceiving the environment is one to which psychologists have not even referred ("Relation of Environment," 133).

I would further align Fiske and the McLuhans on the basis of their mutual interest in coping. For Fiske "the art of popular culture is the art of 'making do'." (*Reading*, 4) Throughout his career Marshall McLuhan sought refuge from fundamental socio-technological change in artistic strategies understood as coping mechanisms (artists create anti-environments, counter-situations or pen counterblasts that allow one to become aware of what is otherwise all but invisible, the environment presently structuring one's experience). A counterblast, McLuhan explained, "does not attempt to erode or explode." It calls for the creation of counter-environments "as a means of perceiving the dominant one [environment]" (*Counterblast*, 5). A counter-environment doesn't destroy, it "controls" and "creates awareness." McLuhan clarifies that art *copes* with environments by creating anti-environments (*Counterblast*, 31). It is a question for Mcluhan, it is fair to say, of the survival of certain valorized artistic practices.

There is nothing very much new in this sense of the receiver as one who copes, however, for it was already present in the groundbreaking work of Richard Hoggart. According to Hoggart, working class people do a great deal of adjusting in the face of the onslaught of massification: "'putting up with things', not simply from a passivity but because that is where one starts from, from the expectation that one will have to put up with a lot; and the maintenance of the traditional corollary of this, to put up with things cheerfully" (*Uses of Literacy*, 270).

Making do, coping, putting up with things: these are passively active responses to incoming messages that are distorted by the specific conditions and situations of receivers. I do not wish to criticize these closely related conceptions of a passive activeness of receivers for even a well-tempered activeness becomes suspiciously weak as it comes into contact with passivity; conversely, the proverbial grin and bear it or stiff upper lip are unbearably strong in their reproductions of class and gender codes. "Making" may be personally and even collectively transformative but it is no straight gate to progressive oppositionality.

Rather, it seems to me that passive activity constitutes a sort of cunning. Cunning preserves; receivers endure. I am reminded here of the very early McLuhan text *The Mechanical Bride* in which the emphasis, while not showing much interest in describing the strategies of coping of individuals within the "whirling phantasmagoria" of the commercial signscape, did proffer a quasi-critical position on the passivity of receivers of mass media through an appeal to Poe's sailor who like McLuhan's industrial man, observes the semiurgical swirling of commercial culture in which he is embedded (sinking) in order to analyze it and ultimately save himself (*The Mechanical Bride*, v-vi).

What McLuhan called strategies of individuals have been refigured by Michel de Certeau, among others, as tactical maneuvers that apparatuses of repression tolerate (turn a blind eye, allow to operate in "dark corners"). In the end, receivers endure and persist, all the while remaining fragile yet mobile targets of innumerable messages. Making is not, in the hands of McLuhan, really a choice at all, though he didn't discount that a decision could be made to match rather than make: "Faced with information overload, we have no alternative but pattern-recognition," as he put it in *Counterblast* (132).

In the conceptual language of de Certeau, which Fiske borrows, users of cultural products "make do" (*Practice of Everyday Life*, 31). These are impure receivers, not exactly non-mirrors of that which is imposed upon them, but perhaps broken or at least cracked mirrors. The break here is salutary: gaps are opened up between users of products and what such products impose upon them. de Certeau elaborates a series of ruses, poaching, quiet diversions, making something else of a message or product through subversive redeployments. "Guile" is a favorite way to describe this repertoire of trickery, though poaching has received a much more elevated status in the literature. A passive activity for de Certeau is a last resort of the weak, by which he means "a calculated action determined by the absence of a proper locus" (*Practice*, 36–7). Weakness is tactical, an art of time, of cleverly used time that has neither means nor options of its own. No illusions, here, de Certeau points out: "The actual order of things is precisely what 'popular' tactics turns to their own ends, without any illusions that it will change any time soon" (*Practice*, 26). This is a position that Fiske accepts wholesale. And the "counter" of blast and environment also puts limits on remaking.

Concluding Remarks: Coping with Matching and Making

My hypothesis is that the social scene of decoding at the telegraphy table, and later at the telephone switchboard, influenced the formulation of problems and solutions in the mathematical model of communication. Telegraphy is a gendered technology, especially after the 1870s in the US and slightly later in Canada when women broke into the hitherto masculine workplace culture. Prior to this time, as one of Thomas Edison's biographers Paul Isreal reminds us, tramp telegraphers such as the young Edison drifted from city to city in search of work and established friendships with operators down the line whose signature "touch" of their keys was known to those sensitive enough to hear (*Edison*, 22). Of course, socializing during down periods would often take place from table to table in a given office; or by operators chatting with one another or with subscribers. The telegraphic scene of decoding on an individual level influences the formulation of problems and solutions around specific practices. There were basically two ways to receive a message: listening to the short intervals (dots) and long intervals (dashes) between clicks and writing out the message in long-hand; or a decoding practice assisted by the registration on paper of the dots and dashes, which would be then translated and written out long-hand for the recipient. The *double-scene* of decoding, without or with a step of paper registration, would require the operator to translate the Morse code and then deliver the message; the final destination being someone *other than the operator* (this suggests the social inequality of the position of the operator in a service economy, and Edison was fired more than few times in the 1860s for various reasons relating to perceived insubordination). A certain level of proficiency is presupposed (that is, in terms of words-per-minute) but more important was the general knowledge that an operator could bring to fill in the inevitable gaps in the message (Edison was constantly consuming newspapers for precisely this reason; although in the telephone exchange women operators were the norm men still made the technical connections). The channel of telegraphy was filled with all sorts of noise fluctuating currents, leakages, etc. The notion of operator discretion must also be considered in its most general rather than moralistic sense because the scene of telegraphic decoding often involved discretionary interpretation even if, in the end, this simply meant informed guesswork that faithfully reproduced the original encoded message (which could be confirmed easily in the case of news stories). The issue of privacy was barely present though it would intensify with the telephonic party line.

Inverse transmission in the double scene of decoding involves supplementation of the message. From the touch of the key to the tone of a female operator's voice, to her familiarity with certain subscribers, to flirting, and eluding the invasive politics of the male foreman, etc., there is a remarkable play at work in the channel that relies upon a relay, a recoder before the decoder proper. Matching cannot be simply contrasted, emptily and unproductively with making, as if the latter was annointed with activeness against an allegedly passive matching operation. Making the link between decoding and lives lived is the hallmark of cultural studies as it has rethought the model of communication and this insight can produce an informed reading of the mathematical model as well. It is evident that the McLuhans overstated the contrast, hypervalorizing creative making, counterblasts and counter-environments. The presence of the qualification 'counter' alone alerts us to the passive-(re)activeness of this conceptualization. Indeed, the sense of "participation" that one finds in McLuhan, which is most fully elaborated in the premises of the cool media hypothesis—low informational media demand greater involvement from receivers—was not by any means absent from the transportation model. In fact, communication was pegged on the participation of a code worker, an active relay. One may only speak disparagingly about the "automata" of the transportation model (poles of sender-relay-receiver) by completely eliding the constraints of the social semiotic scene of decoding. The processes of subjectification that rendered young women telephone operators *active* (*Hello Central?*, 61) nodes in the labor process also gave rise to resistances and strategies of coping (personal and collective) with discipline, standardization, exhaustion, exploitation, etc.

Fiske, McLuhan, and de Certeau specifically alert us to some of the dynamics of coping receivers and these descriptions are some of the richest passages in cultural studies. Yet these insights also need to be brought to the scenes of decoding of the mathematical model. The contrast, in other words, between "matching" and "making" is far from simple.

Works Cited

Ien Ang, *Watching Dallas*, London: Methuen, 1985.

Ian Angus, "From Competitive Capitalism to Consumer Society," in *Primal Scenes of Communication*, Buffalo: State University Press of New York, 2000, pp. 77–88.

Michel de Certeau, *The Practice of Everyday Life*, trans. Steven Randall, Berkeley: University of California Press, 1984.

Umberto Eco, *A Theory of Semiotics*, Bloomington: Indiana University Press, 1976.

John Fiske, *Television Culture*, London and New York: Routledge, 1989.

John Fiske, *Understanding Popular Culture*, Boston: Unwin Hyman, 1989.

John Fiske, *Reading the Popular*, Boston: Unwin Hyman, 1989.

John Fiske, *Introduction to Communication Studies*, Second Edition, London and New York: Routledge, 1990

Gary Genosko, *McLuhan and Baudrillard: The Masters of Implosion*, London: Routledge, 1999.

Antonio Gramsci, "Americanism and Fordism," in *Selections from the Prison Notebooks*, trans. Quintin Hoare and Geoffrey Nowell Smith, New York: International Publishers, 1971, 279–318.

Stuart Hall, "Encoding and Decoding," *Culture, Media, Language*, eds. Stuart Hall, Dorothy Hobson, Andrew Lowe and Paul Willis, London: Hutchinson, 1980, 128–38.

Richard Hoggart, *The Uses of Literacy*, London: Chatto and Windus, 1957.

Paul Israel, *Edison: A Life of Invention*, New York: John Wiley & Sons, 1998.

Henry Jenkins, "*Star Trek* Rerun, Reread, Rewritten: Fan Writing as Textual Poaching," in *Close Encounters: Film, Feminism and Science Fiction*, ed. Constance Penley *et al.* Minneapolis: University of Minnesota Press, 1991, 171–202.

Michèle Martin, *Hello Central? Gender, Technology and Culture in the Formation of the Telephone System*, Montreal: McGill-Queens University Press, 1991.

Marshall McLuhan, *The Mechanical Bride*, Boston: Beacon, 1951.

Marshall McLuhan, "The Relation of Environment to Anti-Environment," in *Innovations: Essays on Art & Ideas*, ed. Bernard Bergonzi, London: Macmillan, 1968, 122–33.

Marshall McLuhan, *Counterblast*, London: Rapp & Whiting, 1969.

Marshall McLuhan and Wilfred Watson, *From Cliché to Archetype*, New York: Viking, 1970.

Marshall and Eric McLuhan, *Laws of Media*, Toronto: University of Toronto Press, 1988.

Claude E. Shannon and Warren Weaver, *The Mathematical Theory of Communication*, Urbana: University of Illinois Press, 1964.

Donald F. Theall, *The Virtual Marshall McLuhan*. Montreal-Kingston: McGill-Queen's University Press, 2001.

CHAPTER TWO

Marshall McLuhan and Media and Cultural Studies

NICK STEVENSON

The modern dissemination of cultural forms has radically restructured the parameters of time and space. From the production of daily newspapers to the electronic transmission of television soaps, the technical forms of mass communication are altering the experiential context of everyday life. Technical media are currently capable of relocating symbolic impressions globally and at an ever-quickening rate. The globe is straddled by competing international news agencies that are capable of cueing in local and national information networks. Some of these "news events" are transmitted in so-called real time. This both recontextualises information across the permeable borders of nation states and gives the appearance of instantaneous communication. The split-second transmission of stories, regardless of their actual content, has made the world a smaller place while correspondingly shrinking human conceptions of time. And yet the mass media's impact upon the construction of horizontal spatial relations and the temporal dimensions of social life remains chronically underresearched. Theoretical problems of this order remain at least analytically separate from the issues related to cultural content that have dominated certain schools of mass communication. Today, given the growing pervasiveness and globalisation of electronic forms of media, such concerns demand further investigation.

The radical impact of new forms of communication upon the dimensions of space, time and human perception are the dominant motifs of Marshall McLuhan.

His work was, initially at least, widely recognised as articulating some of the most profound changes that the new media technologies were ushering in. In cultural and media studies, his ideas were at first warmly welcomed as making a major break-through in articulating some of the dimensions of the emergent electric culture. But the bubble of enthusiasm was soon to burst, and McLuhan's propositions were wide-ly dismissed as exhibiting a form of technological determinism. Such has been cul-tural studies concern to distance itself from technical explanations that it has been neglected to analyse the difference cultural media make. It presumably makes a dif-ference to modern cultures whether they receive most of their information from global television networks, or from a national press printed only once a week. While I shall return to problems in McLuhan's work raised by cultural studies, here I aim to move against the grain of his most vocal detractors and forcibly suggest that his work be critically re-evaluated by cultural theorists of the media. I will defend a version of McLuhan's writing that does not rest well with culturalism: that McLuhan's emphasis on technical media is important for distinguishing between different modes of cultural transmission (oral, literate, electric) and that these media structurate intersubjective social relations. There are nevertheless problems with McLuhan's approach, which I will raise while opening out the importance of the questions he asked.

The Medium Is the Message

Marshall McLuhan is best known for the provocative thesis that the most impor-tant aspect of media is not to be located within issues connected to cultural con-tent, but in the technical medium of communication. The medium, declares McLuhan, is the message. According to him, to attend to the ideological or semi-otic construction of, say, an article in today's newspaper is to miss the point. McLuhan insists, again and again, that the study of the way technical forms of media shape human perception constitutes the most important theoretical issue facing media studies today. The best example he supplies of this process involves the importance of electric light in recontextualising social relations (McLuhan, 1994: 52). The electric light I switch on in my office each morning carries no message, but transforms relations of space and time. For example, it allows me to work late in the evening or early in the morning. This affects the way I structure my public and private life. Of course the electric light has wider consequences in that shop-ping centres, leisure facilities and workplaces can be operable 24 hours a day. Again, it is electric light's capacity to restructure social relations and perceptions that is given analytic priority.

McLuhan, however, was not always of this particular cast of mind. In his first major work *The Mechanical Bride* (1951), he was very critical of the opportunities for manipulation and control opened up by emergent forms of media. Although many of the themes that were to propel McLuhan into wider forms of public recognition were already apparent at this juncture, his writing has much in common with the literary sensibilities of Raymond Williams and the early Frankfurt school (Stevenson, 2002). Consumer society, he argued, echoing more familiar approaches to mass media, imposes a form of passivity upon those subjects who live on an insubstantial diet of canned music and packaged news programmes. Here McLuhan criticises contemporary culture for only offering the illusion of diversity, producing mass uniformity, and eroding the social base of good literature. Advertising both produces social distinctions in order to ideologically mask commercial practices of buying and selling, and has a dehumanising effect on those caught up in the process. The commodification of the most intimate human relations reduces the expression of sexuality to "a problem in mechanics and hygiene" (McLuhan, 1951: 99). The mechanical reproduction of representations of the human body both abstracts from the sensuous nature of human experience and provides a breeding ground for sadistic desires and fantasies. Thus the alienating effect of modern forms of communication both produces pathological side effects and acts as a means of domination. But in McLuhan's subsequent writing he abandoned what might be termed a critical-literary disposition towards consumer culture in favour of a more celebrative mode.

The bulk of McLuhan's later writing is concerned to develop a theory of media that reverses many of his earlier reflections. In the first place, McLuhan no longer takes cultural content as his primary point of concern. In the main, this is due to his attention to the technologies of cultural dissemination. Here modern technologies are no longer viewed as alienating. This is because they are best represented as extensions of the body or, as McLuhan occasionally remarks, the human nervous system. By this he means that the wheel is an extension of the foot and clothing is the technical projection of skin. As a further illustration, and perhaps more importantly in terms of McLuhan's thesis on the media, the book is conceptualised as an outgrowth of the eye, while radio is represented as the technological expression of the ear.

Crucial to an understanding of these processes is the dominance of print culture after the appearance of Gutenberg's bible in early modern Europe (McLuhan, 1962). Following Innis (1951), McLuhan argues that the portable medium of print enabled ideas and perspectives to be circulated across space. In terms of time, the dominance of a writing culture had shortened human memories, because information could now be stored in the durable medium of the book. However, the portability of the book, as Anderson (1983) also shows, allows for the cultural expression of nationalism outside of the control of established forms of religious authority. Anderson argues that the period between 1500 and 1550 combined print capitalism's need to find new markets, the technological advances of the printing press, and the expression of languages other than Latin in print. These factors created new languages of power that helped foster forms of national legitimacy undermining the central authority of the feudal church. While McLuhan makes a similar point, his main emphasis lies elsewhere. The fixing of language into print is important not only because it creates a spatial bias, but because it fosters a bias within human perception. McLuhan argues that "The invention of the alphabet, like the invention of the wheel, was the translation or reduction of a complex, organic interplay of spaces into a single space. The phonetic alphabet reduced the use of all the senses at once, which is oral speech, to a merely visual code" (McLuhan, 1962: 45).

In the medieval period, manuscripts were firmly located in physical space, rarely used punctuation, and were mostly read aloud. Medieval scholarship, in McLuhan's terms, was more for the ear than the eye. With the move towards a predominantly print culture the human senses had become increasingly compartmentalised and specialised. Whereas oral cultures allowed the rich interplay of all the senses, print culture abstracted writing from speech and promoted the visual component of the human organism. The dominance of written forms of communication cultivated a rationalised culture that was linear, uniform and infinitely repeatable. Print culture replaces the sensuous play of oral cultures with a predictable and standardised mode of thought. Further, the hegemony of typography not only "discourages minute verbal play" (McLuhan, 1962: 158) through the unification of grammar, spelling and meaning, but shapes modern forms of individualism. Book culture requires that reading practices are silent and attentive, that the text has an author, and that the translation of a shared collective culture is converted into one dependent upon individual forms of expression. As McLuhan comments, "print is the technology of individualism" (1962: 158). Print supplies the cultural resources for national forms of uniformity, while simultaneously giving birth to notions of individuality. In achieving this, the Gutenberg press converted space and time into the calculable, the rational and the predictable. The linear and logical emphasis of writing was mirrored in the uniform regimentation of clock time. The rationalising impact of the printing press paved the way for geographical maps, railway timetables, and notions of perspective in painting. According to McLuhan, the advent of print culture had both developed certain human senses (sight) rather than others, and shaped a particular form of human rationality. This, however, was all to change with the arrival of electric forms of communication.

The transition to electronic communication can be connected with a change in the experiential nature of modernity. This is best represented through the gradual displacement of hot media with cool media. A hot medium is one that disallows participation and is high in informational content. Conversely, cooler media leave more spaces for the audience to participate, and exhibit lower levels of information intensity. McLuhan explains:

> speech is a cool medium of low definition, because so little is given and so much has to be filled in by the listener. On the other hand, hot media do not leave so much to be filled in or completed by the audience. Hot media are, therefore, low in participation, and cool media are high in participation or completion by the audience. (McLuhan, 1994: 23)

The most obvious example of a cool medium is the telephone. The telephone is a dialogic medium that normally requires at least two people to participate in communication. Conversely, print culture remains a hot medium in that the activity of reading makes fewer demands upon the subject in terms of shaping the flow of information. In McLuhan's terms the telephone "demands complete participation, unlike the written and printed page" (McLuhan, 1994: 267). McLuhan is also aware that the telephone, by making its users constantly available, also has the effect of changing relations of power, and conceptions of the public and the private. Under the previous medium of communication, book culture was dependent upon reading practices that took place in private as opposed to public spaces, and knowledge production was undertaken by a small cast of authors. Cooler media, like the telephone, decentralise the production of knowledge in that they involve a wider range of participants and thereby democratise the formation of opinion. Interestingly, McLuhan argues that it is a characteristic of "bookish" intellectuals to wish to extend so-called enlightened perspectives into societies in more backward regions. This, if the argument is followed, is the effect of an increasingly outmoded form of communication that depends upon centralised forms of knowledge production. The new media, such as the telephone, have ended relations of dominance in communicative relations and have in effect produced a system which no central authority can govern.

Similarly, McLuhan argues that television is cold whereas cinema is hot. The social practice of sitting in a cinema effectively isolated from other members of the audience disallows audience forms of participation. The activity of film viewing, as one might expect, for McLuhan bears a strong family resemblance to the passivity imposed upon the audience by book reading. The medium of film is centralised and authoritarian, requiring the film maker to transform the audience into another world (McLuhan, 1994: 285). Alternatively, where a hot medium like film spells out meanings, the cooler practice of watching television leaves more work for the audience to do. Television, as a more decentred medium than film, allows for the expression of regional dialect, and as the picture quality of most television sets was poor at the time McLuhan was writing, he argued that this converted spectators into more equal partners in the production of meaning. Television, in this respect, cultivated what McLuhan called "depth participation" (1994: 321).

The reconstitution of media into electronic forms of communication also has implications for the reworking of space and time. Previously McLuhan had largely followed Innis by arguing that whereas oral societies were time biased, literate cultures were space biased. However, the displacement of print by electronic circuitry rendered "Innis's" earlier reflections redundant. Space and time had been annihilated. To understand this we would have to reconsider McLuhan's view of the media. Print culture promoted individualism inasmuch as it implied a privatised mode of reception. If an individual wished to read a book she would actively have to seek it out. But under modern conditions, according to McLuhan, cultural forms "pour upon us instantly and continuously" (McLuhan and Fiore, 1967:16). The interaction between modern subjects and communication networks is no longer confined to a few lonely hours before bedtime. Today the lives of the globe's citizens are wrapped around a seemingly endless encounter with material and symbolic modes of communication. Newspapers are read on buses and trains, car radios are tuned to the morning news, joggers listen to talking books while exercising and people make love in front of the television. The mediated experience of modernity is one of "a whirling phantasmagoria" (McLuhan, 1951: v). For McLuhan, modernity is best characterised as the unceasing relocation of information in time and space. Here communication systems put us in constant and immediate touch with different perspectives. The co-ordinates of time and space have vanished, to herald a world where the sense of individualised detachment fostered by a book culture has given way to one where everyone is "profoundly involved with everyone else" (McLuhan and Fiore, 1967: 61). The explosion of the new media has disrupted the visual bias of written forms of communication, returning the globe's citizens to a shared culture that has much in common with that of oral societies. The global village has swept aside the hierarchical, uniform and individualising culture of print production and replaced it with a more tactile culture of simultaneous happenings.

McLuhan, prefiguring much of the current talk on the death of the nation state, comments:

> Department sovereignties have melted away as rapidly as national sovereignties under conditions of electric speed. Obsession with the older patterns of mechanical, one-way expansion from centre to margins is no longer relevant to our electric world. Electricity does not centralise, but decentralises. (McLuhan, 1994: 35–36)

Just as Foucault (1980) and modern feminist movements have argued that power is everywhere, so, McLuhan suggests, are the tentacles of mass communication. A culture driven along by electricity does not flow from any one place or location, but is quite literally organised into networks that have no connecting centre. The technology of communication, therefore, extends our central nervous system into a sensuous global embrace with the rest of humanity. This renders redundant temporal (past and present) and spatial (near and far) distinctions. Those most in touch with the new electronic environment have relinquished the old means of perception delivered by an outmoded print culture. Here McLuhan remains representative of the specific cultural context in which he was writing. The counter culture in the sixties was interested in communication technology due to its perceived capacity to make community. The development of new cultural media like popular music and television created an exciting sense of possibility by potentially reversing the atomising effects of more traditional cultural practices.

These are important points, to which I will return. For the moment, I want to indicate that for McLuhan the elimination of space and time is tied to technological advances in mass communications. If we take a look at our morning newspaper we can immediately see that it inhabits a radically different form to that of the traditional novel. In place of the linear progression of a narrative we are confronted by what McLuhan calls a "communal mosaic" (McLuhan, 1994: 204). A newspaper has a multiplicity of authors and a variety of features and sections (sports page, fashion section, foreign news, editorial) that resist the single point of view evident in the book. The collage-like layout of the modern newspaper will also contain a number of items that have been transmitted from contexts far removed from those who either read or produce the newspaper. The speeding up and globalisation of news-gathering practices mean that temporality and distance will become progressively unimportant in governing newspaper content. Further, McLuhan explicitly argues that, as regards content, it is the consumers rather than those who own and control the means of production who are determinant (McLuhan, 1994: 216). As space and time, as well as patterns of ownership, become irrelevant to the content of the newspaper it is the audience's need for participation that shapes this process. This is nurtured by the fact that modern forms of communication enable audiences to travel through time and space. Before the mass production of photographs, travel was practised "to encounter the strange and unfamiliar" (McLuhan, 1994: 198). Now, returning to our morning paper, we can familiarise ourselves with the Grand Canyon or the Eiffel Tower by glancing at the travel pages. But just as space has been abolished so have been linear conceptions of time (McLuhan, 1969: 122). Under electronic forms of communication the globe has become both historically and spatially visible. When we scan the newspaper we may be moving our eyes across stories from different parts of the world and events from human history. A single newspaper might contain articles regarding a new film on the Russian revolution, photographs of what our city looked like in the 1920s, or a feature on youth culture's attempt to revive the 1970s. This is why McLuhan suggests that the practice of reading a newspaper enables us to travel in time and space without leaving our own home.

These reflections lead on to McLuhan's concept of implosion. In preliterate cultures, he argues, "there is no art in our sense, but the whole environment is experienced as unitary" (McLuhan, 1969: 31). The socially and sensorily integrated world of oral societies, as we have seen, was radically altered by the rationalising impulse of print. This led to the production of a minority, hierarchical and specialised expert culture. The emergence of the public sphere in the eighteenth century, as Habermas (1989) has shown, was intimately tied up with the production of a literate bourgeois society. But while Habermas ambivalently highlights the communicative potential of literate forms of production, McLuhan views this development as creating a centralised top-down culture, which encompasses rigid boundary distinctions. The specialisation of print separated the domains of aesthetics, politics, economics, and the public and the private. The vertical and horizontal relations of these spheres has, however, been radically redrawn through the impact of electronic communication. The new media technologies have restructured social life to the extent that you do not need to be an expert to take part. We now inhabit an overlapping world that has obliterated cultural hierarchies and the separation of spheres. The globe has imploded vertically, temporally and horizontally. Humanity, McLuhan goes on, has collapsed in on itself, returning to the village-like state characteristic of oral societies.

The domain of politics is no longer readily separable from the sphere of communication by which policy is made public. The point about the speeded-up culture of modernity is not that it expands the power of a political establishment that is able to colonise public discourse. Instead the implosion of the media of mass communication into the political domain brings about a society where the media is politics and politics is the media. McLuhan and Fiore (1968) make the point that our political representatives can literally make or invent the news. Further, the corresponding implosion of the public into the private has brought an end to the public sphere. The private realm of critical reflection is continually breached by new media that demand attention, thereby hooking the human organism into the global tides of opinion formation. Cultural implosion has converted a rational public into an interactive mass or, as McLuhan occasionally puts it, an electronic circuit of energy.

Not only has the media imploded into politics, but showbusiness has imploded into education. We could argue that young people's current obsession with video games makes the bookwork associated with traditional forms of education seem unexciting and dull. Educational institutions are now utilising film, television and video as part of the instructive process. According to McLuhan, this will eventually produce hybridised cultural forms that are both entertaining and educational. The notion of the hybrid is an important one for McLuhan. This is because it encourages us to abandon linear patterns of development for the consideration of spatial constellations. Magazine production, has, according to McLuhan and Powers (1989), been transformed by colour television. The emergence of glossy covers, colour pictures and more user-friendly layouts has come about as the medium of magazine production has responded to technological developments in television. This point would have been missed had our analysis been content to trace through the linear emergence of magazine production. McLuhan fruitfully suggests that the historical development of a particular field of media should be related to other fields of cultural production. The technical hybridisation of media forms has produced radical effects, restructuring related fields of production. To enforce this idea, I would draw attention to the hybridisation of music cassettes and the novel into talking books, the merger of television and computers in the development of digital television, the integration of television and video found on MTV, and McLuhan's (1994: 231) own example: that the high production values of the cinema have, changed the nature of advertising. These comments build into McLuhan's overall view of the media as being like a hurricane that has torn apart stable relations of time and space, while the hybridised and imploded culture of post-literate societies are continually shifting the contours of modern experience.

Space and Time: Technology and Cultural Studies

The views of Marshall McLuhan were originally applauded by some and criticised by others. I do not intend to uncritically defend his perspectives here, although they remain germane in mass communication theory because of their concern with issues related to space and time. These themes remain important, given the current lack of attention to them within much media and cultural theory. Along with Adam (1990), I think that concerns around social or media time should avoid positing theoretical dualisms. By this she means that constructed social time should not be pitted against so-called real or natural time. Adam argues provocatively that time is best seen as a multifaceted concept where no absolute distinctions can be made between symbolic and natural time. Adam summarises: "It is not either winter or December, or hibernation time for the tortoise, or one o'clock, or time for Christmas dinner. It is planetary time, biological time, clock and calendar time, natural and social time all at once" (Adam, 1990: 16).

A hermeneutic concern for the way media inform the experience of temporality, that also avoided subject-object dualism, should be concerned to investigate the means by which time structures social action. However, while it is at least arguable that cultural theory has a reasonable pedigree with respect to questions of time, the same cannot be said of spatial relations. Edward Soja (1989) has shown that cultural theory has consistently privileged the investigation of social being and time over that of space. In a theoretical vein similar to that of Adam, Soja suggests that space, when it is considered at all, is often conceptualised as a reified and objective product. Just as time is interwoven with human actions and meanings, so space does not merely act as the undifferentiated background of human interaction but is socially created and transformed by such activity. Space and time are not the *empty containers* of social activity, but both enable and constrain human action. Further, spatial and temporal relations, as McLuhan well understood, do not stand apart from social practices, but are both produced and reproduced by them. This of course does not commit me to defending the specific way in which McLuhan represented the transformation of space and time in his theory of media. But given McLuhan's concern to discuss notions of space and time in connection with the media, and accepting these themes are currently under-represented in the literature, the question now needs to be asked: how do we account for the resistance to his writing within cultural and media studies?

There are two related reasons that are usually offered in opposition to McLuhan's perspectives. The first, which has been most consistently outlined by Raymond Williams (1974, 1985), is the objection that McLuhan's technological determinism acts as an ideological justification of dominant social relations. McLuhan's analysis of the medium of communication, Williams claims, is isolated from broader sociological and cultural contexts. This in effect *desocialises* media analysis in that McLuhan renders invisible the ways in which dominant authority relations structure cultural production, content and reception. In effect, McLuhan renders such questions irrelevant, as the social impact of cultural technology is abstracted from the analysis of specific social relations. The charge that McLuhanism leaves unquestioned global capitalist relations has been a consistent theme of some of McLuhan's sternest critics (Finkelstein, 1968; Nairn, 1969). This strain of analysis can be related to Stuart Hall's (1986) argument that McLuhan's cultural disposition towards the media of mass communication has much in common with uncritical forms of postmodernism. McLuhan's writing turns from the critical-literary perspective evident in his early writing towards a more euphoric position. This stance parallels some of the developments evident within French postmodernism, which has similarly advocated the abandonment of cultural critique. Here the critic is accused of lacking an adequately serious disposition, and of advocating a form of consumerist lying back and enjoying the proliferation of discourses within the global village. There is much in these charges. McLuhan, for instance, has very little to say about the globalisation of capitalist relations that make the global village imaginable. Further, the extent to which the transnational

development of communications technology can be tied into the fostering of capitalist patterns of organisation, control and lifestyle is also neglected. The progressive commercialisation of public space, as Mattelart and Mattelart (1992) have
argued, has meant that hegemonic modes of dominance can be tied into the shift
from public to private operators, and from national to transnational ones. These
issues can also be connected to the realisation of the cultural rather than technical
forms of hybridity that are currently being promoted by globalisation processes. If
on one level we are witnessing the international spread of an homogeneous capi-
talistic culture, at another there has occurred the eruption of different identities. This
is a product of capitalism, in that post-Fordist forms of production need to produce
different lifestyle orientations on the part of consumers, as well as being evidence
of the symbolic capacity of complex, unstable identities to remake themselves
through a global bricolage (Robertson, 1992). The political emergence of hybrid eth-
nic identities has occurred underneath the disciplinary discourses of the nation state,
while articulating connections with a more globally oriented commercial culture. At
the local level, therefore, one can detect a turning away from the uncertain flux of
modernity into more definite social identities, and a more emancipatory, less reactive, recognition of difference (Hall, 1991).

Both Williams's and Hall's criticisms draw our attention to the fact that
McLuhan's attempt to understand the networks of communication is of an overly
technical nature. His concern to address the technical media of communication
means that the meanings that are generated by the intersection of global, national
and local relationships are, to take Williams's phrase, "distinguishable only by their
variable sense-ratios" (Williams, 1974:127). This is a similar point to the one made
by Miller (1971) in his classic study of McLuhan. Meanings, Miller contends, are
not governed by the technical outgrowth of the senses but by linguistic practices.
Following Saussure, linguistic meaning is not determined by technical conditions
(the relationship between signifier and signified is arbitrary) but by the intersubjective nature of language. The interactive nature of, say, a television programme has
more to do with whether it is an open or closed text, or whether the programme is
invested with *relevance* by the audience. The communicative nature of television is
not, therefore, determined by the technical medium. Also like many of the postmodernists who follow him, McLuhan displaces attention from the impact that relations
of power and force have within the social-historical world. His theoretical neglect
of mass communication's role in the production of symbolic meanings and the maintenance of dominant social relations unnecessarily brackets off critical questions
related to the organisation of institutions, culture and ideology.

And yet, while all this is true up to a point, I am left with the impression that
the baby is being thrown out with the bathwater. While the cultural critics are correct to point to the limitations of McLuhan's analysis, their own concerns also con-

tain certain allusions. Critical analysis within mass communication since McLuhan has paid very little attention to those questions which could be deemed central to his engagement. This might, for the sake of convenience, be compressed into a single question. How has the development of media of communication reshaped the perceptions of time and space within contemporary society? The way McLuhan addresses these issues is certainly open to question, and in this respect the charges of technological determinism carry a good deal of critical force. Yet I would argue, along with Carey (1989), Meyrowitz (1985) and J.B. Thompson (1990), that cultural media, regardless of their actual content, have had a radical impact on the nature of social life. The above authors, like McLuhan, argue that media of communication restructure time and space and thereby help shape intersubjective social relations. In this way, viewed less deterministically than McLuhan often presented himself, his writing remains full of insight.

McLuhan offers an interesting analysis of the way in which the introduction of the telegraph transformed human intersubjective relations. He reminds us that, like the telephone, the telegraph makes us continually present and accessible to other persons for communicative relations. The technical medium of the telegraph, for instance, allows us to maintain intimate social relations across time and space, while also structurating those relations. In short, the telegraph does not govern the cultural content of our personal messages, but it does play some part in helping to form them. McLuhan (1994: 256) offers the example of a number of Oxford undergraduates who, on reading that Rudyard Kipling was paid ten shillings for each word he published, telegraphed him. Their telegraph message contained 10 shillings and asked for one of his best words. Kipling promptly replied, "Thanks." We can judiciously argue that while technical media do not determine cultural meanings, as McLuhan implies, they do play some role in helping to form the life-world relations characteristic of modernity.

J.B. Thompson (1990) notes that the transmission of culture in a society dominated by mass means of communication largely takes place without the constant forms of feedback that are distinctive of everyday talk. However, the one-way interactive flow of the television allows new forms of resistance on the part of the audience, in that they are distanciated from the producers of the message. Whereas television makes present the back regions of those who appear on television, my own reactions are absent. When America and Britain decided to invade Iraq without United Nations approval these actions became immediately available to a global television audience, but what is absent is the apparent anger and disdain of the television audience. The cultural technologies and media of everyday life have served to restructure much of modern experience. This discussion should warn against certain trends within poststructuralism that view social and technical relations as radically separable from the production of meaning. Again, while the meaning of last night's six o'clock news is not determined by certain technical apparatuses, it might make a difference to producers and consumers alike whether the information was heard second hand down the telephone, on television while trying to keep up with *Star Trek* on a different channel, or listening to the radio while putting the children to bed. To illustrate these arguments further I will briefly outline the contributions of two other thinkers indebted to McLuhan. Both Jack Goody and Anthony Giddens place at the centre of their analyses of historical change a concern for the media of communication. Arguably, they do this in a way that avoids some of the problems that we encountered with McLuhan.

Oral, Print and Modern Cultures: Jack Goody and Anthony Giddens

The aspects of Goody's (1977; Goody and Watt, 1968) writing I shall view refer to the distinctions he expertly draws between literate and oral societies. The novelty of Goody's approach lies in his insistence that the main differences between the two cultures are to be located within the specific media of communication. Similarly to McLuhan, Goody argues that the significance of these technological factors can be judged independently from ideological considerations. The differences in the communicative acts representative of oral and literate societies have far-reaching consequences for the sociological nature of the respective cultures. Generally speaking, oral societies have a much more pragmatic disposition towards language than is usually evident within literate societies. The social transmission of culture, as one would expect, predominantly takes place in face-to-face interaction, where knowledge is primarily geared towards maintaining the existing set of social relations. Such is the need to maintain tradition across time rather than space that knowledge that does not perform this function tends to be quickly discarded. The transition from a predominantly oral to a literate/oral culture involves the storage of knowledge in written forms. This process allows the emergence of a more critical disposition in that subjects are freed from an overarching concern with the oral transmission of knowledge. The objectification of culture in writing also creates the conditions for critique as it becomes easier for readers to perceive logical inconsistencies and contradictions. If I decided to read this book out to an assembled audience over a number of days it would undoubtedly be difficult for those listening to become aware of some of the problems that remain under-theorised. Conversely, as reviewers and current readers are no doubt aware, the formulation of critical forms of understanding is enhanced, especially given the complex nature of many of the arguments, by the discussion's availability in writing. Further, as most of the people who sit down and read this book will be unknown to the authors, this too enhances the possibility of critical forms of reception. Goody remarks that the advent of writing allowed for the more impersonal means of assessment that are characteristic of modern bureaucracies. Writing will permit those who are distant in time and space from the author to discuss a set of arguments without the results being automatically fed back to the producer of the text. This may produce a certain anxiety within the author, but it also involves a definite break with the more personal forms of interaction evident in oral cultures.

Hence Goody deconstructs the oppositions between the civilised and the non-civilised that are traditionally associated with the contrasting forms of life in literate and oral societies, without advocating a form of cultural relativism. It is, according to him, the distinctions apparent within the means of communication, rather than radically different mind sets, that account for the relatively closed nature of oral societies.

These somewhat compressed reflections throw an interesting critical light on McLuhan's writings. Goody, along with other writers (Chartier, 1989; Thompson, 1990), argues that the transition from a predominantly oral to a print culture is more discontinuous than McLuhan allows. Goody agrees with McLuhan that print had an individualising and specialising effect upon culture, and that it also creates hierarchies of knowledge and social closure. These cultural changes, however, exist alongside the continued importance of an oral tradition. Writing did not so much replace an oral culture as both transform and modify it. Parents still pass on folk memories to their children, and other groups maintain a sense of the past through the performance of popular songs, ballads and stories, not all of which are written down. For all of McLuhan's claims to want to break with the linear grip that print has on the modern psyche, his discussion of the successive stages in the development of the mode of communication (oral, literate, electric) maintains a segmented shape. Print supplements oral culture rather than replacing it.

Goody emphasises the communicative possibilities that are opened up by print. McLuhan, as we saw, tended to view this development negatively as producing sensorily impoverished, uniform and homogeneous forms of life. This bleak reading of print culture unnecessarily discounts some of the more emancipatory opportunities that have flowered in the wake of written communication. As Goody amply demonstrates, the fixing of discourse into print has aided a form of rational, critical consciousness it would be difficult to imagine contemporary life without. Print culture, we may conclude, in opposition to McLuhan, is best represented dialectically. While it certainly had a rationalising impact on the production of knowledge, it also secured the reflexive grounds for counter-factual forms of engagement that have transformed the trajectory of modern cultures.

Anthony Giddens's (1990, 1991) theory of radicalised modernity represents one of the most original and far-reaching attempts to contemplate some of the transformations taking place in the modern world. In pursuing this theoretical project he represents modernity as a runaway juggernaut, where every attempt to order its path produces unintended consequences causing it to spin further out of control. For this reason, we can never gain total control over society. In light of these reflections, Giddens argues that modernity changes at a much faster pace than any prior society, that it has extended its global reach, and finally, that it has had a profoundly transformative effect on traditional social practices. I do not have the space to trace through the wider sets of issues ushered in by these remarks; here I want to concentrate on two areas that have been opened up by modern institutions which are central to Giddens's discussion.

First, contemporary societies have witnessed the development of a time-space distanciation that was not evident in pre-modern societies. By this Giddens means that within the pre-modern period time and space were always strongly located in terms of physical place. The turning of night into day or the passing of seasons served as localised markers of time and space. With the invention of clock time we could say that time has become separated from space, and that time and space have become empty phenomena. The pulling apart of time and space can be visualised in calendars, railway timetables and maps. These devices enable time and space to be co-ordinated without any reference to notions of place—they are abstract means of ordering social activity. The remembering of a birthday does not require the immediate presence of the person in question. The use of calendars helps us to keep track of important social occasions in ways that are not dependent upon concrete local factors.

This leads on to the second aspect of Giddens's contribution I wish to consider—the disembedding of social systems. Modernity, according to Giddens, is a post-traditional social order, where the "emptying out" of time and space allows for the stretching of social relations. If we think for a moment about the globalisation of television networks this should become clear. While global does not yet mean universal, international media organisations are able to transport images and representations across time and space and on to the television sets of the globe's citizens. This tends to convert local wars into global conflicts. In McLuhan's terms the globe has imploded in on itself, eradicating time and space. For Giddens, the relocation of information from localised contexts, evident within modern communication networks, is made possible via the uncoupling of time and space, and disembedding mechanisms such as technical media. These devices involve the separation of social relations "from local contexts of interaction and their restructuring across indefinite spans of time-space" (Giddens, 1990: 21). For example, Giddens argues, expert systems exhibit many of these features, as the knowledge they deploy has a validity independent of the agents who make use of them. Expert systems are part of the fabric of everyday life and have the capacity of extending social relations in time and space. Every time I read a popular feature on health care, expert frames of reference are being recontextualised in terms of certain lifestyle decisions that I might make. The decision to stop eating meat might be informed by an article I read in a women's magazine, a leaflet attacking McDonald's, or my mistrust of the assurances offered by state-employed scientists—these are all examples of the way technical knowledge becomes routinely reconstituted in modernity.

Giddens (1991: 24–7) explicitly recognises the role played by technical media in his short discussion of the cultural make-up of newspapers. It was the invention of the telegraph that allowed the early newspapers to separate space from notions of place. Up until this point, the content of the press had been determined by whether or not news items were close at hand. The telegraph's capacity to disembed information from social location meant that media content was less determined by proximity in space and time, while allowing newspapers to become much more event driven. The transformation brought about by the technical medium of the telegraph reshaped the nature of newspapers. Giddens markedly follows McLuhan by arguing that the restructuring of time and space allows distant events to become part of everyday life, and reshapes modern media content into a collage effect.

The long-term impact of the changing contours of modernity has both unifying and fragmentary effects. The mosaic nature of the newspaper, for instance, both encourages the view that humanity shares a single world while making us aware of its diversity. Again, in a vein very similar to that of McLuhan, Giddens holds that the implosion of global forms of life enhances the notion that human beings currently share a number of opportunities and problems. I agree with Giddens, however, that social forces of unification are also accompanied by processes of fragmentation. As Giddens (1991: 188) argues, the act of reading a newspaper may on one level make us aware of issues related to globalisation, but on another it involves, given the amount of newsprint available, the conscious selection of certain information forms over others. The emphasis McLuhan places on the unificatory implications of communications technology and the relative unimportance of the meanings that these help generate leads him to bypass this point.

In other respects Giddens's remarks suggest similar criticisms of McLuhan to those offered by Goody. Goody and Giddens characterise oral cultures as being in the grip of traditional forms of life that integrate the time-space organisation of the village. The introduction of writing for Goody enables critical reflection whereas for Giddens it has a similar effect in that it contributes towards time-space distanciation. This allows the production of knowledge to be bracketed off from the reinterpretation of traditional codes and practices. The decoupling of time-space from place and the critical appropriation of knowledge from tradition creates the conditions for the reflexive nature of modernity. We have already seen how the routine disembedding of expert forms of knowledge help sustain critical practices. Giddens writes: "In all cultures, social practices are routinely altered in the light of ongoing discoveries which feed into them. But only in the era of modernity is the revision of convention radicalised to apply (in principle) to all aspects of human life" (1990: 38–9).

The reflexive arch of modernity heralds a world where ultimately nothing is certain or free from questioning, including reason. Reflexivity, or the altering of human action in the light of new knowledge, is deeply inscribed in modern institutions. Again McLuhan's reactive reading of the breakdown of tradition, and its quasi-return under electronic forms of communication, should be questioned. The new media of mass communication have not returned modern societies to a form of rationality evident in the pre-modern village. On this point, his writing is irredeemably flawed. McLuhan is right to argue that the media constitute new forms of involvement and spatial connection, but fundamentally mistaken in the extent to which he fails to make the connection between cultural media and reflexive questioning. To follow Giddens, then, we could argue that one of the primary mechanisms that have made new knowledge available has been the medium of mass communication. Various media of communication have flooded audiences' lives with perspectives that have been severed from previous locations within space and time. The critical examination of existing social practices is surely connected to the networks of communication that circulate revised forms of knowledge. Thus, for Goody and Giddens, notions of cultural critique have an intimate connection to technical media of communication. Cultural media act both as storage devices and as a means of relocating information through time and space.

These perspectives imply that technical media have played an important part in helping promote a more reflexive culture within modernity. To offer an example, American talk shows are often concerned with some of the most intimate aspects of modern life. Whether they are discussing child abuse, untidy partners or mixed race relationships they have a function in making public a range of social concerns that have until recently been shielded from the public gaze. While these issues are often dealt with in a sensational manner (in America intense network competition means that a variety of means of holding audiences is utilised) talk shows have recontextualised relations between the public and the private. The fact that these shows can be stored on videotape enables researchers to look at the ways sexuality and race are represented. This would of course be difficult if one could view the programme only once. The transportable nature of culture, in a global television market, means that such shows are potentially viewable by a vast audience. Talk shows, as Giddens indicates, offer a popular mix of expert opinion and audience participation. This enables viewers, in contexts radically different from the United States, to encounter discussions of issues that may be more repressively framed in their own national context. The recontextualisation of "what constitutes a healthy relationship" partially takes such questions out of the hands of professional bodies and lays it open for public reflection. Yet the major problem with this analysis is that concerns with the way technical media serve to democratise reflexivity within modernity are overly separated from the ways talk shows mobilise powerful discourses.

Recent research by Joshua Gamson (1998) has suggested viewing talk shows through the binary opposition of discourses of trash television and democratisation represses more ambivalent features. The popularity of the talk show format is poorly captured by high cultural concerns about dumbing down and the idea they at least give a voice to the marginalised and disempowered. Talk shows, argues Gamson, are undoubtedly cheap, populist forms of television that depend upon a mainly working class audience. Those who complain about the shows from an elitist perspective are often concerned with the "explicitness" and "vulgarity" of much of the material that is represented. Here Gamson sharply observes the shows are being criticised for failing to live up to middle class notions of respectability. Further, the cultural democratisation thesis poorly appreciates the narrow range of stereotypes which encode participants on talk shows. Yet, even this view, can be pushed too far. Resisting the call for more "responsible" forms of television, Gamson argues that the overtly populist nature of talk shows allows for the representation of difference. In other words, sometimes the shows do indeed represent the participants through degrading stereotypes, but at other moments the desire to shock allows for more unregulated moments of queer difference. That is, the progressive edge of popular talk shows represent working class and gay cultures in their awful diversity. These reflections suggest that cultural studies are perhaps best served by the development of more ambivalent frameworks that move debates beyond the forms of dichotomous thinking that so readily dismissed McLuhan's theorisation of technical media.

Conclusion

This chapter has argued that the work of Marshall McLuhan continues to ask a number of critical questions that until relative recently have become partially repressed within cultural and media studies. The continued capacity of technical mediums of mass communication to shape the flow of our common cultures in the global arena is reason enough to keep reading McLuhan. It is true his views grew out of a particular culture that was excited by the new possibilities being offered by new media, but we need to remember here that McLuhan's time was different from our own. This, however, is not to dismiss McLuhan out of hand. However, at the chapter's close, I want to argue that cultural analysis is better served by more multiperspectival and ambivalent frameworks than those occupied by either McLuhan or the majority of his critics. The task is not to "return to McLuhan" but to relate his many insights to the rapid changes sweeping through our shared media cultures. It is building on McLuhan's suggestive insights and comments in new contexts that best respects his genius. For example, beyond the scope of this current essay, we might investigate how McLuhan's insights might be linked to the growth of cyber-feminism. Notably Sadie Plant (1997) has sought to explore ways in which the world wide web has broken with the forms of linear logic evident in masculinist thinking. Like McLuhan, albeit in a different setting, we could argue that what is being explored is how different cultural mediums imprint different cultural values. Yet, it is also noticeable, that the feminist voices raised against this mode of thinking have suggested it merely replaces one essentialism with another (Squires, 1996). Feminists have continued to point to the ways in which women remain marginal amongst internet users, and of the cultural dominance of masculinity on-line. Yet within these debates, unlike those that dismissed McLuhan, there is the beginning of a new sensibility that both recognises technological capacity of cultural mediums while linking these concerns to issues of political economy and meaning. It is to these more ambivalent and less dogmatic frames of reference that cultural studies is urged to return.

Bibliography

Adam, B. (1990) *Time and Social Theory*, Cambridge, Polity Press.

Anderson, B. (1983) *Imagined Communities*, London, Verso.

Carey, J.W. (1989) *Communication as Culture: Essays on Media and Society*, London, Unwin Hyman.

Chartier, R. (ed.) (1989) *The Culture of Print: Power and the Uses of Print in Early Modern Europe*, Princeton, NJ, Princeton University Press; Cambridge, MA, Polity.

Finkelstein, S. (1968) *Sense and Nonsense of McLuhan*, New York, International Publishers.

Foucault, M. (1980) *Power/Knowledge: Selected Interviews and Other Writings, 1972–1977*, New York, Pantheon.

Gamson, J. (1998) *Freaks Talk Back: Tabloid Talk Shows and Sexual Noncomformity*. Chicago: University of Chicago Press.

Giddens, A. (1990) *The Consequences of Modernity*, Cambridge, MA, Polity.

Giddens, A. (1991) *Modernity and Self-Identity: Self and Society in the Late Modern Age*, Cambridge, Polity.

Goody, J. (1977) *The Domestication of the Savage Mind*, Cambridge, Cambridge University Press.

Goody, J. and Watt, I. (1968) "The consequences of literacy," in J. Goody (ed.), *Literacy in Traditional Societies* (pp. 27–68). New York, Cambridge University Press.

Hall, S. (1986) "Postmodernism and articulation," interview by L. Grossberg, *Journal of Communications Inquiry,* 10 (2): 45–60.

Hall, S. (1991) "Old and new identities, old and new ethnicities," in A. King (ed.), in *Traditional Societies,* Cambridge, MA, Cambridge University Press.

Innis, H.A. (1951) *The Bias of Communication,* Toronto, University of Toronto Press.

Mattelart, A. and Mattelart, M. (1992) *Rethinking Media Theory: Signposts and New Directions,* trans, J.A. Cohen and M. Urquidi, Minnesota, MN, University of Minnesota Press.

McLuhan, M. (1951) *The Mechanical Bride: Folklore of Industrial Man,* New York: Vangaurd.

McLuhan, M. (1962) *The Gutenberg Galaxy; the Making of Typographic Man,* Toronto: University of Toronto Press.

McLuhan, M. (1969) *Counterblast,* New York, Harcourt, Brace and World.

McLuhan, M. (1994) *Understanding Media: the Extensions of Man,* London, Routledge.

McLuhan, M. and Fiore, Q. (1967) *The Medium Is the Message,* New York: Bantam.

McLuhan, M. and Fiore, Q. (1968) *War and Peace in the Global Village,* New York: Bantam.

McLuhan, M. and Powers, B.R. (1989) *The Global Village,* Oxford, Oxford University Press.

Meyrowitz, J. (1985) *No Sense of Place: The Impact of Electronic Media on Social Behavior,* New York, Oxford University Press.

Nairn, T. (1969) "McLuhanism: The myth of our time," in R. Rosenthal, *McLuhan Pro and Con,* Harmondsworth, UK, Penguin.

Plant, S. (1997) *Zeros + Ones: Digital Women and the New Technologies,* London, Fourth Estate.

Robertson, R. (1992) *Globalisation: Social Theory and Global Culture,* London, Sage.

Soja, E. (1989) *Postmodern Geographies: The Assertion of Space in Critical Social Theory,* London: Verso.

Squires, J. (1996) "Fabulous feminist futures and the love of cyberculture," in Dovey, J. (eds.) *Fractural Dreams: New Media in Social Context,* London, Lawrence and Wishart.

Stevenson, N. (2002) *Understanding Media Cultures,* London, Sage.

Thompson, J.B. (1990) *Ideology and Modern Culture: Critical Social Theory in the Era of Mass Communication,* Cambridge, MA, Polity.

Williams, R. (1974) *Television: Technology and Cultural Form,* London, Fontana/ Collins.

Williams, R. (1985) *Towards 2000,* London, Penguin.

CHAPTER THREE

Waking Up to the Call Girl

GLENN WILLMOTT

What does "McLuhan" stand for? Certainly not a theory. Perhaps a discourse, a certain mode of attention, and thus an expression of critical values, regarding media, mind, and culture; or even more likely, perhaps, a less coherent, more fluid practice of counter-discourse, predicated on existing clichés of media, mind, and culture. Discourse or counter-discourse, its keywords and much of its detail seem linked to fashion (it doesn't take long before readers will wonder who "Jack Parr" is, though these are the first two words of the paperback edition of *Understanding Media: The Extensions of Man* in 1964), and to the idea of an era (be it the television age, the computer age, the sixties, the millennium, etc.). The present essay begins from the intuition that there is, in fact, a coherent cultural theory to be found in McLuhan's work, but that this theory is not marked as a theory or directly expressed as such. It is not found in the content of the work, then, but in the social and material life intended for the discourse itself, which is to say in a kind of implicit narrative of the "coining" and value of McLuhan's stated interests (i.e., in the *media* as keys to the hidden modes of production proper to any historical totality) as a cultural cliché. For there is a coherent theory at work in McLuhan's initiating a certain sub-cultural field, an anti-environment, a multifarious probe, a happening, that retains the stamp or signature of "McLuhan" even as it escapes his own intentional or moral direction (as in the French expression for Pop Art: *mcluhanisme*).

To retrace this narrative field is beyond the means of the present essay. As a starting point, however, I wish to outline in brief, the production of "McLuhan" as a media celebrity and commodity in the 1960s, then argue that this very production is justified, and takes on profound meaning, in the context of McLuhan's long understanding of modern culture as a fantasy world—that is, as a social formation plunged into unconscious processes that determine the political, psychological, and sociable limits of individual life. This view, which sees modernity as something like a vast fantasy factory into which we are all plugged, as producers and consumers alike, may recall the dystopian romance of *The Matrix* (dir. Larry and Andy Wachowski, 1999), and indeed this film's roots reach down through the decades into a similar dystopian romance (with its call to awake from a technologically-induced, politically-exploitative world of dream) of *The Mechanical Bride: Folklore of Industrial Man* (1951). To be sure, the latter work was in the later McLuhan's view anachronistically addressed to an "industrial" rather than "digital" world, and so was properly superceded by *The Electronic Call Girl* (his private title for *Understanding Media* [Marchand, 1989, p. 169]). But I will argue that this dystopian vision remains the same. Only the solution to this vision—the means of waking, and the prospect upon waking, digitally—must change. This last is the current value of "McLuhan."

The moment at which McLuhan made his entrance onto the world stage was a matter of difference among his contemporary chroniclers. His publication in 1964 of the primary scripture, *Understanding Media: The Extensions of Man,* was necessary to his popular success, but was generally acknowledged to be insufficient without the media and cultural hype which—beginning early in 1965 with the first "McLuhan Festival" in Canada, and with the first commercial promotions of his discourse by Generalists, Inc. in the United States—transformed "Herbert Marshall McLuhan, 53-year-old Canadian English Professor," as Tom Wolfe put it, into "*McLuhan*" (1969, p. 108). The present section provides an overview of his many public masks in this diverse media context: his engagement in the business world outside the university, his mediatization into a public image, and his absorption into the radical aesthetics of art and alternative education in the counter-culture of the sixties.

The Gutenberg Galaxy filled out and gave coherence to McLuhan's work in the experimental journal *Explorations,* and although it received the Canadian Governor General's award for non-fiction in 1962, McLuhan remained known only within prescribed circles—as an avant-garde intellectual or a "scholarly nuisance"—until he published *Understanding Media* with the trade publisher McGraw-Hill in 1964 (Stearn, 1967, p. 1). By early 1966, the two books together had sold more than 55,000 copies, and by 1969—the height of McLuhan's success—*Understanding Media* alone had sold more than 9,000 in hardcover and more than 100,000 in soft, and was described as "the fastest-selling nonfiction book at Harvard and at Ann

Arbor." Hugh Kenner tells us that the book descended from paperback to a "drug-store" dime-novel edition. It is to be expected that McLuhan's subsequent book, the first to be published during his period of celebrity, would be a bestseller. And indeed, *The Medium Is the Massage*—a photo-pictorial collage designed by Quentin Fiore, and featuring much of the same textual material in simplified form (actually a bricolage of McLuhan's discourse, "co-ordinated" by Jerome Agel)—sold over 100,000 copies in its first three print runs in 1967, and eventually nearly a million copies worldwide (Pollack, 1966, p. 56; Diamond, 1967, p. 54; Marchand, 1989, p. 193).

By 1974, McLuhan was able to boast of this global success to a disparaging academic milieu (satisfied to see the McLuhan craze die out by the early 1970s), claiming a "much bigger interest in the Latin world than in the Wasp world": "My biggest following is in Mexico, and South America, and then, next, in Paris and Japan. *Understanding Media* and *The Gutenberg Galaxy* have been translated into 22 languages, and are about to appear in several other languages" (Molinaro, C. McLuhan and Toye, 1987, pp. 505–6). *The Gutenberg Galaxy* was translated into at least twelve languages, and in France, Claude Cartier-Bresson's Maison Mame published translations of four of McLuhan's major texts as well as a selection of short essays, between 1967 and 1974 (p. 452n). The German translation of *Understanding Media* first appeared in 1968 from Econ Verlag, under the title *Die Magischen Kanäle*—"the magic channel" (p. 337n).

It is true that "McLuhan" failed to die out around the world, as it seemed to do as a fad in America. His persistent afterlife in French poststructuralist and cultural theory has ironically allowed "McLuhan" to haunt the academy which had thought him gone. For McLuhan is inextricable from the fabric of French critical theory since the sixties: Jean Baudrillard and Paul Virilio recognize themselves as inheritors of his catastrophic view of the global, postmodern media. Derrida's valorization of the material forms of signification (e.g., the *gramme*), and Foucault's studies of bio-technology and social power (e.g., the *panopticon*), participate in a historical-epistemological formalism inaugurated by McLuhan. Canadian critic John Fekete, whose Marxist *Critical Twilight* had raked McLuhan over the coals in 1977, redeemed him in an article of 1982 as an important (if still critically wanting) and indigenous producer of poststructuralist insights then being imported enthusiastically from France. The French connection has not dried up. An April 1991 front page of the "Livres-Idées" section of *Le Monde* proclaims "Régis Debray saisi par McLuhan," in his new *Cours de médiologie générale*. To the McLuhanist tradition of media theory, the review tells us, "Régis Debray apporte un effort de systématisation et de généralisation très français, qui culmine dans un tableau synoptique [not reproducable in this note—but about as totalizing and systematized as Joyce's key to *Ulysses*] décrivant les trois âges de la 'médiasphère': l'écriture (logosphère), l'imprimerie (graphosphère), et l'audiovisuel (vidéosphère)" (Jean-Louis Missika, review of *Cours de médiologie générale* by Régis Debray [*Le Monde*, 19 Apr 1991], p. 17). This translates to: "Regis Debray makes a very French effort to systematize and generalize that culminates in a summary table describing the three ages of the 'media world': writing (logosphere), printing (graphosphere) and audiovisual (videosphere)."

But the explosive dissemination of his work in North America had its limits, and by about 1970 they had been reached. Most of his books from 1969 to 1972, such as the slender *Counterblast*, the stylistically frustrating *From Cliché to Archetype*, *Culture Is Our Business*, and *Take Today: The Executive as Drop-Out* received either little or adverse contemporary response and remain relatively unknown today.

The apparent contradiction between McLuhan's tangible production as a literary academic (with a message) and his ideological position as a media formalist (against the message) was heightened by the very mediatization of "McLuhan" in the years 1965–70. McLuhan's books became supplementary to his mass-media image. "I have seen customers of an entirely unbookish aspect," reported one commentator, "typical mass-media folk, enter bookstores as though treading on foreign territory and ask the clerk, in the hesitant tones one uses with strange, semimagical beings, for the 'latest book by McLuhan.' They too want to know what's happening to them and they think, or at least they've heard, that McLuhan can tell them." "Like Andy Warhol," Hugh Kenner wrote, "whose works we don't need to see to appreciate their point, McLuhan is the writer his public doesn't need to read." For there were other channels. "The media were hell-bent," Kenner later recalled, "on making a media phenomenon of the Media Sage; thus hardly anyone really knows what Marshall McLuhan had to say." Large circulation magazines began to run articles on McLuhan in 1965, beginning with Harold Rosenberg's discussion in the "Books" section of the *New Yorker* in February. Although properly a review, it discussed his work as a whole and dubbed him the first Pop philosopher—an epithet that would stick to him throughout his period of celebrity. By November of that year, *Harper's* was running an article on "Canada's Intellectual Comet," speaking of McLuhan as a "cult" phenomenon both attracting the credulity of "Poppers," "Camp Followers," and "converts and disciples" "eager" for such technological miracles as computerized ESP; and attracting the serious attention of leading intellectuals. By 1966, "McLuhan" was a full-scale media event—which justified to McLuhan his view of the new power of the media, in which "any yokel can become a world center who thinks up a few phrases" (Rosenthal, 1969, p. 5; Kenner, 1969, p. 24; Schickel, 1965, pp. 62, 64; Howard, 1966, p. 95).

In 1964, *Time's* unsigned review, "Blowing Hot and Cold," blasted *Understanding Media* as "fuzzy-minded, lacking in perspective, low in definition and data, redundant," and "just the right combination of intelligence, arrogance and pseudo-science" to become that summer's "fad . . . or parlor game" (Crosby and Bond, 1968, pp. 43–44). *Newsweek* redressed this wrong early in 1966 with a featured interview which enumerated McLuhan's penetrations into art and business cultures and recounted his ideas without critical commentary, and with a kind of distanced awe. A year later McLuhan's face appeared—in chiaroscuro multiple exposures—on the cover of *Newsweek*, accompanied by a lengthy article. He subsequently appeared on the cover of *Saturday Review,* and was either featured in or wrote articles for *Glamour, Look, Vogue, Family Circle, Fortune, Life, Esquire, Nation, Playboy, Harper's, New Yorker, Miss Chatelaine,* and *Mademoiselle.* McLuhan may be the only literary intellectual to have been submitted to a statistical analysis of magazine and periodical citations: "Post-Mortem on McLuhan: A Public Figure's Emergence and Decline as Seen in Popular Magazines," provides interesting data, including a chart showing McLuhan's relative newsworthiness as a subject for articles in 1967, compared with eleven other public figures from Robert McNamara (the most popular) to Jean-Paul Sartre (the least). McLuhan finds himself slightly less favoured than Cassius Clay, but slightly more so than Martin Luther King. Press cartoons about McLuhan also abounded. They began to appear in *The New Yorker* in 1966, such as the one reproduced in Marshall McLuhan, *The Medium Is the Massage* (1967, pp. 56–7), which shows a youth (electric guitar momentarily propped against the wall) explaining "McLuhan" to his father (surrounded by bookshelves, reading). A cartoon from the same magazine four years later depicts "a young woman saying to a man as they left a cocktail party, 'Ashley, are you sure it's not too soon to go around to parties saying, "What ever happened to Marshall McLuhan"?'" (Marchand, 1989, p. 220). Time-Life Inc. and *Newsweek* both offered this English professor an office in their American headquarters, for "anytime he was in need of one" (p. 173).

McLuhan's mediatization was not limited to the popular press. He had earlier experimented with new media formats—the report of a study McLuhan prepared for the National Association of Educational Broadcasters in 1960 included a video which was telecast as part of the Canadian Broadcasting Corporation's series "Explorations" on May 18 of that year, according to what appears to be a transcript from this telecast (Stearn, 1967, pp. 137–46). However, McLuhan attained his real media dissemination when the radio, record, and television industries "turned on" to his image as a Pop philosopher. The high point was in 1967: CBS Records released an LP version of *The Medium Is the Massage* nearly simultaneously with the publication of the book, part postmodern sound collage and part McLuhan lecture. Having entered the image bank of the times, there were television references— Goldie Hawn giggling "Marshall McLuhan, what are you doin'?" on *Laugh-In*— and actual television appearances. CBS interviewed him "at length on its top-rated Sunday night public affairs show," and NBC produced an hour-long "experimental" special promoted in *Newsweek* as "eschew[ing] the usual sequential reporting in favor of quick cuts, overlapping images and out-of-focus shots of McLuhan," and explained by its producer with the one word: "Mysterioso" (Compton, 1969, p. 107; Diamond, 1967, p. 53). This last has been described as:

> complete with the full Pop ritual of flashy, splashy lighting, electronic sound, fancy cut-
> ting, zooms, lots of stop action—in fact, the whole art director's kit of exciting-visual-
> effects: go-go girls zazzing away but as if the film ran sideways (why do they never show
> go-go girls dancing straight up, the way their mothers would want them to?), and,
> toward the end, a cute little bit of I-can-be-as-cool-as-you-are-buddy contemporary
> graphics, showing an H-bomb exploding in the shape of an exclamation point. . . .
> [McLuhan] appeared sometimes in darkness, sometimes with a red light flickering on
> his face. He appeared, disappeared. Sentences hung in the air. Print. Electronics.
> Technology. The alphabet. Western man. Life. Death. Pop Art. The motorcar. The
> Beatles. Gutenberg. Civilization (Arlen, 1969, pp. 82–83, 86–87).

Like Rauschenberg on the air, "McLuhan" became the signature of a postmodernist aesthetic in television and other popular media in America, just as it became the label—*mcluhanisme*—for Pop art and culture in France.

So that "McLuhan" was not only *on* television; he was *in* television. "Norman Felton was the most important television producer of his age," said NBC vice-president Paul Klein: "He used to make his shows—*The Man from U.N.C.L.E.*, for example—the way he thought McLuhan would envision them. The rule was, the more you made it so that viewers had a challenge figuring out what was going on, the more you didn't tell them, the more they wanted to watch what was going on" (Marchand, 1989, p. 200). And there were more rules than that, said Klein, suggested by "McLuhan." Not that McLuhan may be thought of as an origin for any of this aesthetic production: he was apparently the namer, the giver of language, for a postmodern *techne* already at work in sixties popular culture. What was new and to be named was the translation of technics from the modernist art film to the television medium, where its rhythmic integration with the commercial schedule of advertisement, its enframing in the form of the serial, its new relationship to a domestic audience, and other differences severed its ties to the high-art situation of modernist formalism.

Who first discovered "McLuhan"? Commentators variously claimed that McLuhan was first "discovered by young people and the artists, not by the literary crowd," or instead by Madison Avenue, according to the publisher of the periodical *Books*, Jerome Agel (Diamond, 1967, p. 54). Where did Count Basie first hear of him, that he composed "Afro-Eurasion Eclipse" to express and explore in musical terms, McLuhan's idea of the loss of identity in the Global Village? It is probably better to say that he was discovered by no one, by no particular group or institution first, but by all of them at once—an unconscious effect of the mysterious sort of social life engendered by the mass media. All were equally entranced by "McLuhan."

McLuhan's name was often linked to those of sixties artists, and we shall see that he encouraged the association of his own work with the art of the postmodern Happening. Aside from George Steiner, quoted later on in this chapter, there are the examples of Theodore Roszak, who complains of the "cultural millions American society can now afford to lay out on 'exploding plastic inevitables' . . . the entertainments provided by the Andy Warhols and Marshall McLuhans" (Roszak, 1969, pp. 258–59), and Hugh Kenner, who similarly draws a parallel between McLuhan and Warhol (Kenner, 1969, p. 24). The "pop" in the epithet, "first pop philosopher," came to refer to Pop Art as well as to popular culture. Rosenberg's original 1965 *New Yorker* review, "Philosophy in a Pop Key," had praised McLuhan for having found meaning in the *popular* culture of everyday life, some "positive, humanistic meaning and the color of life in supermarkets, stratospheric flight, the lights blinking on broadcasting towers" (Rosenberg, 1965, p. 136). Richard Schickel's review, soon after, drew this "pop philosophy" under the rubrics of Pop Art and Camp as "do-it-yourself attempts to resolve the conflict between our pretensions to the finer things and our visceral adoration of the less fine. Pop, as a mode of expression, Camp as a shorthand style of appreciation, are both means of giving some sort of aesthetic-intellectual rationale to the fascinated attention we pay the mass media." Critical or not, McLuhan shared with Pop Art a symptomatic "desire to move beyond the attitudes of cultural criticism as it is customarily practiced by literary people," those able to condemn the popular aesthetic, but unable to admit or explain the ineluctable desire for what it offered. "Often," Schickel remarks, "we reject the documentary show in favor of the trash. Audience surveys bear this out; the very people who claim to desire more elevated fare are also the ones who ignore existing programs which critics regard as the medium's finest hours" (Schickel, 1965, pp. 63–64). Like Pop Art, McLuhan appealed to a sense of inadequacy in cultural-critical understanding.

He was not merely compared to radical art culture; "McLuhan" was absorbed into it. A *Newsweek* article of 1966 reports the most high-profile products of this aesthetic dissemination, beginning with two events advertised as "McLuhan Festivals":

> At the University of British Columbia, the faculty—in the name of McLuhan—set up a sensory fun house in which professors walk through a maze of plastic sheets hung from the ceiling of an armory while slide projectors splashed images on floor and ceiling and loudspeakers blared weird noises. They also rigged up a "sculptured wall"—a frame covered with a stretch fabric behind which a girl writhed. The idea: Touch the girl and learn all about tactile communication. In San Francisco last month, McLuhan was invited (but did not go) to a three-day sensorium at Longshoremen's Hall that included nude

projections, a God box and jazz mice. And last week, at the 3rd Rail Time/Space Theater off-off Broadway in New York's East Village, a series of happenings happened under the title, "McLuhan Megillah" (Pollack, 1966, p. 56-57)

The University of British Columbia McLuhan Festival was indeed the first event of a "McLuhan craze" in the Happenings of experimental art culture. Philip Marchand tells us that:

> Gerd Stern, prominent in a collective of artists in New York, was one of the most ardent promoters of McLuhan in the early sixties. He spread the word through the work of his collective, which pioneered the multimedia, 'total theater,' psychedelic, environmental art performances (they went by a variety of names) that became a fixture in artists' lofts in the late sixties. McLuhan, on a couple of occasions, spoke at such performances. By 1968 he was being acclaimed in the pages of the *New York Times Magazine* as the "number one prophet" of this consciousness-expanding art; one Greenwich Village enthusiast, at about the same time, staged a multimedia event that was climaxed by his singing quotations from McLuhan's works (1989, p. 172).

Experimental art culture was but one expression of a more general radical aesthetic movement which I return to in chapter nine. Suffice it here to say that around 1968, when McLuhan met cultural revolutionaries Abbie Hoffman and Timothy Leary, both of them approved of him—Hoffman concluding, "The Left is too much into Marx, not enough into McLuhan" (Marchand, 1989, pp. 172, 207). McLuhan was not himself enthusiastic for experimental art; he had difficulty staying awake at the multimedia events he attended (p. 200).

Despite his seduction of a sixties counter-culture, McLuhan's most shocking achievement as a mediatized intellectual, as "McLuhan," was his penetration of the business community—and his financial success in doing so (Alderman, 1966, pp. 16–19). Magazine articles from 1966 onward never fail to enumerate McLuhan's business activities. For example, *Newsweek* tells us:

> Industrialists travel from as far away as Japan and India for audiences in his disheveled, book-lined office at the University of Toronto. American executives pay him fees of up to $1,000 to come to their luncheons of stringy roast beef and preach his often impenetrable sermons on communications. . . . Recently, seventeen Canadian executives— including two presidents and five vice-presidents—paid $150 apiece for the privilege of a two-day seminar with McLuhan in Toronto (Pollack, p. 57).

Similarly, *Life* reported that "Businessmen . . . view McLuhan with awe. Advertising agencies, confused by the changing markets of consumers, implore the professor to tell them what they're doing wrong. . . . Urgent letters from vast corporations beg him to preside at seminars, enlightening their executives on humanity, on commerce, on their products" (Howard, 1966, pp. 92, 95). Another issue of

Newsweek relates what happened when "in 'Understanding Media,' McLuhan needled Bell Telephone's research department for being 'oblivious to the real meaning of the telephone.' Stung, the Bell people recently journeyed up to Toronto for a séance"; and that "he signed—at a handsome fee—with the Container Corp. of America to give a lecture to Container executives and selected customers" (Diamond, p. 53)—actually two lectures, for $2,500 apiece, despite his disgust for a business he called responsible for a "massive garbage apocalypse" (Marchand, p. 185).

The press did not exaggerate. In 1966 alone, according to his biographer, McLuhan spoke to the Container Corporation of America, to a management consulting conference, to "the American Marketing Association, the American Association of Advertising Agencies, and the Public Relations Society of New York. He gave a talk in Washington, D.C., before approximately twenty assistant secretaries in the Johnson administration, under the auspices of the United States Civil Service Commission. He gave numberless interviews to magazine and newspaper reporters, appeared on television and radio talk shows," and gave a press conference. He also maintained regular contact with a member of the research department of Bell Canada, while one advertising and communications firm even gave him the title of "Senior Creative Consultant and Director" for its company (Marchand, pp. 175, 185). "There were many studs of the business world," observed Tom Wolfe, "breakfast-food-package designers, television-network creative-department vice presidents, advertising 'media reps,' lighting-fixture fortune heirs, patent lawyers, industrial spies, we-need-vision board chairmen—all sorts of business studs, as I say, wondering if McLuhan was . . . right" (Wolfe, p. 109).

What this "dialogue" with the business community produced is uncertain. "Such seminars," said McLuhan, "take a great deal out of you because you are dealing with people who don't know what you're talking about." But he also held that "in many ways, businessmen are more receptive to new ideas and approaches than academics." Perhaps there is something in the latter impression, since one outside observer at such an event rankled at the "uncritical adulation" of its audience. And it is certainly difficult to imagine any other contemporary academic having an advertising agency publish a pamphlet on him or her titled, "I'm the only one who knows what the hell is going on" (Pollack, p. 57; Howard, 1966, p. 95).

In fact, McLuhan had begun to court the business world long before his mediatized celebrity as a pop philosopher—and with no little success. In 1955, McLuhan joined forces with a neighbour in public relations to form "Idea Consultants," intending to sell ideas for products and advertising to needy companies. Such ideas ranged from the distasteful, "transparent potties for use in toilet training children," to the prescient, "the manufacture and sale of taped movies for replay on television sets." But the ideas did not sell. By the later 1950s, however, McLuhan had begun to realize his own idea of the consultant business. He began to speak regularly to the General Electric (GE) Management Center at Croton-on-Hudson, New York, on the subject of contemporary communications. The GE talks lasted at least from 1959–64. "The [GE management] school, the first of its kind, had been set up under the influence of the doctrines of still another academic-turned-management theorist, Peter Drucker. Prior to its establishment, promising executive talent had been sent off to regular academic courses at various universities to put the final touches on their intellectual development. Now similar courses would be administered by a school run exclusively by and for the company. GE was prepared to spend whatever money was necessary to bring the best lecturers—academics from Harvard and Yale, high-priced consultants like Drucker, and even Ronald Reagan, then a television spokesman for GE" (Marchand, 1989, pp. 150–51). Believing that untutored businessmen were "like children" in their innocence of print culture and their plasticity before change, McLuhan hoped to see them become the "erudite men of ready and eloquent speech" which the new corporate bodies of the postmodern age seemed to promise, a kind of late-capitalist *Childhood's End!* (Marchand, pp. 100–101, 139, 151).

In addition to speaking engagements, McLuhan made connections in the business world which led either to sponsored projects or to the further promotion of his name. One friend at IBM arranged for him a large grant for a media research project; he also counseled him on the consulting fees he should ask from interested businesses. Ironically, despite the original *Time* review which called *Understanding Media* a pseudo-scientific fad with the lasting significance of a parlour game, a management planner for Time-Life Inc. brought (and bought) McLuhan into his projects, and later initiated a psychological study to test McLuhan's hypotheses with regard to the aesthetic form of their magazines and their audience response (Marchand, pp. 162–3, 156–7).

The most important colleagues McLuhan made in the business world were two Californian entrepreneurs, Howard Gossage and Gerald Feigen, who ran several ventures including Generalists, Inc.—"acting as consultants to people who can't get what they need from specialists because what they need is the big picture." The enterprise was a modestly successful version of McLuhan's own, earlier Idea Consultants. They also engaged in "genius scouting," and they discovered McLuhan, a self-advertised generalist, early in 1965. They were well-connected in important advertising and magazine publishing circles, and in the same year they arranged two rounds of social events—in New York and San Francisco—at which their new "investment" met powerful persons in the local government and culture industry. The first of these trips marked, according to Tom Wolfe, the pivotal point in McLuhan's mediatization, his transformation into "McLuhan" (Wolfe, pp. 128,

108). Gossage and Feigen invested an initial $6,000 (and later "a lot more") into promoting the Pop philosopher and media guru, organizing their own "McLuhan Festivals" and other events which mixed the consulting session with the cocktail party. One of their guests, Tom Wolfe—himself promoted by his publisher as "America's foremost pop journalist"—was also instrumental in spreading the word.

But the promotional efforts of Gossage and Feigen were nothing as compared to the full commercialization undertaken by the New York entrepreneur, Eugene Schwartz. With Schwartz, "McLuhan" became the product of Marshall McLuhan, Inc., under the direction of Schwartz's Human Development Corporation. At the height of McLuhan's success—and marketability—between 1967–68, Schwartz launched the *Marshall McLuhan DEW-LINE Newsletter*, in which he packaged "McLuhan" in a medium, as he put it, "that could be delivered faster than a book but had more inherent depth than television." McLuhan's son Eric, then 26 years of age, found himself on the top floor of 200 Madison Avenue in New York, editor of the *DEW-LINE*. Advertisements for it were not geared towards a sophisticated intellectual audience. An ad in the *New York Times* began: "This is an invitation to join a select group of business, academic and government leaders who are about to receive what must be the most startling newsletter ever printed." Hard-sell aside, the newsletter really was unconventional. McLuhan himself merely contributed fragments of text—mostly recycled from other work—while Eric McLuhan and Schwartz came up with unusual forms in which to purvey it (partly to prevent it from being photocopied and distributed to nonsubscribers): posters, vinyl recordings, projection slides, and in one issue, a deck of playing cards with a McLuhanist message on each card, to be used to inspire business or personal decision-making. The newsletter ran from 1968–70, with more than 4,000 subscribers, mostly "top-flight executives in advertising, in firms like IBM," as well as in the White House, "an obscure Nixon aide named Fred Panzer." Others of Schwartz's schemes which never got off the ground were a "Marshall McLuhan Bookshelf" of McLuhan's favourite books reprinted as a series under his name, the "Marshall McLuhan Show," a network talk-show, and McLuhanesque "sensory retraining centers" for the "rehabilitation of individuals with hopeless sensory biases." In 1970, Schwartz organized a high-profile "McLuhan Emergency Strategy Seminar" on Grand Bahama Island, "strictly limited to 500 top executives," the ads said, and designed to "explore the most frustrating breakdowns in your organization, your market and your environment—and restructure them into the kind of breakthrough you may have been waiting for for years. [Price: $500 per customer.]" Marshall McLuhan, Inc. helped to brush aside the last vestiges of intellectual credibility—as a "neutral observer" of the environment—that clung to the tweedy image of "McLuhan" (Marchand, pp. 198–9, 216–17). From the mid-1960s onward McLuhan required the services of professional accountants.

One cannot miss, in nearly any account of McLuhan's career, his commentator's fascination with the various price tags attached to him. With the exception of Tom Wolfe, who slyly made illuminating fun of McLuhan's commodification as "McLuhan," it purely maddened his critics. His value-neutral "'probing' has served [him] well," one of the more ireful expressions went,

> It has allowed him to pose as a cultural lion while ingratiating himself with IBM and *Time* magazine. . . . *Time* magazine is pernicious crap. But no one who says as much winds up with his face on the million-dollar cover. "Probing" has allowed McLuhan to go barnstorming the country as a Container Corporation of America lecturer and—so the *London Observer* reports—to pin down a hundred-thousand-dollar-a-year super-professorship at Fordham University. His most recent literary effort, *The Medium Is the Massage* (sic.)—a gimmicked-up non-book—is fetching $10.95 a copy in the hardbound edition. He should worry about intellectual respectability? About as much as Andrew Ure or Samuel Smiles, who long ago discovered the secret of becoming successful "fee-losophers" in an exploitative social order (Roszak, p. 268–69).

The most controversial price tag came with the $100,000 "jet age academic chair" offered by Fordham University to McLuhan for the year 1966–67—initially to be funded by New York State's Albert Schweitzer Professorship in the Humanities. "You've heard money talking? Did you get the message?" one critic quoted caustically, from McLuhan's own *Mechanical Bride*. No doubt McLuhan was unnecessarily demonized for his financial successes; but the fact of his commodification, as a supposedly critical approach to modern life, was the deeper issue. And McLuhan did occasionally speak candidly of his works as commodities—an example of his "put-on." The *Newsweek* cover story reports with enthusiasm, for example, that "he considers statements in his books and his speeches as tentative probes—disposable as Kleenex" (Compton, p. 107; Ricks, 1969, p. 100; Diamond, p. 57; Marchand, p. 154). Even before his celebrity, to a friend "who asked about his progress in writing *The Gutenberg Galaxy*," he had answered that "he was in the process not of writing it, but of 'packaging' it." But academe was not ready *consciously* to affirm the value of a consumable critical ideology with a price tag.

Of course, the real issue is how well McLuhan could use this "affirmative" form of critical ideology as an uncanny and disturbing—dislocating, he would say—mirror of a postmodern *technical* subjectivity. All that can be said for certain is that the extent to which such a formalist, *dialogic* mask—his "put-on"—might have worked *cannot* be judged by how favourably or unfavourably it was received in its milieu. It can only be judged by what it produced, which need neither encorporate his critical discourse, nor bear his signature. While contemporary critics generally felt McLuhan to be corrupt and wrong, grating as he did against the most essential, humanistic and scholarly values of his intellectual audience, all the antipathy thus inspired was unable to ground itself in an alternative critical practice supposed to be proper to the postmodern world space he had chosen for his lists. So that while most of the criticism effectively demolishes McLuhan, it leaves no critical space left over for itself, and reduces itself in McLuhan's landscape to a parody of itself, to the purveyor of merely another printed and published, commodified and alienated, critical gesture. A curious result of reading essays on McLuhan by a wide variety of intellectuals of the period—some quite influential and distinguished—is a sense of the *anonymity* these intellectuals achieve. For few attempt to offer more than a negative critique.

Kenneth Burke, for example, tells us (along with a series of unremarkable observations upon McLuhan's scholarly mistakes and simplifications) that McLuhan does not understand the "Dramatic"—Burke's privileged paradigm—and so truncates all dramatic agency into mere physiological instrumentality. Burke is compelling; he is even, I would say, right. But once we stand on the ground where McLuhan *was*, that of critical agency in a postmodern world, then what *is* the Dramatic? In Burke's critique, we merely circle back to an abstraction that is indifferent to historical modes of the social production of meaning and its communication (Burke, 1969, p. 166). Similarly, Left criticisms contemporary with McLuhan demolish him at the expense of cutting away their own ground in the material history of aesthetic orders of language and representation; I am thinking, in particular, of Dwight Macdonald and Sidney Finkelstein, the latter authoring the Marxist-based, *Sense and Nonsense of McLuhan* (1968). An impressive exception is John Fekete, who in 1978 authored the most extensive Marxist critique of McLuhan to date, and who turned in 1982, after contact with French poststructuralism, to a more "friendly" reading—in which he discusses McLuhan's productive affinities and differences with Derrida and Foucault (Fekete, 1982, p. 64).

But the fact that so many able critics missed McLuhan's critical strategy suggests not that they were blinded by "print," as McLuhan would have had it, but that he lost control of the irony in his rhetoric, the satire of his mask: he "put on" or entered the other, the mass, the double of his social existence, and *lost* this game played on the edge of extinction. "Large corporations," Tom Wolfe wrote pessimistically in 1965, "were already trying to put McLuhan in a box. Valuable! Ours! Suppose he *is* what he sounds like, the most important thinker since Newton, Darwin, Freud, Einstein, and Pavlov, studs of the intelligentsia game—suppose he *is* the oracle of the modern times—*what if he is right?*—he'll be in there, in our box" (Wolfe, pp. 109–10). But this is the very problem for which "McLuhan" is the archetype, and which concerns us still: can the projection of critical knowledge be arrested, projected, and retraced in its postmodern production as a commodity form? Is "McLuhan" merely the *reverse* image of ourselves, of the critic today?

McLuhan's contemporaries were horrified by his entry into the commodified discourse of popular culture, into the dangerous, mimetic game of its media. Here are the voices of but two critics:

> His famous slogan, "the medium is the message" (or "massage") has already become as proverbial as "nice guys finish last" or "history is bunk," part of American folklore. And though he disapproves of the medium of print, four of his books have become best sellers, while his theories have been expounded in universities and seminaries as well as on TV and the radio and in all the mass magazines. Most of the converts to McLuhanism came with minds already well-equipped with the latest thought-saving ideas, from *Angst* to Zen, and accepted it as a new and shinier intellectual gadget (Klonsky, 1969, pp. 126–7).

> To attach some significance to the clarion call from Canada that "the medium is the message," we must be given something more than a worn cliché (Wagner, 1969, p. 154).

Critics were generally intolerant of the superficiality they perceived in McLuhan's style—that electrified, "cool" discourse which spun itself from a vast tissue of clichés and popular phenomena, formulaic effects, aphorisms, slang, jokes, myths, and icons current to youth culture, Pop Art, and the mass media—all the while seeming to dismiss outright (as "obsolete") the rules and values of traditional critical expression. "Up go posters of Batman and Bogart on living-room walls all over America, and onto the bookshelf goes McLuhan. The Campbell's soup can becomes an object of art and the Jack Paar show a subject of deep philosophical analysis. If we are to have pop art, why not pop metaphysics too?" (Roszak, p. 258) Suspicion of McLuhan's cliché discursive style extended beyond his texts to his disseminated image, which Tom Wolfe helped to produce:

> I first met Marshall McLuhan in the spring of 1965, in New York. The first thing that I noticed about him was that he wore some kind of a trick snap-on neck tie with hidden plastic cheaters on it. He was a tall man, 53 years old, handsome, with a long, strong face, but terribly pallid. He had gray hair, which he combed straight back. It was a little thin on top, but he could comb it into nice sloops over the ears. Distinguished-looking, you might say. On the other hand, there were the plastic cheaters. A little of the plastic was showing between his collar and the knot of the tie. I couldn't keep my eye off it (Wolfe, p. 135).

Wolfe's fascination is tell-tale, for while he emphasizes in McLuhan's self-presentation the inauthenticity of this "trick" element, whose duplicitous "cheaters" are meant to be "hidden," he also records its persistently obvious—almost willful—visibility. The sartorially-minded Wolfe is fixated upon a danger that the cliché tie does not pretend, that it is somehow *the real thing*. This dangerous possibility is transferred to McLuhan himself: when the Canadian longhair offers the outrageous prophecy that "New York is obsolete," that "people will no longer concentrate in great urban centers for the purpose of work" and that "New York will become a Disneyland, a pleasure dome," Wolfe can only whisper to himself, "what if he is right?"—what if he is the real thing? The assertion of the fake tie punctuates McLuhan's every revelation: "Just before he made this sort of statement—and he was always analyzing his environment out loud—he would hook his chin down over his collarbone. It was like an unconscious signal—*now!* I would watch the tie knot swivel over the little telltale strip of plastic. It was a perfect Rexall milky white, this plastic" (Wolfe, p. 107–9). But for "McLuhan," the cliché *is* the real thing.

Cliché is at once the most revealing and the most obscure term invented by McLuhan to refer to media and their effects upon us. Why obscure? Because when we recognize a cliché, according to McLuhan, it no longer functions as a cliché (but is rather a sign, symbol, quotation, or *archetype* of itself). Essential to the paradoxical nature of the actual *cliché* is that it is never recognized for what it is, but like a *mirror* reflects the image of something else; it is "cognized" or absorbed without being "recognized" or realized for consciousness, like the medium behind its message. The mirror is a metaphor for the medium that is an extension of ourselves, and provides a fantasy of wholeness and self-sufficiency, but is misrecognized as an external object of mastery, an other. This difficult metaphor is explained in *Understanding Media*, where McLuhan uses the myth of Narcissus to describe the imaginary mistaking of the *self* embodied in an extended medium for *another*.

In *Understanding Media: The Extensions of Man* (1964), McLuhan defines a primary psychological relationship of human subjectivity to its media environment: "The Greek myth of Narcissus is directly concerned with a fact of human experience, as the word *Narcissus* indicates. It is from the Greek word *narcosis,* or numbness. The youth Narcissus mistook his own reflection in the water for another person. This extension of himself by mirror numbed his perceptions until he became the servomechanism of his own extended or repeated image. The nymph Echo tried to win his love with fragments of his own speech, but in vain. He was numb. He had adapted to his extension of himself and had become a closed system" (51). The image given back to Narcissus appears to be that of another, but is really a misrecognized fragment of himself. Paradoxical results follow. The deafness to Echo and the misrecognition of himself form a kind of unconscious self-alienation for the Narcissan subject, in which his consciousness abstracts itself from its field of perception—even though this field will remain as a labyrinthine hall of mirrors in which he is doomed to wander without knowing it, veritably blind. The mirror "numbs" the subject to his parts; it is "narcotic." This, ironically, yields a felt wholeness. What is felt is the coherence not of an ego identity but of a fantasy relationship with the mirage of an "other" object. The medium as mirror offers to the subject the closure of its own form, the "closed system" to which the subject will narcissistically (or as one may suppose, at the point of psychosis, schizophrenically) "adapt." The work of adaptation is the work of repression, a reduction of consciousness to the felt wholeness of a closed system. McLuhan compounds into his own psychological discourse his reading of the collective psychology of Carl Jung, the social psychology of Alfred Adler and Karen Horney, and the gestalt psychology of Wolfgang Kohler—the latter probably introduced to him through his reading of I. A. Richards. Freudianism, he believed, was too focused upon individual narratives and experiences circumscribed by the Oedipus complex and its libidinal economy.

In *From Cliché to Archetype*, McLuhan radically redefines a cliché to be any "unit extension of man," that is to say, any "medium, technology or environment." The cliché is taken for "transparent," whether it is the text behind the idea, the tool behind the work, or the market behind the product. It is "a coin so battered by use as to be defaced." No matter whether the "coin" is linguistic or technological, it acts as a form of social currency, an intersubjective medium of power and value. The cliché is represented or "archetypalized" in this aspect by the dramatist Ionesco, who "declined to see language as an instrument of communication or self-expression, but rather as an exotic substance secreted—in a sort of trance—by interchangeable persons" (McLuhan with Watson, 1970, pp. 21, 54, 204).

Here we must be reminded of Lacan's description of "empty speech" in similar terms drawn from Mallarmé:

> The art of the analyst must be to suspend the subject's uncertainties until their last mirages have been consumed. . . . Indeed, however empty [the subject's] discourse may seem, it is so only if taken at its face value: that which justifies the remark of Mallarmé's, in which he compares the common use of language to the exchange of a coin whose obverse and reverse no longer bear any but effaced figures, and which people pass from hand to hand "in silence" (Lacan, 1977, pp. 43).

In this passage the "value" referred to by Lacan can arise only in the symbolic dialogue of the analytic situation, that is, in a certain, transformative exchange in which "empty" speech becomes "full" or "true speech"; otherwise, it seems to me, the "coin" merely continues its exchanges, *méconnu,* in the subject's imaginary. One might suppose that Lacan refers merely to a function of speech in the quiet remove of the analytic situation, where media and technology would never want to tamper. But it is precisely here, where "the subject is spoken rather than speaking," that Lacan discovers the extensions of cultural, material media. The cliché substance of empty speech is a "language-barrier opposed to speech" whose mediating "thickness" should be measured "by the statistically determined total of pounds of printed paper, miles of record grooves, and hours of radio broadcasting that [our] culture produces per head of population." Lacan sees this material, linguistic "thickness" producing, paradoxically, an emptiness—that which constitutes, for example, "empty speech"—and he marks this paradox in an evocation of T. S. Eliot: "We are the hollow men / We are the stuffed men," he says of our "language-barrier" culture, "Leaning together / Headpiece filled with straw. Alas!" Here the substance of the emptiness, the straw, is that language-barrier of cultural media as cliché. Speech may be made of it, or it made of speech, but it is the speech of an other: "the subject is spoken rather than speaking" (Lacan, 1977, pp. 70–71).

To retain this material and historical sense of the real in giving particular form to the individual work and social matrix of the imaginary is to respect the social critique which polarizes Lacan's work in the late 1940s and 50s, a critique which he characterizes as an intervention of the quiet, symbolic function of psychoanalysis in the imaginary "madness that deafens the world with its sound and fury" (Lacan 1977: 7). It is in the clinical form of his symbolic intervention, rather than in his modernist social vision and critique, that Lacan's critical practice significantly diverges from McLuhan's. My justification for comparing McLuhan to Lacan is grounded in this vision and critique, not in any truth-value supposed by either of them. Lacanian concepts will be used, not to provide any external authority (indeed I am rather skeptical on this matter), but to describe and illuminate the subtleties of a modernist, psychoanalytic aesthetic that is congruent, in McLuhan's vision, with the better-known Lacanian model.

It is only in its misrecognized or *imaginary* function, described above, that McLuhan views the medium as a cliché—the *techne* in which the "subject is spoken rather than speaking." McLuhan sees a social and historical world organized by the cliché as praxis: the "cliché is not necessarily verbal . . . it is also an active, structuring, probing feature of our awareness." It is "an act of consciousness" deployed to extend its mastery over an environment, "serving to enlarge man's scope of action" along with "his patterns of association and awareness" (McLuhan with Watson, 1970, pp. 55, 150, 57). It is a practical as well as epistemological form of power and desire—power that is experienced as an imaginary mastery of its objective environment, and desire that is experienced as a play of aggressivity. McLuhan sees the "driving emotion in all technological cliché development" as the type of willful and aggressive, chaotic desire punned upon in Joyce's *Finnegans Wake:* "'A burning would is come to dance inane,' and of course, 'the willingdone musiroom'—a massive collection of human cliché and weaponry by which a 'burning would' manifests itself in ever new environments and power" (p. 124). The *weapon* appears here as a privileged example and metaphor for the cliché in McLuhan's text, since it represents the direct extension of power as an act of closure in the creation of mastery (the apparently complete conquest of what or who is other to the self). For the cliché as an extension or probe not only transforms its environment, but destroys it—the knife, for instance, which is the medium of Macbeth's imaginary aggression:

> Macbeth thinks in terms of the cliché-technologies of the knife and trammel net as means of murdering and creating, of probing and retrieving. His knife will destroy Duncan, that is, monarchy itself. "We will proceed no further in this business." The cliché of the knife as an instrument of ambition will destroy monarchy and order and all the political clichés of society. By scrapping all order, he will set up a school in which all will learn "bloody instructions." There will be nothing left to retrieve but the scrapped clichés of violence (p. 45).

The knife as clichés-weapon reduces all clichés (otherwise invested by archetypes of moral and political order) to their common denominator, in which Duncan is interchangeable with Macbeth is interchangeable with all others in the transitive chaos of imaginary power by "bloody instructions, which, being taught, return / To plague th' inventor." Macbeth's cliché act of betrayal not only "creates" the mirage of mastery which informs his ego fantasy, but the real forms of destruction and vulnerability around him, for which he must take tragic responsibility. And Macbeth's tragedy is an archetype of a cliché that is our own: "The very techniques by which one achieves desirable innovations, destroy most of the pre-existing achievements and require a new creation. The 'tragic flaw' is not a detail of characterization . . . but a structural feature of ordinary consciousness" (p. 45).

The work of the artist, already announced as such in *The Mechanical Bride*, is to reverse and retrace this tragic experience for others. One possibility is for the artist to do it for him or herself, then to offer this aestheticized self as a "mask" for others—so that others might retrace and recognize their imaginary selves (for example, in the cliché "self-portraits" of Cindy Sherman). In his consideration of the "author as cliché," McLuhan uses the example of "Montaigne" as a personal "body" which has extended its "members" into the "outerings and utterings" of a public book—that is, as a self-image "circulated as a public probe." This extension of the body and image, with its secrecies and obscenities, is also a mirror or mask in which the public "other" alternates as intimate confidant and victim of abuse. The same author-public couple McLuhan sees in Baudelaire, whose spleenful envoy to the readers of *Les fleurs du mal* he quotes—"*hypocrite lecteur, mon semblable, mon frère*"—and explains: "One is probe for the other. Both are clichés. Joyce put it in a phrase: 'My consumers, are they not my producers?'" (McLuhan with Watson, 1970, pp. 25–26, 27–28).

This is the Narcissan image of the author which Wyndham Lewis criticized in Joyce, whom he called a mere "craftsman," a "medium" or instrument of his environment, who could record no perceptions of his own but only channelled those of others, a world of mere "clichés" (Lewis, 1957, pp. 90, 96). This is the danger of the artist who plays a game on the edge of extinction in the *techne*. All artists and authors are, like Macbeth, inventors in the imaginary: "Perhaps all authors have to 'play God' in some degree for their public. After all, they do make a world. In *The Apes of God* Percy Wyndham Lewis queries the very essence of authors as godlike probes. He portrays them as essentially apes or manipulators of other people's archetypes" (McLuhan with Watson, 1970, p. 28). The artist is the ambivalent hero of McLuhan's media universe because his or her function is to invent new, whole worlds. But these worlds are not, like God's, ex nihilo. The artist merely recycles his or her environment, a process McLuhan calls "retrieval" and which works ironically against the "chaos" of the imaginary. For the artist's environment is none other than that vast "waste land" of the real, thrust out of normal perception by a culture's dominant clichés—whether these clichés are technologies or ideologies. The artist is its archeologist. McLuhan conceives of history as the real residue of imaginary *praxis*, the hidden, unimaginable ground of its exploits, taking whatever form—the junkyard, the waste land, the middenheap, the garbage, the repressed, the anonymous, the unconscious, the forgotten, the "dirt." This historical product is retrieved in symbolic form for the subject as a kind of *mirror on a mirror*—still a cliché, therefore, but one which reflects an image of the subject *and* its history or other scene. Such a retrieved or *reversed* image—such a "retracing" of imaginary projection— defines the *archetype* of McLuhan's idiosyncratic lexicon. It re-creates the real otherness of the cliché as fragment, psychic part, extension, and intersubjective medium of an anonymous, historical other.

The archetype is by definition always also a cliché: "The archetype is a retrieved awareness or consciousness. It is consequently a retrieved cliché—an old cliché retrieved by a new cliché." So retrieval does carry with it a danger, for if clichés are not retrieved as symbols but, in a great abstraction of the mind from history, as transcendental clichés annexed to a new imaginary, then the archetype is destined to fulfill the "cliché" definition set for them (mistakenly) by Northrop Frye. Always ready to contradict his perceived rival, McLuhan argues that Frye entirely mistakes the symbol for its opposite number, the cliché, and so encloses his students in a critical imaginary. "The student might easily find himself in a world of chaotic and conflicting suggestions if he were to attempt to use Northrop Frye's definition of a symbol as an exploratory probe: 'Symbol: Any unit of any work of literature which can be isolated for critical attention. In general usage restricted to the smaller units, such as words, phrases, images, etc.'" Archetypes for McLuhan are always historical and local. "But for the literary archetypalist," he says with respect to Frye, "there is always a problem of whether *Oedipus Rex* or *Tom Jones* would have the same effect on an audience in the South Sea Islands as in Toronto." Cliché and archetype have *real* historical limits. For similar reasons, McLuhan's understanding of the archetype should not be confused with that of psychoanalyst Carl Jung. The Jungian archetype is primarily of interest to McLuhan in its relation to psychic structure, not its relation to "race memory," which he admits has a "shaky scientific basis." (McLuhan with Watson, 1970, pp. 21, 36, 118, 23).

The world of the archetype, McLuhan repeats too many times to cite, is a "rag-and-bone shop" in which history returns upon the subject in symbolic form. But whereas the ego is coherent only in its images, and its images must remain closed within the felt wholeness of the imaginary extension of desire, the whole subjectivity is embedded in and with a history, never to be contained in a "masterful image" of itself. "Rag-and-bone shop" and "masterful image" are phrases McLuhan borrows from W. B. Yeats's "The Circus Animals' Desertion," which he analyzes in *From Cliché to Archetype* (pp. 126–7). This history can be retrieved or retraced because, while the cliché is "incompatible with other clichés, . . . when we consciously set out to retrieve one archetype, we unconsciously retrieve others; and this retrieval recurs in infinite regress" (p. 21). The archetype is caught up in the circulation of signifiers, of signifiers folded by associative implication with other signifiers according to an intersubjective order similar to the Lacanian symbolic. Lacan provides a good example of what McLuhan understands by archetypalization, in the work of re-creation forced upon the analytic subject in his or her session with the analyst: "In this labour which he [the subject] undertakes to reconstruct *for another* [the analyst], he [the subject] rediscovers the fundamental alienation that made him construct it *like another,* and which has always destined it to be taken from him *by another*" (Lacan, 1977, p. 46). It is as if the clichés of the subject spoken-rather-than-speaking suddenly appeared, by dint of repetition, in quotation marks—in a language not invented within the imaginary closure of the subject but easily circulated, as quotation or citation, slipping out of the subject's hands. For Lacan, this slippage is guided by the form of language in general, one drawn from a familiar model of speech. For McLuhan it is guided by forms of language media which are different and conflicted, so there is no general "discourse of the Other" which might totalize the relation of the subject to the world. This "archetypal unconscious" is the present form, extending well beyond the conscious self, of his or her retrieved history. The more radically consciousness is "dislocated" by symbolic interference from cliché—from, for example, the "centralizing imagery" of a period—the more it will be problematized by a differently sensed historical identity. This archetypal work is the highest function of art.

For McLuhan, art is not the specialized craft of an artist, but a general, cultural function. In *Understanding Media,* he defines the artist as "the man in any field, scientific or humanistic, who grasps the implications of his actions and of new knowledge in his own time." Correlatively, art is defined as "exact information of how to rearrange one's psyche in order to anticipate the next blow from our own extended faculties." The ideal "rearrangement" of the psyche in art becomes, in *From Cliché to Archetype,* the fissuring of the subject's consciousness by "gaps or intervals" open to the archetypal interpellation of contents repressed or abandoned to the junk-yard of a cultural, technological, ecological, and political unconscious. Despite its idealism, such a relation between the subject and the symbolic order which circu-lates the residuum of the real is yet less evasively idealized than the relation of "true speech" advanced by Lacan. Recall that the latter is meant, in the speaking situa-tion of psychoanalysis, to set up a kind of symbolic interference in the imaginary subject and its media. Its "goal is to restore in them [the 'slaves' of imaginary mas-tery] the sovereign freedom displayed by Humpty Dumpty when he reminds Alice that after all he is the master of the signifier, even if he isn't the master of the sig-nified in which his being took on its form." But for McLuhan, "the master of the signifier" is never more than an "ape of God," and the symbolic order of the arche-type has no meaning except in the imaginary play of cliché *praxis.* "Initially any cliché is a breakthrough into a new dimension of experience," while the archetype is only a repetition of the breakthroughs and breakdowns which transform reality, a retracing of its comings and goings (McLuhan with Watson, 1970, p. 58).

Modernist poets and artists, McLuhan would have us believe, turn the violence of their historical subjectivity away from the ego and its imaginary relations with the world, absorbing it instead in their archetypal or symbolic activity, their art. Through a kind of mimesis or symbolic repetition of this violence (with its echoes of ritual scapegoating or sacrifice), the artist momentarily dissolves his or her ego in the shattered image of its unconscious. McLuhan champions James Joyce for hav-ing, like Alice, "pushed all the way through the Narcissus looking glass" of being-in-media, and "moved from the private Stephen Dedalus to the Finnegan corporate image." If this Finnegan, like Humpty Dumpty, becomes visible in the "mirror of language," he says, it is not as a general, Lacanian *master of the signifier* but, he says, as a *symbolic* character, an image of selfhood *thrown together* from "the 'magazine wall' of memory and all human residue" (McLuhan with Watson, 1970, p. 163). The dif-ference between these two mirror images is given for McLuhan in the irreducibil-ity of the symbolic order to any essential form of language. The differences between various historical and material forms of language will always restrict the "master of the signifier" to a local field of power, to one corner of his or her junkyard. Once recognized as such, once historicized, the "master of the signifier" can only "ape" mastery—that is, can only project an *image* of it.

McLuhan's own public image of the sixties may be seen as just such a situation-al cliché, a product of his imaginarily conceived *praxis* as the master of signifiers proper to the Global Village. If modernist critics as diverse as Leavis, Innis and Lacan tried to discriminate and define a medium for critical self-knowledge in a her-metic and enduring, verbal situation—screened off from the background noise, the sound and fury of the "language-barrier"—McLuhan tried to invent more transient clichés which might do so from within the "language-barrier" itself. The latter critical art, as George Steiner recognized, is radically anti-essentialist in its pragmatism: "[As readers of McLuhan] we belong to an awfully important radical group. As Nietzsche says, 'I hope nobody will call himself a philosopher after this.' Certain op sculpture and op art has a built-in time bomb which says, 'You've seen me, it's a happening.' McLuhan is related to our present sense of those important thinkers who are deliberately subverting their own case" (Steiner, Miller and Forge, 1967, p. 239). McLuhan's art is an art of the Happening—an invention of his public image and critical rhetoric as self-destructing clichés.

In a chapter devoted to it in *From Cliché to Archetype,* McLuhan describes the Happening as an art formed out of the archetypal materials of Camp described by Susan Sontag: "Camp sees everything in quotation marks. It's not a lamp, but a 'lamp'; not a woman but a 'woman.' To perceive Camp in objects is to understand Being-as-Playing-a-Role. It is the farthest extension, in sensibility, of the metaphor of life as theater." The Happening uses Camp by depopulating it, subtracting the supposed actors from its metaphorical theatre, to produce an environment of objects and caricatures whose proper subjects—individuals and their imaginary hold on the environment—are missing. The critical process then begins, because "with the Happening the exploratory and probe functions have to be assumed by the audience directly. . . . It expects the audience to immerse itself in the 'destructive element,' as it were" (McLuhan and Watson, 1970, pp. 188, 198). The unrecognized, real media of individuality—its extensions in cliché imagery and technologies—becomes the message. The same reversal aesthetic McLuhan found in the interior landscapes of poetic form and its solitary reader, is here translated to theatrical form and its collective audience.

A very few critics, such as George Steiner and Raymond Williams, cautiously advanced the notion that the effect of McLuhan's clichés and contradictions, the short half-life given by his rhetoric to his ideas, was essential to the significance of his work (Williams, 1967, pp. 186–89; Steiner, Miller and Forge, 1967, p. 239). It was more than essential. It is the stylistic key to his peculiar, collective psychotherapeutic project of the sixties, which may now be seen as the attempt to channel as much of the unconscious "junkyard" of present historical waste—ideological, technological, social—through the symbolic orders of his time, the mass media and the university—to its destination in the imaginary powers of the "cliché" individual subject of that history. McLuhan was of course limited by his own, inescapable rivalries and fixations. His career, if in some ways really tragic, is yet the tragedy of an uncompromising self-satirist, of a Humpty Dumpty who masters the signifier of a period at the cost of relinquishing his ego to the signifieds informing its power and waste. The sixties presented to McLuhan a kind of bloating of the unconscious grounds of existence by the detritus of modernity, the returning shapes of oppressed races and genders (oppressed classes he imagined had already reversed their position in modernity), repressed myths and ideologies, suppressed industrial environments of pollution and actual garbage. "For great stretches of cultural time the unconscious has been the environment of consciousness. The roles of guest and host are tending to reverse at present" (McLuhan and Watson, 1970, p. 200). Under these conditions, McLuhan saw individual consciousnesses also as tired clichés, overwhelmed and recontained by the "destructive element" of their own, hidden historical residuum in their mode of production.

Rather than produce, like other sixties intellectuals, a "theory" of his time, McLuhan tried to adhere to what he perceived to be the truth of the "Mess Age" as mediating, for its subject, an infinite regress of possible clichés and grounds irreducible to theorization. "The medium is the message" was one such cliché, "cliché" and "archetype" themselves, less successful ones. The effect may be compared with advertising, which McLuhan considered a paradigmatic discourse of his time: "Ads are the cave art of the twentieth century. . . . They are vortices of collective power, masks of energy invented by a new tribal man." The statement appears in his 1970 book of advertisement analyses, *Culture Is Our Business,* which asserts that art cannot easily be distinguished from commercial arts or advertising, since "business and culture have become interchangeable" (McLuhan, 1970, p. 7). McLuhan's critical art (and business) thus tends towards the social-psychological program of that author he read more than any other, Wyndham Lewis: "You must talk with two tongues, if you do not wish to cause confusion. . . . / For, the Individual, the single object, and the isolated, is, you will admit, an absurdity. / Why try and give the impression of a consistent and indivisible personality?" (McLuhan and Watson, 1970, pp. 161–62). This modernist self-reversal McLuhan likened to "standing on both sides of a mirror simultaneously." The journey through the looking-glass is a prescription for self-satire, the insertion of the subject into a junkyard of his or her own "extended" history or being-in-media. This is a modernist view of the critic, which perhaps persists in the social dimension of Lacan's discourse. In *Television* (1990), he describes the psychoanalytic critic as a kind of saint, whose "business" is to "embody," to sacrifice him or herself to, the "trash" of unconscious subjectivity (Lacan, 1990, p. 15).

The packaged "McLuhan" is now nearly extinct. But the retrieval of McLuhan's tarnished *image* may provide a conscious mirror in which to view archetypes of the cliché implications of our own critical practice today.

As I initially suggested, these processes are all spelled out in the pre-digital *Mechanical Bride* (1951). In one of the book's many mass cultural "exhibits," titled "Woman in a Mirror," McLuhan compares a magazine advertisement for nylon stockings (Berkshire Knitting Mills, 1947) to Picasso's oil painting, *Girl Before a*

Mirror (1932). He tells us that the modernist "technique" of "juxtaposition and contrast," of "withholding syntactical connection," is used by both to express a hidden "symbolic unity among the most diverse and externally unconnected facts or situations" (McLuhan, 1951, p. 80). But whereas the advertisement is meant to work its expression unconsciously, in effect to insert its dream logic of signs seamlessly and subliminally into the similarly symbolically-structured, fantasy life of the individual, the work of modern art is meant to do just the opposite, to retrace and reveal this unconscious structure and process as a wake-up call to the individual, to display what has been repressed. In the ad, the "mirror" to which McLuhan refers is both a squared-off archway that separates the image of a model from that of a rearing horse, and the frame of the ad itself in relation to the gaze of the reader. In the painting, the mirror is more explicitly the linear figure that separates complementary images of a woman—in McLuhan's words, "setting a conventional day-self over against a tragic night-self" (p. 80)—so that the painting self-reflexively represents the mirror, and perhaps the painting itself, as a psychological form. Picasso turns the "conventional day-self" of the *cliché* advertising image into an *archetype* of the "tragic night-self" of the consumer. The discourse of sexual desire and aggressivity that determines the latter *via* the former, is explored throughout *The Mechanical Bride* as the product of a sensationalist, profit-driven marketplace that has thoroughly industrialized—through technological production, media production, and market research—the modern psyche.

In 1970, then, McLuhan envisioned the same world, at least in this dystopic dimension: a social and political world plunged in what he had earlier described as somnambulism, and now figured as dreaming awake (McLuhan and Watson, 1970, p. 200). In the later vision, however, two new considerations arise. Firstly, the "industrial" and "mechanical" discourse is gone, and with it most of the anti-capitalist critique. In its place we have respectively the "digital" and the "electronic," and an ambiguously (I have argued, in a neutral sense, "duplicitous") affirmative citation of capitalist processes in (high and low) culture. Secondly, it is not clear that waking into a consciousness of this condition—that is, restoring the mastery of an authentic self over the externally manipulated unconscious and over its signifiers—can be so clearly distinguished from dreaming.

The confident psychological program of *The Mechanical Bride*, burning with anti-modernist (and true to the period type, masculinist) energy, is to restore the proper ego, the mature consciousness, the authentic individual self, in a public (i.e., commercial mass media) world of mechanical, mesmerized, and otherwise somnambulant others. But the program of the later "McLuhan" scatters or lacks this energy and confidence, and does not seem to promise any restoration from categories of artifice to those of authenticity. Precisely this breakdown of distinctions, between artificial and authentic experience, is what Dean MacCannell (1976) once argued defines modernity. The modern seeks endlessly for the "real" in a world of cultural productions, whose only authenticity (what Benjamin called aura) is itself artificial. By all accounts McLuhan never explicitly affirmed or identified with his own (in part) productions of "McLuhan." I suspect he retained a distance of modernist transcendence characterized by Eliot, that of a spiritual and timeless still point (albeit one recognized and accessed, paradoxically, through temporal moments of experience, and for McLuhan, specifically, through fault lines in media as such); this enabled McLuhan to distance himself (he would say, as a "detached observer") at a third point, away from the postmodernist collapse of a reality-simulation dualism. Authenticity, in other words, is not a temporal concern; at best it is a dialectical one, whose spiritual (and perhaps properly mystical) recognition depends upon a leap of faith with respect to a Baudrillardian postmodern condition. Such an authenticity is more absolutely humble (if I can use such a phrase) than even that humility characteristic of Eliot, whose repeated projection of a masterful if abject visionary point of view admits both explicit lamentation over the progress of history and direct cultural critique. The later McLuhan can affirm waking, without reference to any ground of self or society that is outside the dream, because waking and dreaming become one indivisible spiritual process—and in the processes of cliché and archetype, one structured like a language!—rather than hierarchically maintained psychological states.

Indeed, McLuhan's most startling quality is his deconstruction of the conscious/unconscious discursive hierarchy upon which *The Mechanical Bride* and modern cultural criticism more generally had been based. Hence the *archetype* must not be understood merely as the "coming to consciousness" of a cliché, but as an ongoing *retracing* of that very process itself as it stages itself, as it plays itself out in series of cultural productions of the "authentic" (conscious) self and "real" (basic) social forms. Such a retracing is not wholly conscious, nor guided by conscious or individual mastery. When McLuhan says, as he occasionally does, that everything he says is quoted or borrowed, or he emphasizes collective dialogue over individual argument, there is something to it that goes to the heart of his intellectual project in the sixties and beyond. The authorial ego is sacrificed—it is tempting to say, even in the religious sense—to the explosion of cultural productions of the "real" and the "self" in media. So it is, I have argued, that "McLuhan" retraces its own signature in the media. This may be understood as the archetype of what Paul Mann calls "masocriticism," the pathetic and aggressive cliché of modern critical practice:

> Like everything else in culture, criticism is driven by obscure identifications, attachments, revulsions, by forces of desire and aggression that its various representations always conceal and displace.

> Whatever semblance of mastery one manages to project, and whatever critical distance one arrogates to oneself, writing entails orders of submission that cannot be reduced to operational, ideological, or linguistic protocols alone. The something else to which one's discourse is always subjected, and which one seeks to control through myriad proxies, is in the end the master that can never be mastered, least of all by the hapless (ethical, postcolonial, psychoanalytic, etc.) discourse of the Other (Mann, 1999, p. 24).

While Mann is thinking mainly of literary criticism here, and the relationship of the critic to the figure of an author, the suggestion is equally compelling for the critic of mass culture considered as a text, whose "author" figure will represent a power and mastery that, if admittedly less determinate, will be felt to be that much more present and concrete. "McLuhan" is an unsettling (because uncanny) image of the intellectual "ape of God," the writer or teacher who pretends to master the language of the world, who projects the image of a waking consciousness, ready to decode the signs of its dream—but who must in doing so produce another discourse plunged in the cultural field, another commodity plunged in the commodity world, another fiction plunged in the factory of modern dreams. Because such waking must go on and on ("I can't go on, I'll go on") there is no end to this waking (as the temporal, diverse production of wakings rather than as a determinate, ideal state); there is no end to dreaming either. But if waking can never rid itself of this supplementary dreaming, and both must go on, then what happens to cultural critique, and to the force of McLuhan's earlier, dystopian vision of the exploitative organization of fantasy by a capitalist world? How can one distinguish between "dreaming awake" this world, and never waking to it at all? What is the good of what increasingly appears, in the archetypal dissemination of "McLuhan," nothing more than an act of faith?

Returning now to my initial suggestion that McLuhan's darker view of modernity in *The Mechanical Bride* underlies his later work, I would not deny that such an aesthetic of retracing may for McLuhan be just that: a spiritual exercise, whose good lies in a transcendental negation. This is certainly implied, for example, when McLuhan comments in *From Cliché to Archetype* upon Yeats' having to "lie down where all the ladders start." McLuhan brilliantly inverts the realist irony of the assertion by reading the ladder as Jacob's ladder: "Jacob lay down only to climb a ladder, or to dream, at least, of a ladder of angels ascending and descending in heavenly hierarchy" (p. 127). Here the poet's ironic denial of the transcendental cliché, of masterful dreams in relation to the world, are turned into an alternative transcendence based on negation of that world by the humble dreamer. According to this spiritual logic, one must lie down and dream in order properly to rise and wake, i.e., to one's relationship to an Other beyond history. This, too, is what McLuhan says Milton's Satan is initially conscious of, but soon represses and forgets: "his subordination to God as created Being to uncreated Being," and the primal "defeat which had been inflicted upon him" (p. 15). And accordingly, the modern dream factory may be retraced and its imaginary ladders pulled down, only in order to dream this final, mortifying dream of an absurd ladder—one that, if pulled down, would collapse in the opposite direction (from whence it began), and negate the meaning of all the dreamer's temporal world, everything the dreamer knows and is, but the dream itself. Surely, McLuhan's many critics of the sixties and seventies saw in "McLuhan" this kind of negation: a kind of incoherent or volatile morality, whether euphoric or apocalyptic in tone, and an implicitly resigned, transcendental distance from social problems and the need for social change, which was typically ascribed to an overly conservative Catholicism. Whether there is something to this reading of McLuhan or not, it remains too simple on its own, and cannot account for McLuhan's willful participation in a McLuhan industry, or the dissemination of a "McLuhan" that has exceeded whatever intentions and interests were his own.

The sacrificial insertion of McLuhan's own image into the dream factory of mass culture is not merely masocritical with respect to some ultimate Other, even according to Mann's secular account of modern criticism. I refer to sacrifice because of the destruction of a self-projection of the ego, initiated for the good of others in relation to some transcendental Other, that is involved in the loss of control of a prestigious or even coherent identity and author in "McLuhan," letting loose the signature to accumulate and disperse meanings, to initiate divergent productions, to "ape" wholeness and presence in so many disseminations, and to represent thereby its subjection to and distortion by, violently perhaps, other organizations of force and meaning. To retrace the dream factory is to interrupt and penetrate its dream work, as Freud knew at the very start: dream analysis *feeds back* into dream thoughts and dream work. In this way modern media may reveal themselves, even within the fantasy work of the capitalist world factory, as the repressed or cliché engines of cultural (in)authenticity. Where authenticity, the real of self and world, is recognized as labouriously created and consumed as such, rather than essentially given in the reified form of humanist values, psychic drives, or market emotions, the nature of fantasy itself must change, perhaps unimaginably, and reality with it. The process of psychological feedback is key, because for McLuhan it defines cybernetic—what I have more handily called digital—as opposed to mechanical media. Feedback "means introducing an information loop or circuit, where before there had been merely a one-way flow or mechanical sequence," he announces in the last pages of *Understanding Media*: "Feedback is the end of the lineality that came into the Western world with the alphabet and the continuous forms of Euclidean space" (McLuhan, 1964, p. 307). Waking is becoming vulnerable to feedback, not finally getting it right.

In other words, you can awake from the dystopian dream world of *The Mechanical Bride*, but never to a non-mechanical bride. Everything is already mechanical, in the expanded sense of a total penetration of the artificial and the authentic (hence the collapse of the bride/prostitute distinction, and embedded within it, the inalienable/alienable property or good/commodity distinction). This last condition is now called cyborgian, fusing the categories of human and machine, and it belongs to the world no longer named mechanical but digital. What "McLuhan" explores and retraces for us is this digital dystopia, the fantasy factory from which we can no longer escape but within which we may lodge images of our own subjection and enthrallment, that might lead to new kinds of fantasy, and ritual signs, no longer desirous of—as if according to the kind of overdrawn reality principle that Marcuse associates with surplus repression (Marcuse, 1966, p. 35)— the kind of oppressive drive to mastery unleashed by the individual and institutional Macbeths of the modern world. To wake up to the digital call girl rather than to the mechanical bride is to submit the call girl, and the waking self, to a new dream work, in which prostitution—along with the alienation and exploitation of a modern capitalism of which, in modern art, she has been mirror image and archetype—is no longer desired.

References

Alderman, T. (1966, August 6). The all-at-once world of the management hootenanny starring Marshall McLuhan. *Canadian* [Ottawa] *Citizen*, 16–19.

Arlen, M. J. (1969). Marshall McLuhan and the technological embrace. In R. Rosenthal (Ed.), *McLuhan: Pro and con* (pp. 82–87). Baltimore, MD: Penguin.

Burke, K. (1969). Medium as "message". In R. Rosenthal (Ed.), *McLuhan: Pro and con* (pp. 165–177). Baltimore, MD: Penguin.

Compton, N. (1969). The paradox of Marshall McLuhan. In R. Rosenthal (Ed.), *McLuhan: Pro and con* (pp. 106–124). Baltimore, MD: Penguin.

Crosby, H. H., & Bond, G. R. (Eds.) (1968). *The McLuhan explosion: A casebook on Marshall McLuhan and Understanding Media*. New York: American.

Diamond, E. (1967, March 6). The message of Marshall McLuhan. *Newsweek, 69*(6), 54–57.

Fekete, J. (1982). Massage in the mass age: Remembering the McLuhan matrix. *Canadian Journal of Political and Social Theory, 6*(3), 50–67.

Finkelstein, S. (1968). *Sense and nonsense of McLuhan*. New York: International Publishers.

Howard, J. (1966, February 25). Oracle of the electric age. *Life, 60* (8), 92–95.

Kenner, H. (1969). Understanding McLuhan. In R. Rosenthal (Ed.), *McLuhan: Pro and con* (pp. 23–28). Baltimore, MD: Penguin.

Klonsky, M. (1969). McLuhan's message or: Which way did the Second Coming went? In R. Rosenthal (Ed.), *McLuhan: Pro and con* (pp. 125–139). Baltimore, MD: Penguin.

Lacan, J. (1977). *Ecrits: A selection*. (A. Sheridan, Trans.) New York: Norton

Lewis, W. (1957). *Time and western man*. Boston: Beacon.

MacCannell, D. (1976). *The tourist: A new theory of the leisure class.* New York: Schocken.

Mann, P. (1999). *Masocriticism.* Albany, NY: State University of New York.

Marchand, P. (1989). *Marshall McLuhan: The medium and the messenger.* New York: Ticknor and Fields.

Marcuse, H. (1966). *Eros and civilization: A philosophical inquiry into Freud.* Boston: Beacon.

McLuhan, M. (1962). *The Gutenberg galaxy: The making of typographic man.* Toronto: University of Toronto Press.

McLuhan, M. (1964). *Understanding media: The extensions of man.* New York: McGraw-Hill.

McLuhan, M. (1951). *The mechanical bride: Folklore of industrial man.* New York: Vanguard.

McLuhan, M. (1970). *Culture is our business.* New York: McGraw-Hill.

McLuhan, M., & Fiore, Q. (1967). *The medium Is the massage: An inventory of effects.* New York: Bantam.

McLuhan, M., with W. Watson. (1970). *From cliche to archetype.* New York: Viking.

Missika, J. L. (1991, April 19). Review of Cours de Mediologie Generale by Regis Debray. *Le Monde*, 17.

Molinaro, M., McLuhan, C., & Toye, W. (Eds.) (1987). *Letters of Marshall McLuhan.* Toronto: Oxford.

Pollack, R. (1966, February 28). Understanding McLuhan. *Newsweek, 67*(9), 56–57.

Ricks, C. (1969). McLuhanism. In R. Rosenthal (Ed.), *McLuhan: Pro and con* (pp. 100–105). Baltimore, MD: Penguin.

Rosenberg, H. (1965, February 27). Philosophy in a pop key. *New Yorker*, 129–36.

Rosenthal, R. (Ed.) (1969). *McLuhan: Pro and con.* Baltimore: Penguin.

Roszak, T. (1969). The summa popologica of Marshall McLuhan. In R. Rosenthal (Ed.), *McLuhan: Pro and con* (pp. 257–269). Baltimore, MD: Penguin.

Schickel, R. (1965, November). Marshall McLuhan: Canada's intellectual comet. *Harper's Magazine, 231*(1386), 62–66.

Stearn, G. E. (Ed.) (1967). *McLuhan: Hot and Cool, a critical symposium.* New York: Dial.

Steiner, G., Miller, J., & Forge, A. (1967). The world and Marshall McLuhan. In G. E. Stearn (Ed.), *McLuhan: Hot and Cool, a critical symposium* (pp. 236–242). New York: Dial.

Wagner, G. (1969). Misunderstanding media: Obscurity as authority. In R. Rosenthal (Ed.), *McLuhan: Pro and con* (pp. 153–164). Baltimore: Penguin.

Williams, R. (1967). Paradoxically, if the book works it to some extent annihilates itself. In G. E. Stearn (Ed.), *McLuhan: Hot and Cool, a critical symposium* (pp. 186–189). New York: Dial.

Wolfe, T. (1969). *The pump house gang.* New York: Bantam.

CHAPTER FOUR

Studying Media *as* Media:
McLuhan and the Media Ecology Approach

Lance Strate

Let me begin with a story about a professor at my university. This professor was a senior faculty member and an accomplished scholar, and he had a no-nonsense approach to education. He regularly taught a large, impersonal lecture course. It was a required course, which meant that the professor was free to make it as difficult and demanding as he liked. And he relished the reputation he gained for his strict and severe grading. His final examinations were especially tough, and at the beginning of the exam period, the professor would warn his students that they must stop writing when he announces that the test is over. Otherwise, they would be given a failing grade for the final, and fail the course.

One semester, one of his students ignored this warning, and continued to work on his essay after the professor announced that time had run out. All of the other students obediently put their pens down, and dropped off their examination booklets in a great pile on the desk at the front of the room. As the rest of the students walked out of the room, the one student finished writing, and walked to the front of the room with his booklet. The professor looked at him sternly, and told him that he would not accept his exam, and that the student would receive a failing grade. The student looked the professor squarely in the eye and said: "Do you know who I am?" The professor responded: "No, I do not, and frankly I couldn't care less!" The student then said "Good!" and stuck his final into the middle of the pile of booklets, and ran off.

Now, I must confess to you that this is not a true story. I took it from a book of urban legends written by the American folklorist Jan Harold Brunvand (1986). Actually, Brunvand refers to this particular story as one of the legends of academe, but the important point is that it is truly a legend, a story passed on and preserved by word of mouth. It is told on many different college campuses in the United States, but always told as a true story that happened right here, at our school, at some time in the recent past. Nowadays, when so much of our attention is captured by our electronic technologies and digital communications, it is both important and humbling to recall that speech is still the foundation of human culture, and that oral traditions have yet to be extinguished altogether. At the same time, it is clear that the urban legends of today are but a faint echo of the orality that existed before writing took hold. We have no living tradition of orally composed epics such as the *Iliad* and *Odyssey, Gilgamesh, Beowulf,* the *Elder Edda,* or the *Kalevala.* We have no non-literate singers of tales whose bardic performances maintain cultural continuity from generation to generation. We do not depend on collective memory alone for the preservation of knowledge. And poetry, proverbs, and other such oral media no longer serve as our dominant mode of public communication.

The legend of the professor and student originates as an oral form of communication, but its content is very much derived from literate culture. The setting of the school represents the institutionalization of literacy, and the university symbolizes literacy in its highest form. The professor is an embodiment of the literate mindset, demanding that his students proceed by the book, and that his instructions be followed to the letter. In other words, his rigidity mirrors the fixity of the written word, in contrast to the flexibility and multiformity of oral traditions. Also, the professor is an elitist, treating his students as if they were beneath contempt. The word "elite" comes from the same root as "literacy," both referring to the distinction between the lettered and the unlettered. And, of course, the legend revolves around an examination, where the main activity is writing, and it is the student's refusal to stop writing that gets him in trouble.

The student's ultimate triumph is derived from the fact that the examination booklets are mass-produced products, each one identical to the other, insuring his anonymity. They are, in fact, print media, a point we tend to overlook because most of what is printed does not consist of words, or pictures, but of straight lines to guide our handwriting. In one of my own classes, I use a piece of ruled paper as a test for my students. I show them the paper and ask them to write down what they see. Some students write that it is a blank piece of paper. To them I say that they need to shed their preconceptions and use their powers of observation. Other students write that it is lined paper, sometimes also noting the color of the lines and the paper. To them I say that they are using their senses, but need to think more about the meaning of what they see. And finally, a few students will say that they see lines *printed* on paper, or even that they see a *print medium*. And to them I say that you are ready to study media, that is, to study media *as* media.

The professor in our legend does not understand media *as* media. He is fully immersed in literate culture, and dismisses alternatives, or cannot imagine them in the first place. The student, on the other hand, is the central figure in an oral narrative, and very much resembles the trickster character of oral myth and legend, such as the Native American Coyote god, the ancient Greek Titan Prometheus, or the Norse pantheon's Loki. The student has much in common with these oral heroes (Strate, 1994, 1995, 2008), but at the same time he is literate enough to pursue higher education. And given the fact that this legend is a contemporary one, I think it safe to assume that the student is in fact postliterate, a product of the electronic media environment. Much like the computer hacker, he steps outside of the system, uncovers its code, and alters it to his own benefit. The literate culture that the school manifests is an invisible environment to the professor. But literate culture's structure, and its flaws, stand exposed to the students of the electronic era.

The student is the hero of the legend, and the story is told so as to foster our sympathy for him. Of course, those of us who are educators may feel guilty for taking sides against our colleague, the professor. But I want to suggest to you that it is in fact appropriate for us to identify with the student. As students ourselves, we need to use our powers of observation to reveal our otherwise invisible media environments. And as scholars, we need to use our powers of understanding to make meaning out of our media environments, and their effects. After all, consider just some of the fields of study that have arisen in response to innovations in communication technology.

Alphabetic writing, by virtue of its ability to make speech visible, gave rise to the discipline of rhetoric in ancient times, and to the study of language and poetics, which was also known as grammar; the alphabet also set the stage for what was known as dialectics, or logic, as codified by Aristotle. Rhetoric, grammar, and logic together became known as the trivium, the basis of the medieval university curriculum, and what became known as the liberal arts. In the nineteenth century, innovations such as the steam-powered printing press and telegraphy led to both the modern newspaper and also to journalism as an academic pursuit, while the addition of the motion picture gave birth to film theory and cinema studies. The introduction of broadcasting in the form of radio, following on the heels of mass circulation newspapers and magazines, and the movies resulted in the study of mass communication. The invention of photography, film, and sound recording suggested the studies of interpersonal communication and nonverbal communication. Sound recording technology was also instrumental to the discovery of primary oral cultures and the beginning of orality-literacy studies (Lord, 1960; Ong, 1982; Parry, 1971). Electricity and electric devices, especially the electric media of communication were essential to the development of technology studies (Carey, 1989, 1997), and information theory, cybernetics and systems theory (Bertalanffy, 1969; Wiener, 1950). In many ways, the modern field of communication established in the aftermath of World War II went hand in hand with the development of television, information technology, and the digital computer (Shannon & Weaver, 1949; Wiener, 1950).

These very same media and technologies had much to do with the sudden interest in studying language and symbols that is characteristic of the late nineteenth and early twentieth century, which includes the new fields of linguistics and semiotics, in analytic philosophy, general semantics, and of course in media ecology, the intellectual tradition with which I am associated. In this essay, my focus will be on Marshall McLuhan, but I want to make it clear that media ecology is more than McLuhanism. Its roots can be traced to the studies of technology produced by Lewis Mumford, Jacques Ellul, and Peter Drucker; the research on oral tradition, writing systems, and typography associated with Eric Havelock, Walter Ong, Jack Goody, and Denise Schmandt-Besserat, as well as Lucien Febvre, Henri-Jean Martin, and Elizabeth Eisenstein; the studies of media and culture of Harold Innis, Edward T. Hall, Edmund Carpenter, and James Carey; and the investigations into symbolic form carried out by Alfred Korzybski, Suzanne Langer, Dorothy Lee, and Neil Postman (for an extended review of the literature in the field of media ecology, see Strate, 2006; see also Lum, 2006).

Media ecology is the study of media *as* media, which follows from McLuhan's (1964) famous maxim, "the medium is the message" (p. 7). "The medium is the message" is McLuhan's wake up call to individuals like the professor who, like most people, tend to ignore the medium and only pay attention to content. McLuhan was trying to say that, "it's the medium stupid!" McLuhan's goal was the liberation of the human mind and spirit from its subjugation to symbol systems, media, and technologies. This can only begin with a wake-up call to pay attention to the medium, because it is the medium that has the greatest impact on human affairs, not the specific messages we send or receive. It is the symbolic form that is most significant, not the content. It is the technology that matters the most, its nature and its structure, and not our intentions. It is the materials that we work with, and the methods we use to work with them, that have the most to do with the final outcome of our labors.

Of course, there are some who disagree with this point of view. For example, in the United States there is the National Rifle Association, a pressure group that opposes all attempts at gun control. Their slogan is "guns don't kill people, people do." If you disagree with this argument, and believe that there is greater potential for violence with firearms than without them, then you believe that the medium is the message. The idea has been expressed in any number of ways. It is inherent in

Henry David Thoreau's (1980) observation on the building of the railroads: "we do not ride on the railroad; it rides upon us" (p. 67). The idea is also implied in Mark Twain's wonderful remark that when you have a hammer in your hand, everything looks like a nail (quoted in Eastham, 1990, p. 17).

The medium is the message because content cannot exist without a medium. Words can take the form of speech, or writing, for example. Or they can exist as internalized speech within the mind, the product of nerve impulses in the brain. But there must be some physical basis for them, in matter or energy. And the different forms that they take determine what their meaning and impact might be. The words we think to ourselves seem different when we utter them out loud. The words we write down take on a permanence, distance, and impersonal quality in comparison to speech.

Along the same lines, information does not exist in a vacuum. It can be found riding radiowaves or the electric current running through wires, or stored in magnetic or optical form. Or information can be found in the sequences of chemicals that make up strands of DNA and RNA. The code and the mode of information that is used will determine who has access to the data and who controls its dissemination, how much information will be distributed, how fast it will be transmitted, how far it will travel, how long the information will be available, and the form in which it will be displayed. As these variables change, so does the message that is being communicated.

Artists have long understood that the medium is the message, that the same subject will yield an entirely different effect if the image is rendered in oil paints or watercolors, or sketched in charcoal. Sculptors likewise know that the decision of whether to chisel a bust out of stone, carve it from wood, or mold it in clay will have a major impact on the end product. And musicians will tell you that when the same melody is played on violin, trumpet, and xylophone, you have three different pieces of music.

The medium is the message as well because the medium precedes the message. Before we produce the finished product, we must first have the raw materials we need, and the means to shape them. Before we can encode a message, we must first have the code with which to construct it. And before we learn how to talk, we first must babble. The sounds that babies make, goo-goo, ga-ga and the like, are the sounds of the medium of speech without the linguistic content. First we learn how to recognize and make the significant sounds of our language, and only later do we learn how to make the significant symbols, that is, spoken words.

McLuhan (1964) also argued that the medium is the message because the content of a medium is, in a certain way, another medium. For example, the medium of speech becomes the content of writing, the medium of writing becomes the content of print, the medium of print becomes the content of hypertext. Jay David

Bolter and Richard Grusin (1999) refer to this process as *remediation*. And they point out that the computer and computer networks remediate just about every other medium in existence, turning written documents, books, magazines and newspapers, paintings and photographs, sound recordings and telephone conversations, as well as radio, movies, and television into content for websites and multimedia presentations. At the same time, computer displays and interfaces are themselves remediated as content for older media such as motion pictures and television. When one medium becomes another medium's content, it becomes the code, symbolic form, or aesthetic style used to create specific messages.

McLuhan explained that another reason why the medium is the message is because the user is the content. What he meant was that audiences and readers must interpret the messages that they receive, process the sensory data that they take in, make meaning out of their environments, the artifacts that exist in them, and the events that occur within them. This coincides with such approaches to the study of communication, media, and culture as reader response theory, uses and gratifications research, ethnographic research of audiences and consumers, and studies of the decoding process; it also is consistent with contemporary research on the biology of perception and cognitive science. The point here is that if the message is largely constructed on the receiving end of communication, then its effect on us is limited. Therefore, it is the medium and not the message that has the greatest influence on the user and the audience. Put another way, it is the context that determines the content.

McLuhan's critics have been fond of making the counter-statement that the medium is *not* the message, to the point that this denial has become an academic cliché. And of course it misses McLuhan's point entirely. We all know that medium and message are separate categories. That is our starting point, and dismissing McLuhan simply leaves us back at square one. The critics seem to think that we are dealing with a mathematical equation, which says, "let x equal medium, let y equal message, such that x equals y." But "the medium is the message" is a metaphor not a mathamatical problem and, it also is a contradiction in terms, an oxymoron—Ray Gozzi, Jr. (1999) calls it an oxymetaphor. Its purpose is to call our attention to the complex, dialectical relationship between medium and message.

McLuhan's critics have also taken him to task for denying the existence of content altogether, which would certainly be an absurdity. In point of fact, he was merely trying to put content in its place, a secondary role in relation to the medium. Whatever the consequences of the messages we send, it is the media we use that play the leading role in human affairs, it is our technologies that shape us individually and collectively.

McLuhan's emphasis on media effects has led some of his critics to label his approach as technological determinism. Technological determinism is a straw man used to caricature McLuhan as some sort of media Calvinist, and to dismiss his arguments without serious consideration. After all, most people get upset at the denial of free will, in theory as well as in practice. But McLuhan never actually used the term determinism, nor did he argue against human agency. In his best selling book, *The Medium Is the Massage,* he wrote, "there is absolutely no inevitability as long as there is a willingness to contemplate what is happening" (McLuhan & Fiore, 1967, p. 25). John Culkin (1967) summed up McLuhan's position with the quote, "we shape our tools and thereafter they shape us" (p. 52), suggesting a transactional approach to media.

Free will does not mean freedom from limits, constraints, and outside influences. As diffusion researcher Everett Rogers (2003) puts it, innovations have consequences, and while some of the consequences may be desirable, others may be undesirable. And while some consequences may be direct effects of the introduction of a new technology, these in turn may lead to further indirect effects. And while some consequences may be anticipated, there will always be others that are unanticipated. Along the same lines, it may be true that a good part of what we call reality is a social construction, but the construction we end up with is not necessarily one that we intended to build. Moreover, only an intellectual divorced from everyday life could forget that construction begins with raw materials and the tools to shape them. Media are the stuff with which we build our social realities.

Other critics complain that media ecology scholars like McLuhan, Havelock, and Ong put forth a "Great Divide" theory, exaggerating the difference between orality and literacy, for example. And it is true that they see a great divide between orality and literacy. And a great divide between word and image. And a great divide between the alphabet on the one hand, and pictographic and ideographic writing on the other. And a great divide between clay tablets as a medium for writing, and papyrus. And a great divide between parchment and paper. And a great divide between scribal copying and the printing press. And a great divide between typography and the electronic media. And now a great divide between virtuality and reality. I could continue to add to this list, but the point is that there are many divides, which suggests that no single one of them is all that great, after all.

The critics miss the point that media ecology scholars often work dialectically, using contrasts to understand media. Additional examples would include Mumford's (1934) organic and mechanical ideologies, Innis's (1951) heavy and light media, and space and time biases, and McLuhan's (1964) categories of hot and cool. Theorists such as Donald Theall (2001) and Daniel Czitrom (1983) have described McLuhan's method as a form of dialectics, while Judith Stamps (1995) and Paul Grosswiler (1998) have traced the parallels between McLuhan's implicit dialectical system, and the explicit dialectics of critical theorists. McLuhan (2006) was critical of dialectics in the classical sense, it should be noted, arguing that the emphasis on logic originating with Socrates, Plato, and Aristotle, was in conflict with approaches that favor rhetoric and grammar, with which he was aligned. But the concepts of the dialectician that Stamps and Grosswiler discuss represent a significant movement towards McLuhan's ideal of the grammarian. In general, media ecology represents a less mature body of theory than critical theory (if media ecology is to be considered theory at all), but also one that is more open-ended and adaptable, and more concrete, less prone to *the hardening of the categories*, as McLuhan was wont to say. Ultimately, dialectics is not an end in itself for media ecology scholars, but rather a step that brings us closer to a truly ecological perspective.

Media ecology scholars also use broad categories like oral, scribal, print, and electronic cultures. They are alternatives to divisions such as agricultural, industrial, and information societies, based on the notion that it is communication, not economics, that most influences social life. In this sense, we would view the evolution of speech and language as intrinsically related to the origin of the human species. The development of systems of writing from various forms of notation is associated with the transition from tribal societies to what has traditionally been called civilization, that is, the founding of cities in Egypt, Mesopotamia, India, and China. The substitution of paper for parchment, and the printing revolution that began with Johann Gutenberg is tied to the shift from the medieval period in Europe to modernity. And as electronic and audiovisual media have been introduced over the course of the nineteenth and twentieth centuries, we recognize that we have entered into a new period of history, one that we have yet to understand, so that the best we can do is to term it postmodern.

Each of these broadly defined historical periods can also be understood as a basic type of media environment, that is, the oral, scribal, print, and electronic media environments. But media ecology scholars also recognize that any given society at any given time has its own unique media environment. Whether we focus on the general or the specific, what is essential is to understand that media *are* environments. It is more common to think of media in terms of a pipeline or transportation, something that links or bridges two points. Media ecology scholars have long been critical of the transportation model, McLuhan (1995) arguing that we should replace transportation with *transformation*, Tony Schwartz (1974) that we should use the concept of *resonance*, James Carey (1989) that we substitute *ritual*, and Walter Ong (1982) that we simply use *human communication*.

All of these possibilities have ecological connections, but the term in question, "medium," is also defined as a substance that surrounds or pervades, that goes between two points not by drawing a straight line between them, but by drawing a circle around them. For example, fish swim through the medium of water, just as we move through the medium of air. Bacteria such as acidophilous live in the medium of milk, which they transform into yogurt. And we call that colony of bacteria a culture. In other words, as Neil Postman (2000) has explained, cultures are formed within media, rather than media simply being produced by cultures.

One of the dictionary definitions for the word "medium" is "an environment," and understanding media as environments is the antidote to thinking of media in terms of cause-and-effect relations. A medium is not like a billiard ball, producing its effects by striking another ball. Rather, it is more like the table on which the game is played. Put another way, a medium is not an actor, it is a stage on which human agents play their parts. As environments, media do not determine our actions, but they define the range of possible actions we can take, and facilitate certain actions while discouraging others.

Media function as environments, ecologies, and systems. Content is what happens within the system, and it may or may not affect the system. Technological innovation is a change that occurs to the system itself, and its impact will be profound and far-reaching. And from a systems perspective, we can understand that media do not cause certain effects in a linear manner, but rather particular forms of communication, consciousness, and culture emerge out of particular media ecologies.

While McLuhan viewed media as environments, he is better known for using the popular notion that technologies are extensions of our bodies and our capabilities. But these two conceptions differ only in emphasis, not essence, and McLuhan's emphasis is on the human end of technology. In extending ourselves, our technologies come between ourselves and our environment, and thereby become our new environment. In shielding and protecting us from our old environment, our media numb our bodies and our minds, which is why McLuhan said that every extension is also an amputation. Or as Max Frisch (1959) put it in his novel, *Homo Faber*, "technology is the art of never having to experience the world" (p. 178). But keeping the world out also allows us to establish a sense of order and a degree of control. Niklas Luhmann (1989, 1995) emphasizes the importance of closing a system off from the chaos that surrounds it in order for that system to organize itself, and maintain its structure. In other words, the medium is the membrane.

It is no secret that I am using a variety of biological metaphors for media and technology, but it may come as a surprise to you that some media ecology scholars consider them to be more than metaphors. For example, Lewis Mumford (1952) argues that technology is not unique to human beings. In particular, he points to beaver dams, bird nests, anthills, and bee hives as some of the most elaborate technological constructions in the animal kingdom. Technology is not only an extension of man, but also an extension of nature. All living things adapt to their environments in order to survive, and they also modify their environments in order to make them more survivable. The drive to remake one's environment is the technological imperative, and it is present in bacteria and viruses just as it is in us.

Technology is natural, and that is why human speech is a medium. It is true that we are born with the genetic predisposition for language use, which is then activated by interaction with others. But we are also born with the genetic predisposition towards tool use, an instinct we share with other species, a trait that natural selection seems to have favored in us as much as human evolution has favored language use.

The human body is our primary medium, which is why Mumford (1967) argued that the first machines were made of flesh and blood, and appear early in antiquity. Mumford called them invisible machines, because they were based on the coordination of human labor, for engineering, architectural, or military purposes. The building of the pyramids, of temples and palaces, of irrigation ditches and canals, as well as the building of empires, all were accomplished by invisible machines. Such complex coordination only became possible after the introduction of writing as a medium of organizational communication. Eventually, the fallible human parts of early machine technology would be replaced with the more reliable inorganic components we associate with modern machines. But the important point is that today, as in the past, human techniques and procedures, human organizations and institutions are technologies comparable to tools, machines, and computers.

But today, unlike the past, we are overwhelmed by our technologies, and uncertain about what will emerge out of our electronic media environment. McLuhan (1951) found inspiration in Edgar Allan Poe's short story, "A Descent into the Maelstrom," in which a shipwrecked sailor is trapped within a whirlpool, but escapes death by finding the pattern hidden within the vortex. The maelstrom is our media environment, and the only way out is through synthesis or pattern recognition. We cannot get out through linear logic and cause-and-effect thinking alone. We need to work dialectically and ecologically, riding through complex systems on the edge of chaos.

At this point, I would assume that you expect me to tell you how we might go about doing this. And now I must confess that my reach exceeds my grasp, and I cannot do much more than provide you with some preliminary thoughts. In contrast to print media, which maintain a sense of distance between reader and writer, electronic technologies, through their speed and audiovisual form, bring us together. At the same time, in contrast to face-to-face communication, the electronic media keep us apart. We are simultaneously together and apart. Consequently, we demand commitment from each other, and we run away from the demands of commitment. We expect each other to behave responsibly, and yet refuse to take responsibility for our behavior. We seek intimacy and depth, but find only surfaces. The synthesis of together and apart is a constant sense of connection, for example, as the cell phone makes us available at all times, and a constant sense of dislocation, as the cell phone call interrupts and disrupts the pre-existing situation and imposes a new set of conditions upon us.

As individuals as much as in relationships we are both together and apart. We project ourselves through the Internet, creating alter egos, electronic doubles, shadow selves. Kenneth Gergen (1991) explains how, through the multiplication of mediated-interactions, we increase the number of roles that we play, the number of selves that we put on. We create aliases and avatars, which result in identity diffusion. And we leave traces of ourselves behind for others to encounter, multiplying ourselves over time to a degree unprecedented in human history. We may meet our past selves online or stored as data, further fragmenting our self-image. And we may even find our identities hijacked by others, a truly horrifying violation of our personal integrity.

McLuhan (1995) suggested that the loss of identity results in violence, not just out of frustration, but in an effort to form a new identity. And terrorism may in fact be a response to the theft of identity that occurs when the electronic media environment absorbs primarily oral cultures. But are our aggressive tendencies intensified or reduced when identity is not lost, but multiplied? Also, are we experiencing a permanent breakdown along the lines of a multiple personality disorder? Or might we eventually come to terms with our legion of selves, and create a new synthesis, a new integrated mindset, a new form of consciousness?

As societies, we are also coming together and falling apart. McLuhan (1962) coined the term "global village," another example of dialectical thinking as the globe is the largest possible social unit, and the village or tribe is the smallest. He argued that this new form of social organization, the global village, is emerging out of the electronic media environment. The old media environment, dominated by typography, had seen the birth of nationalism and the emergence of the nation-state as the only legitimate form of social organization. This occurred in part because print made possible coordinated systems of government, for example, by the printing of law books and bureaucratic forms. And it facilitated the creation of homogenous cultures, through the production of literature and the establishment of universal schooling. In the electronic era we see nations coming together to form a global community, in the form of the United Nations and the European Union. But we also see nations breaking apart, as has been the case throughout the former Soviet bloc, in the developing world, and much to our chagrin in Iraq. But it is also happening in stable western countries like Belgium, Spain, and Great Britain.

Both from above and from below, the nation-state is under assault, and not just from larger and smaller political units. We have long known of the revolutionary potential of multinational capitalism. And we now know of the appalling possibilities presented by terrorist networks such as Al Qaeda. Virtual tribalism in forms both benign and threatening is undermining social stability. I fully expect the United Nations to emerge from this turmoil not as the champion of globalization, but as a conservative force protecting the nation-state against these assaults. In the end, we may find ourselves in a world where multiple affiliations are possible, and power and status is measured by the number of associations or citizenships we can claim.

I think it is no secret that the city too has been under attack since the Second World War. Death has come from the skies to London, and Dresden, and Hiroshima, and New York. The airplane and missile is to the city as firearms were to knights in armor. The concentration of populations into urban centers once served the function of mutual protection, but it now renders us vulnerable to attack. It is important to understand that the city was one of the most important and most powerful technologies human beings have ever created. The city was the first supercomputer, the first medium for gathering, storing, and processing information on a scale that transcends human experience. And like the electronic computer, the city-computer could not function without a special, artificially constructed language, a language for creating programs and processing data. That special language was writing. But the electronic media have not been kind to literacy, and the development of the digital computer in the aftermath of World War II has rendered the city-computer obsolescent. This does not mean that the city will disappear. I certainly have no intention of moving away from the New York Metropolitan Area despite the patterns I have recognized and related to you. But the future belongs to new forms of social life, new media of communication, whether I am a part of it or not.

And so, in the end, I fear that I am not all that different from the professor giving the exam in our urban legend. I have my habits and expectations, and cannot help but be taken by surprise by that student, who represents the future, as the professor represents the past. But what I can do is embrace that student and enter into a dialogue with him. I believe we can create a dialectic within ourselves, between the student and the professor. I believe that we can create a new synthesis, so that, like the student we can find the freedom to step outside of the system and understand our media environment, and like the professor we can find the discipline to systematize that knowledge and make it available to others. And maybe then we will be able to find our way out of McLuhan's maelstrom.

References

Bertalanffy, L. v. (1969). *General system theory: Foundations, development, applications.* New York, G. Braziller.

Bolter, J. D., & Grusin, R. (1999). *Remediation: Understanding new media.* Cambridge, MA: MIT Press.

Brunvand, J. H. (1986). *The Mexican pet.* New York: W. W. Norton.

Carey, J. W. (1989). *Communication as culture: Essays on media and society.* Boston: Unwin Hyman.

Carey, J. W. (1997). *James Carey: A critical reader* (E. S. Munson & C. A. Warren, Eds.). Minneapolis: University of Minnesota Press.

Culkin, J. (1967). Each culture develops its own sense ratio to meet the demands of its environment. In G. Stearn (Ed.). *McLuhan: Hot and cool* (pp. 49–57). New York: New American Library.

Czitrom, D. J. (1983). *Media and the American mind : From Morse to McLuhan.* University of North Carolina Press.

Eastham, S. (1990). *The media matrix: Deepening the context of communication studies.* Lanham, MD: University Press of America.

Frisch, M. (1959). *Homor faber: A report* (M. Bulloock, Trans.). San Diego: Harcourt Brace Jovanovich.

Gergen, K. J. (1991). *The saturated self: Dilemmas of identity in contemporary life.* New York: Basic Books.

Gozzi, R. Jr. (1999). *The power of metaphor in the age of electronic media.* Cresskill, NJ: Hampton Press.

Grosswiler, P. (1998). *Method is the message: Rethinking McLuhan through critical theory.* Montreal: Black Rose Books.

Innis, H. A. (1951). *The bias of communication.* Toronto: University of Toronto Press.

Lord, A. B. (1960). *The singer of tales.* Cambridge, MA: Harvard University Press.

Luhmann, N. (1989). *Ecological communication* (J. Bednarz, Jr., Trans.). Chicago: University of Chicago Press.

Luhmann, N. (1995). *Social systems* (J. Bednarz , Jr. with D. Baecker, Trans.). Stanford: Stanford University Press.

Lum, C. M. K. (Ed.). (2006). *Perspectives on culture, technology, and communication: The media ecology tradition.* Cresskill, NJ: Hampton Press.

McLuhan, M. (1951). *The mechanical bride: Folklore of industrial man.* New York: Vanguard.

McLuhan, M. (1962). *The Gutenberg galaxy: The making of typographic man.* Toronto: University of Toronto Press.

McLuhan, M. (1964). *Understanding media: the extensions of man.* New York: McGraw-Hill.

McLuhan, M. (1995). *Essential McLuhan* (E. McLuhan, & F. Zingrone, eds.). New York: Basic Books.

McLuhan, M. (2006). *The classical trivium: The place of Thomas Nashe in the learning of his time.* Corte Madera, CA: Gingko Press.

McLuhan, M. & Fiore, Q. (1967). *The medium is the massage: An inventory of effects.* Corte Madera, CA: Gingko Press.

Mumford, L. (1934). *Technics and civilization.* New York: Harcourt Brace.

Mumford, L. (1952). *Art and technics.* New York: Columbia University Press.

Mumford, L. (1967). *The myth of the machine: I. Technics and human development.* New York: Harcourt Brace and World.

Ong, W. J. (1982). *Orality and literacy: The technologizing of the word.* London: Routledge.

Parry, M. (1971). *The making of Homeric verse: The collected papers of Milman Parry* (A. Parry, Ed.). Oxford: Clarendon Press.

Postman, N. (2000). The humanism of media ecology. Proceedings of the Media Ecology Association 1, 10–16 [online] http://www.media-ecology.org/publications/proceedings.html.

Rogers, E. M. (2003). *Diffusion of innovations* (5th ed.). New York: The Free Press.

Schwartz, T. (1974). *The responsive chord.* Garden City, New York: Anchor Books.

Shannon, C. E. & Weaver, W. (1949). *The mathematical theory of communication.* Urbana: University of Illinois Press.

Stamps, J. (1995). *Unthinking modernity: Innis, McLuhan, and the Frankfurt School.* Montreal & Kingston: McGill-Queens University Press.

Strate, L. (1994). Heroes: A communication perspective. In S. Drucker & R. Cathcart (Eds.). *American Heroes in a Media Age* (pp. 15–23). Cresskill, NJ: Hampton Press.

Strate, L. (1995). The faces of a thousand heroes: The impact of visual communication technologies on the culture hero. *The New Jersey Journal of Communication* 3(1), pp. 26–39.

Strate, L. (2006). *Echoes and Reflections: On Media Ecology as a Field of Study.* Cresill, NJ: Hampton Press.

Strate, L. (2008). Heroes and/as Communication. In S. Drucker & G. Gumpert (Eds.). *Heroes in a Global World* (pp. 19–46). Cresskill, NJ: Hampton Press.

Theall, D. F. (2001). *The virtual Marshall McLuhan.* Montreal & Kingston: McGill-Queens University Press.

Thoreau, H. D. (1980). *Walden or, life in the woods and on the duty of civil disobedience.* New York: Signet.

Wiener, N. (1950). *The human use of human beings: Cybernetics and society.* Boston: Houghton Mifflin.

Section Two: McLuhan and Critical Theory

Radical or Reactionary? A Closer Look at Critical Theory, Media Ecology and Marxisms

DONNA FLAYHAN

Introduction

This essay highlights the compatibility between dialectical materialism and media ecology. I begin by summarizing the works of Judith Stamps (1995) and Paul Grosswiler (1998) as sound scholarship that demonstrates commonalities between seemingly disparate theoretical traditions of critical theory, Western Marxism, and media ecology. I will then discuss the differences between the traditions while highlighting the similarities in activist Marxist scholarship that not only documents the dialectic in action (as do critical theory and Western Marxism) but also enacts a dialectical method of scholarship that is apparent in the works of media ecologists and those writing in the activist Marxist tradition (such as Leon Trotsky and Rosa Luxemburg). Thus while I agree with the general work of Stamps and Grosswiler that a medium theory or media ecological approach to studying communication is indeed more radical than many have recognized, I will actually argue that the traditions of critical theory and Western Marxism may be "radical" in the sense of critical/criticism, but that they are not radical or revolutionary tools for theoretical insight, as are media ecology and activist Marxism.

Critical theorists are anything but radical either in research method or in political implications. It is not that media ecology is similar to the Frankfurt School or Western academic Marxism that makes it a radical methodological approach that also has radical political implications; it is that media ecology has much in common with an activist Marxist tradition that is not ashamed to use dialectical materialism both to understand (a radical method) and to change (a radical political tool) the world. Cultural criticism is often both conservative and wrong, whereas dialectical investigations are often radical and accurate.

Marxism and Media Ecology: More than the Dialectic as Method in Common

One of the great strengths of the ideas of media ecologists such as Marshall McLuhan (1951, 1962, 1964, 1988), Harold Innis (1950, 1951, 1952, 1954), Walter Ong (1982), Joshua Meyrowitz (1985, 1993), and James Carey (1989) is that their analyses of media—while out of sync with their contemporaries—are accurate analyses of the dynamic interplay between communication technologies, culture, and consciousness. All of these media ecologists employ, with varying degrees of consciousness regarding their underlying method, dialectical materialism in their work. The Frankfurt School theorists Theodor Adorno, Max Horkheimer, Leo Lowenthal, Walter Benjamin, and Herbert Marcuse claim to all that they are employing the dialectical method; they are not. All of their work is straight cultural criticism of content and nothing more.

In Judith Stamps's (1995) *Unthinking Modernity: Innis, McLuhan, and the Frankfurt School*, Stamps does an outstanding job of demonstrating how Innis and McLuhan were both much more radical in their methodological approaches to the study of media than they have been given credit for in critical studies of media. While Stamps discusses that Innis, McLuhan, Horkheimer, Benjamin, and Lowenthal all employ a method she refers to as "negative dialectics," I find that her examples of Innis and McLuhan employing the method arise from a look at their actual studies, whereas she relies on the words of what Horkheimer, Benjamin, Lowenthall, and Marcuse are actually doing in their work which is very different from a dialectical approach to media studies (Stamps, 1995).

The scholars of the Frankfurt School engage in straightforward critical analyses of media content. Whether analyzing the radio and music with Adorno, or analyzing the changing type of heroes in American Magazine Autobiographies with Lowenthal, or looking at the one-dimensional man in the West with Marcuse, all of the Frankfurt School theorists espouse that they employ the Marxist dialectic, yet they do not analyze inherent contradictions and driving forces of change in mass communication. Instead, they look at how it is only the ruling class ideas in society that appear in modern mass media (not much of an insight) and they predict that those ideas will lull the society into confusion and submission.

The media ecology work of Innis, McLuhan, Ong, Meyrowitz, and Carey all use a dialectical method that sees unity in opposing historical forces, and most often examines the contradictory material force of a new communication technology interacting with human beings in society.

While I agree with Stamps that McLuhan's *Mechanical Bride* shares much in common with the method employed by the Frankfurt School, yet this work was done before McLuhan read Innis and began to focus on media form rather than content and employ a dialectical method of investigation. McLuhan's *Mechanical Bride* is simply an analysis of advertising content as being uniform and deadening to the soul. This is all true enough but rather obvious and nothing like McLuhan's later media ecology work that is astonishingly insightful about the roles played by media and changes happening in the social world.

In McLuhan's later works that were influenced by Innis, we see McLuhan employ dialectical materialism when analyzing how shifts in media alter sense ratios. We also see him employ the dialectic when studying the interaction between vernacular languages and the printing press providing necessary conditions for the emergence of the modern nation state. Paul Grosswiler's (1998) *The Method Is the Message: Rethinking McLuhan Through Critical Theory* is an admirable work that looks at the dialectic method employed by Marx and McLuhan. Grosswiler is also very careful to demonstrate that McLuhan did not like Marx's work and was a conscious anti-Marxist. Yet in a thoughtful scholarly fashion, Grosswiler ignores what the theorist is saying and instead examines what the theorist is doing. McLuhan employs the same dialectic method of investigation as does Karl Marx (Grosswiler, 1998).

While Grosswiler, like Stamps, does a great job of demonstrating how the dialectical method is employed by McLuhan, Grosswiler also takes the words of the critical theorists of the Frankfurt School at face value rather than seeing the dialectical method alive in their work. Grosswiler himself is a scholar who enacts negative dialectics as a way of seeing, but the Frankfurt School theorists and Western Marxists do not do so.

Media ecologists employ a dialectical materialism that examines the interplay of the material forces of (inherent biases of) new communication technologies and focuses on how they transform, often in a revolutionary way, the social order. Whether Innis is examining the rise and decline of empires, or McLuhan is examining nationalism and the rise of the modern nation state, or Ong examining oral versus literate modes of consciousness, or Meyrowitz examining changing social behavior among men, women, adults, children, and politicians and the citizen, or Carey examining the way that the telegraph altered the structure of language and ushered in the change in the stock market from speculation based on place to speculation based on time bias and information. With the above list, it is clear that when these media ecologists, who employ the dialectical method, examine revolutionary changes fostered by communication technology, they are enacting radical methodological approach that leads to accurate insights. Employing dialectical materialism in such a way provides great insights into the role that communication technologies play in restructuring consciousness and culture, yet it is not the entire picture. In the last section of this essay, I will suggest that the scholarship of Carey, Meyrowitz, and Ong could be extended using a more holistic sense of material forces including class position as a factor affecting and helping to asymmetrically structure the alterations in consciousness and culture ushered in by dialectical material forces.

For now it is important to note that the works of the media ecologists are more insightful than the work of the Frankfurt School because they focus on media form (materialist) not media content (idealist). The works of the media ecologists reveal that when the material force of a new communication technology is introduced into an existing social order, that order is restructured in fundamental ways. It is not radical ideas, or the lack thereof, that drive for change, it is the self-activated dynamic of the dialectic forces unfolding with the material forces of a new technology of mass communication. This approach has much in common with the dialectic method as employed by Karl Marx in his life's works. Paul Grosswiler (1998) does a nice job of highlighting Marx's use of the dialectic.

In the next section I will examine how the lack of understanding of the dialectic method, due to a blind acceptance that Western academic Marxism or the Frankfurt School of critical theory are dialectic in their analyses, robs media theory of conscious use of the radical method and the subsequent insights. I will show that it is the activist Marxist tradition that emerged in the struggles in the streets, not the Western Academic Marxist tradition that we should look to for useful ways to apply dialectical materialism. Straight cultural criticism is not dialectical or radical; media ecology and the activist Marxist tradition are both.

For an Activist Marxist Tradition: Class & Dialectics, Not Criticism, as Radical

As indicated above, in this section I argue for a specific type of Marxism, the activist Marxist tradition, to be merged with media ecology: I argue against a (re)turn to the Frankfurt School or British cultural studies. I argue for a look at a very different Marxist tradition than the one described by Hardt below (1992, p. 7):

Marxism has embarked on the long march through history, from Marx and Hegel to critical theory and French structuralism. Its power has resided in a capacity for self-criticism and the seemingly endless creative energy of an intellectual commitment to reconstituting Marxism in different historical moments.

This trip from Hegel to Marx to the Frankfurt School to Althusser's influence represents only the academic strain of Marxism, ignoring the wealth of Marxist theory developed in the context of actual involvement in social struggle: a journey that takes us from Marx and Engels to Lenin, Luxemburg, and Trotsky to Howard Zinn and Dave Zairin.

I argue in this section that the versions of critical theory (Frankfurt School) and Althusserian influenced Marxism (Stuart Hall's brand of British cultural studies) slight the importance of class and dialectics in their analyses.

One of the major proponents for bringing Marxism into communication theory in the United States is Hanno Hardt. Hardt's 1992 book, *Critical Communication Studies: Communication, History, and Theory in America,* indicates just what type of theory he considers to be Marxist and thinks would be useful to include in North American communication theory. As indicated above, Hardt is referring mainly to the Frankfurt School and British cultural studies when he is discussing Marxism. I will argue in this section that these schools of thought tend only to be critical theories of ruling class ideological domination without a revolutionary sense of dialectical contradiction and class struggle. The Frankfurt School and Western academic Marxists are not Marxist theorists in the tradition of Marx and Engels. Marx and Engels do not stop at an analysis of ruling class domination of ideas; they recognize that social struggles and resistance to oppression are real historical phenomena that will exist as long as inequality and exploitation exist, and that our theoretical understanding must reflect and highlight these phenomena in order for us to play a valuable role in struggles when they do break out. I argue that theorists in the activist Marxist tradition help us to more accurately understand the world as it is and how to best intervene to push it in the direction of democraic socialism. The Marxists and Marxism described and advocated by Hanno Hardt and Stuart Hall emphasize ideological domination and the role of radical thought in breaking out of ideological domination.

The tendency to equate the Frankfurt School's critical theory with Marxism is common and is illustrated in comments by Hardt such as (p. 133) "Max Horkheimer and Theodor Adorno with their introduction of critical theory to an American environment that was not particularly receptive to Marxist theorists, especially foreign ones." This tendency is also apparent in Hardt's discussions surrounding the 1983 *Journal of Communication* "Ferment in the Field" with "recent debates concerning critical theory and other Marxist approaches to communication research." James

Carey has gone so far as to argue that critical theory is the code name for marxist theory as a result of McCarthyism and the stigma of anything Marxist. Yet the assumption that the Frankfurt School represents the best and most sophisticated Marxist theory fails to see that an adequate emphasis on political struggle, class struggle, and contradiction are central to a Marxist project. The static theoretical view of ideological domination advocated by the Frankfurt School's major proponents is perhaps critical (one could argue that it is actually conservative), but certainly not revolutionary.

As Leszek Kolakowski (1978) put it in *Main Currents of Marxism: The Breakdown*, critical theory in general and Marcuse's work in particular are forms of Marxism without the proles. Kolakowski calls Marcuse's thought (1978, p. 413),

> Marxism without the proletariat [irrevocably corrupted by the welfare state], without history (as the vision of the future is not derived from a study of historical changes but from an intuition of true human nature), and without the cult of science, a Marxism furthermore in which the value of liberated society resides in pleasure not creative work.

When we examine the ideas developed by the Frankfurt School with their critique of the culture industry and enlightenment philosophy, we are led into an arena of struggle, or lack thereof, that exists only in the realm of ideas. Far from being Marxist materialists providing a "radical" critique of society, Theodor Adorno, Max Horkheimer, and Herbert Marcuse simply describe the methods of political domination of the ruling class and assume that they are all powerful for dominating conscious thought and criticism. The goal of their theory is to raise consciousness through radical criticism of the dominant ideology.

As Horkheimer and Adorno describe their goal in *The Dialectic of Enlightenment* (1972, p. 265),

> the chief aim of such criticism is to prevent mankind from losing itself in those ideas and activities which the existing organization of society instills in its members.

In the famous chapter in which they critique "The Culture Industry," Adorno and Horkheimer are often attacked for their elitism, but rarely does the critique logically extend to the criticism that their theory is ultimately far from "radical" and revolutionary, but rather a dismal distress over ideological domination. They write (p. 147), "The culture industry tends to make itself the embodiment of authoritative pronouncements, and thus irrefutable prophet of the prevailing order." Thus their theory leads only to cynicism, pessimism, and criticism, not to contradictory dialectical forces that lead to struggle and allow for a potential opening for meaningful change.

Just as I argue that the Frankfurt School's "Marxism" is a form of critical theory of ideology with no sense of class and contradiction, so too is Althusserian-influenced British cultural studies.

British cultural studies began with activist-informed Marxist theorists such as Raphael Samuels, Richard Hoggart, Raymond Williams, and E.P. Thompson, all of whom had a strong sense of class and an active engagement in the social struggles of the day. Unfortunately, that strain of bottom-up history in British cultural studies was abandoned for Althuserrian Marxism with a de-emphasis on class by the time of the "Ferment in the Field" discussion in 1983 in the United States.

Stuart Hall describes the early work in British cultural studies, such as Richard Hoggart's *The Uses of Literacy* and Raymond Williams's *The Long Revolution*, as a break from (1980, p. 60) "vulgar materialism and an economic determinism." Yet the vulgar materialist and economic determinist Marxists are never identified, and thus it is unclear who the early British cultural studies scholars are breaking with. As British cultural studies moves away from the bottom-up history influence of Hoggart, Samuels, Williams, and Thompson and toward Althusserian Marxism in the late 1970s and early 1980s, it moves away from the materialism with a strong sense of class that was insightful, but not unique to, those early Marxist theorists in British cultural studies.

In the turn from bottom-up history to ideological studies in British cultural studies, Stuart Hall argues that now Althusser can save Marxism from crude determinism. Again it is not clear who the crude determinists that Althusser is breaking from are; what is clear is that British cultural studies moved further away from a strong sense of class and social struggle and closer to the Frankfurt School's fetishizing of ideology. Hall argues in "Signification, Representation, Ideology: Althusser and the Post-Structuralist Debates" that (1985, p. 92)

> Althusser was the key figure in modern theorizing on this question who clearly broke with some of the old protocols and provided a persuasive alternative which remains broadly within the terms of the Marxist problematic.

Again we are left to wonder who represented the "old protocols." And as we are pondering that, Hall moves on to claim that Althusser is a true renegade because he enabled Hall to (p. 92) "live in and with *difference*." Hall explains (p. 92):

> Althusser's break with a monistic conception of Marxism demanded the theorization of difference—the recognition that there are different social contradictions with different origins; that the contradictions which drive the historical process forward do not always appear in the same place, and will not always have the same historical effects.

This unique break attributed to Althusser is something that already appears quite clearly in activist Marxist theory, as early as 1903 in Lenin's *What Is To Be Done?*

I will return to *What Is To Be Done?* later. For now I simply want to indicate that what Hall and others consider theoretically subtle about Althusser's multiple social contradictions is actually not unique to him at all. Moreover, because of the form that this analysis takes in Althusser's work, and then in Hall's, it slights the importance of inherent contradictions and class struggle. Instead of "adding" a new dimension to Marxist theory (which had actually been added to by Lenin decades earlier), Althusser subtracts class altogether. So with Althusserian Marxism we get analysis of ideological domination, not resistance. Thus when the turn to understand and theorize resistance in Althusserian-influenced British cultural studies takes place, resistance is limited to the ideological struggle over the meaning of texts. With little sense of class and too strong a sense of ideological domination, British cultural studies was left nowhere to turn for resistance to oppression other than a disastrous turn to the resistive reader in the 1980s.

It will be demonstrated below that Lenin argued against crude economism determinism and reformism in his debates with influential German socialist Eduard Bernstein in the late 1890s. None of what is considered new in Althusser as far as avoiding economic determinism is new at all. Moreover, the move to fetishize the realm of ideology is not only not new, but it was the first point in Marx's critique of the Young Hegelians. In a sense, with the Frankfurt School and British cultural studies we are right back at the Young Hegelian idea that change comes from radical thought—a point that Marx argued was bankrupt over 150 years ago.

We see this Young Hegelian idea of radical criticism leading to liberation in the Frankfurt School and Althusserian-influenced British cultural studies, and it is clear in the call for the future of the field by Hanno Hardt in the last sentence in *Critical Communication Studies* (p. 227):

> The dilemma of American communication studies continues to lie in its failure to comprehend and overcome the limitations of its own intellectual history, not only by failing to address the theoretical and methodological problems of an established academic discipline, but also by failing to recognize the potential of radical thought.

This idealist, not materialist, philosophy has inherited the title of Marxism in academic arenas but is stripped of its revolutionary spirit in linking ideas of philosophers with the struggles of the day, including but not limited to class struggles, in order to push struggles in a revolutionary direction. The idealist tradition described above that is credited with "rethinking Marxism" and saving it from crude determinism has really drained Marxism of the central elements of dialectics, contradiction, and class struggle that make it a theory of working class revolution. This is a consequence of ignoring the activist Marxist theoretical tradition that is materialist but not mechanical. Left out is the activist Marxist tradition that recognizes but does not fetishize ideological domination, and is much more nuanced in its understanding of struggles in general, and economic struggles in particular, than is the crude economic determinism that Western academic Marxism is credited with breaking with.

Central to Marx's theory is the contradiction between the drive for profit inherent in the capitalist system and the needs of ordinary working people—the inevitability of class conflict and the potential for the struggle to push history in the direction of socialist revolution. An understanding of class contradiction and the inevitable outbreaks in struggle (but clearly not inevitable victory and certainly not inevitable socialist revolution) is central in all of Marx's work and should be central still. While it is central in the activist Marxist theory of Lenin, as stated above, it is not the only element.

Activist Marxist theorists did not become crude economic determinists with a blind faith in the working class as they are so often characterized. Theorists such as Lenin, Luxemburg, and Trotsky identified "different social contradictions with different origins" long before Althusser did, and they were able to keep a sense of the importance of class at the same time.

Lenin's (1903) arguments in *What Is to Be Done?* demonstrate that far from economic determinism, Lenin the activist Marxist theorist, was arguing for Social Democrats (Marxists) at the dawn of the twentieth century to recognize the dangers of "economism" and reformism.

Lenin wrote *What Is To Be Done?* in 1903: it was a culmination of ideas that had developed over a series of debates published in the more economic determinist *Rabochneye Dyelo (Worker's Cause)* magazine and Lenin's newspaper *Iskra (Spark)*. *Iskra* had called for support for university students in demonstrations in 1898. Workers did eventually join in support of the students. Yet "economists," as Lenin labeled them, felt that the only role for a socialist was in the local trade union agitating around economic questions.

Lenin found this limiting and argued that the economists were simply tailing the most reactionary edge of workers' struggle. As historian Roland Pipes described the economists in *Social Democracy and the St Petersburg Labor Movement 1885–1897* (1963, p. 124),

> The roots of Economism are best sought in the agitational method of Social Democratic work. The socialists who had devised this method acknowledged the indifference of labour to politics and proposed to overcome it by demonstrating the allegedly indis-

soluble link between economic interests and the country's political order. Whereas in theory agitation was political, in practice it remained confined to economics. From agitation, which pushed politics into the background as a matter of tactical expedience, it was only one step to Economism proper, which subordinated politics to economics as a matter of principle. Economism thus came into being in Russia in 1896–1897, in the wake of the emerging mass labour movement.

Thus economic determinism was the main difference between this group of socialists dedicated to worker struggles only and Lenin's theory that calls for political agitation against all acts of tyranny. Those against students, religious sects, peasants were important sites of struggle.

Lenin argued in *What Is To Be Done?* that socialists should help different religious sects write newsletters spreading their cause. Clearly this is not a simplistic, mechanical understanding of "religion is the opiate of the masses." Instead it recognizes the need to defend oppressed religious sects, broadening the political struggle, and link it with economic struggle. Exposure to political, not just economic, struggles was central to Lenin's theoretical and political project. He writes (1903, 1969, pp. 68–69):

> for decades the very economic struggle before which all economists grovel to be the preferable, particularly important, and "most widely applicable" means of rousing this activity and its broadest field. This error is characteristic, precisely in that it is by no means peculiar to Martynov. In reality, it is possible to "raise the activity of the working masses" *only* when this activity *is not restricted* to "political agitation on an economic basis." A basic condition for the necessary expansion of political agitation is the organisation of *comprehensive* political exposure. *In no way* except by means of such exposures *can* the masses be trained in political consciousness and revolutionary activity.

Clearly Lenin is not even close to an economic determinist approach in his Marxist theory of struggle. In fact, Lenin overstates the idea that there is a strong separation between economic struggles spilling over into struggles for political demands. Scholars debate whether Lenin did not understand the political potential that can stem from struggles beginning with economic demands, or if he was just overstating the case as a needed corrective measure to the rampant economic determinism in social democracy in Russia at that time (Cliff, 1986, p. 60).

Indeed the crude economic determinist and reformist strains in Social Democracy that Lenin was responding to were not unique to Russia. In Germany, Eduard Bernstein wrote an influential book in 1899 titled *The Preconditions of Socialism and the Task of Social Democracy* that advocated economic determinism and reformism as the road to socialism. These strains ultimately won out in the German Social Democratic Party, and became the philosophy of Karl Kautsky and the Second International which argued that socialism was inevitable and would come through a series of reforms to capitalism from above, from the party and politicians, not from workers power from below, as Lenin and the activist Marxist tradition argues.

Perhaps it is this economist strain of Marxism that accounts for the widespread idea that Western Marxists were escaping the crude economic determinism of Marxism. As should be clear from the discussion above, Lenin understood the importance of struggle at "multiple points of rupture" (as it may be put in the academic jargon of today). So too did Luxemburg and Trotsky. All three of these activist Marxist theorists understood the dynamic of the dialectic and have a strong sense of class, but do not fall into the trap of economic determinism. In the next section I analyze the dynamic understanding of dialectical contradictions, class, and political struggle in the works of Trotsky and Luxemburg.

Class and Dialectics

In order to discuss the need for a sense of class in a media ecology approach to cultural studies, a clear understanding of the notions of class and dialectics central to Marxist theories should be explored. This is a particularly important discussion in the context of the United States, where many intellectuals either slight class or discuss it as a rigid ontological category based on income and job prestige. The different understandings of class and dialectics by American reformists and Marxists is clarified in the debate over morality between John Dewey and Leon Trotsky.

In his analysis of the debate over morality between Russian Marxist Leon Trotsky and American pragmatist John Dewey, George Novack points out that the main differences between the two over moral theory "revolved around disagreements over the agents and the means of social advancement." Both Dewey and Trotsky are sincere in their desire to make the world a better place; one sees the road to travel as reform, the other, revolution.

Novack is one of the few intellectuals in the United States to join an activist revolutionary socialist organization and it is clear in his scholarship that he understands and has a strong sense of the difference between Trotsky and Dewey. In essence, Novack argues, the dispute between Dewey and Trotsky was over *method*: "both method of thought and method of conduct" (Novack, p. 81). Dewey argues that Trotsky's method of reasoning is incorrect because, as Novack paraphrases (Novack, p. 81), "he deduced the means (the class struggle) from his reading (or misreading) of the course of social development."

Novack explains why Trotsky's evaluation of means by reference to needs of the class struggle is not the product of deductive processes alone (p. 82):

The impressive array of factual materials regarding class conflict and its crucial role in history from which these laws are derived were observed and recorded long before Marx arrived on the scene. For instance, many ancient Greek writers and historians (Thucydides, Aristotle, Plato) noted and described them. What the historical materialists did was to give the first adequate and correct explanation of them. They explained how classes originated through the growth of the productive forces, the division of social labor, and the existence of a sizeable surplus of products, and why class conflicts have revolved around the mode of appropriation of this expanding surplus of wealth.

Marxists did not invent class struggle; they recognized and described it as a historical phenomenon.

Even members of revolutionary socialist parties in the United States often fail to have a strong sense of class and the historical reality of class struggle. American intellectual and member of the Socialist Worker's Party James Burnham fails to understand that Marxist dialectics are more than ideas in the heads of Marxists when he writes (Rees p. 116):

> There is no sense *at all* in which dialectics (even if it were not, as it is, scientifically meaningless) is fundamental in politics, none at all. An opinion on dialectics is no more fundamental for *politics* than an opinion on non-Euclidean geometry or relativity physics.

Trotsky responds to and explains this lack of understanding of contradiction and social struggle of American socialists with a materialist analysis (Trotsky quoted in Rees, p. 117):

> American 'radical' intellectuals accept Marxism without the dialectic (a clock without a spring) . . . The secret is simple. In no other country has there been such a rejection of class struggle as in the land of 'unlimited opportunity'. The denial of social contradictions as the moving force of development led to the denial of the dialectic as the logic of contradictions in the domain of theoretical thought.

Trotsky goes on to argue that it is absurd to claim that arguments concerning method are not central to correct political analyses and conclusions (Trotsky quoted in Rees, p. 117):

> What is the meaning of this thoroughly astonishing reasoning? Inasmuch as *some* people through a bad method *sometimes* reach correct conclusions, and inasmuch as some people through a correct method *not infrequently* reach incorrect conclusions, therefore . . . the method is not of great importance . . . Imagine how a worker would react upon complaining to his foreman that his tools were bad and receiving the reply: With bad tools it is possible to turn out a good job, and with good tools many people only waste

material. I am afraid that such a worker, particularly if he is on piece-work, would respond to the foreman with an unacademic phrase.

This is not to argue that the dialectic tool is a mirror to be held up to reflect the dialectic of nature. Phrases like those of Walter Benjamin and Bertolt Brecht in their opening of the journal *Krise und Kultur (Crisis and Culture)* capture the spirit of dialectical materialism with the call for studies conducted "with the purpose of demonstrating to the bourgeois intelligentsia that the methods of dialectical materialism are dictated by their own necessities."

Yet such a description still leaves Marxists open to the charge of crudely applying "natural laws" to society. Trotsky deals with this problem by stating that (Trotsky quoted in Rees, p. 124) "public life is neither a chemical nor a psychological process, but a social process which is shaped by its own laws." Trotsky writes (quoted in Rees, p. 124):

> Dialectical cognition is not *identical* with the dialectic of nature. Consciousness is a quite original *part* of nature, possessing peculiarities and regularities that are completely absent in the remaining part of nature. Subjective dialectics must by virtue of this be a distinctive part of objective dialectics—with its own special forms and regularities.

As Rees writes (p. 124), "Trotsky's differentiation between the form of the dialectic appropriate in nature and that adequate for the study of society both preserves the unity of the dialectic (thus avoiding dualism) and also prevents deterministic interpretation of Marxism." Just as class struggle is a consequence of dialectical contradictions, the approach that Marxists take to analyse and evaluate the appropriate role in a particular struggle is a dialectic between objective conditions and subjective responses to those conditions that may then alter the objective conditions.

Trotsky's interactionist understanding of the relationship between theory and practice are similar to Marx's term "practical-critical activity" (Trotsky quoted in Rees, p. 125):

> The dialectic of consciousness (cognition) is not thereby a *reflection* of the dialectic of nature, but is a *result* of the lively interaction between consciousness and nature and—in addition—a method of cognition, issuing from this interaction.

The theoretical explanation of the use of the dialectic describes the interactive use by Trotsky of the dialectical method in his own work, particularly in his theory of permanent revolution. Trotsky's discussion of the theory of permanent revolution recognizes that socialism is not inevitable and that revolutions do not take place in a uniform manner. Just as the global spread of capitalism itself follows a path of combined and uneven development throughout the globe, so too do theories of revolutionaries need to highlight the importance of a nuanced understanding of social struggle.

Marx, Lenin, Trotsky, and Luxemburg all move back and forth constantly between what is actually happening in the social world and how that connects to the possibilities for revolutionary change. Luxemburg's analysis of the character of the mass strike in St. Petersburg in January 1905 illustrates the point of recognizing that sometimes economic struggles do break out into larger struggles for political change.

Trotsky's activist Marxist informed theoretical understanding of the dialectic is similar to Rosa Luxemburg's use of the dialectic in her study of *The Mass Strike*. Luxemburg demonstrates how the mass strike (not the revolutionary party as Lenin argued and as represented in the discussion above) can also overcome the separation of economic and political struggles inherent in reformist theory. She demonstrates how the mass strike fuses together the struggle for reforms within capitalism with the struggle for the revolutionary overthrow of capitalism. She writes (Luxemburg, p. 6):

> And this awakening of class feeling expressed itself forwith in the circumstances that the proletarian mass, counted by millions, quite suddenly and sharply came to realise how intolerable was that social and economic existence which they had patiently endured for decades in the chains of capitalism.

Thus Luxemburg demonstrates how the struggle to win economic reforms can spill over into political activity. She also argues, conversely, and based on historical example, that struggles for political demands can trigger struggles for economic demands. This is important since reformists see what Tony Cliff refers to as "a 'Great Wall of China' dividing partial struggles for economic reform and the political struggle for revolution" (Cliff, p. 7). Luxemburg writes (p. 7), "The movement does not go only in one direction, from an economic to a political struggle, but also in the opposite direction."

This phenomenon described by Luxemburg applies as much to the specific situation in St. Petersburg in January of 1905 (where economic demands spread to political) as it does to the situation in Paris in May of 1968 and December of 1995 (where political demands of students spread to a general strike throughout the nation). While these struggles did not inevitably lead to socialist revolutions, they demonstrate the two-way interaction for potentially revolutionary struggles originating "at multiple points of rupture." This nuanced and dialectical understanding of sites of potential struggle was not first identified and articulated by Althusser, but by Lenin, Luxemburg, and Trotsky.

Yet this *potential* does not mean an inevitable or automatic road to socialist revolution, instead it indicates potential sites for revolutionary activity.

Unfortunately, the vulgar Marxism of Karl Kautsky and the Second International took such claims to indicate that socialist revolution was inevitable and that a series of stages must be followed. This type of mechanical Marxism was embraced by Stalin as he led the counter-revolution within the Soviet Union in the 1920s and dictated the policies of Communist parties around the world. Trotsky demonstrates how this type of mechanistic "Marxism" fails to grasp the world as it operates, therefore, missing revolutionary opportunities. In response to Stalinists accusing him of skipping over historical stages, Trotsky writes (quoted in Rees, p. 131):

> It is nonsense to say that stages cannot in general be skipped. The living historical process always leaps over isolated 'stages' which derive from theoretical breakdown into its component parts of the process of development in its entirety, that is, taken in its fullest scope . . . It may be said that the first distinction between a revolutionist and a vulgar evolutionist lies in the capacity to recognize and exploit such moments . . . One stage or another of the historical process can prove to be inevitable under certain conditions, although theoretically not inevitable. And conversely, theoretically 'inevitable' stages can be compressed to zero by the dynamics of development, especially during revolutions.

Thus the crude Marxism of the Second International, and the later atrocity of Stalinism, worked to simplify and mechanize Marxist analyses of class and dialectics.

Perhaps these are the crude economic determinists that Hall refers to in his argument that Althusser has saved us from a reductionist Marxist history. If so, Hall and British cultural studies have missed the theoretically sophisticated side of activist Marxist theory for far too long. It is this tradition that medium theorists working in the North American cultural studies tradition should look to for insights into potential "points of rupture." If we understand the activist Marxist theoretical insights as to possibilities for struggle and change, we necessarily must at some point move out of the realm of ideas and actually engage in the active struggles of the day.

What Is To Be Done?

The critique of academic Marxism above is set out as a note of caution against an idealist approach to Marxism that fails to see how material contradictions in everyday life lead to struggle and resistance. Indeed, I have demonstrated that the radical method and the politically radical uses of that method are embodied in dialectical materialism, not critical analyses of ideas in media content. Rather than theorize why there has been little or no resistance to ideological domination by ordinary working people, activist Marxists have been engaged in the struggles that do break out, even when small, in order to influence them with ideas and have their ideas influenced by the struggles.

Praxis, theory-informed action and action-informed theory, is the basic premise of an activist Marxist tradition. It allows for nuanced analyses that see more than the dichotomy of ideological domination or working class resistance: it allows for an examination of the possibilities and problems in the struggle for revolutionary change.

We left the twentieth century the same way that we entered it, now the sense of urgency for revolutionary change has intensified. The choice is still between socialism and barbarism, and barbarism appears to be winning. With all of the horror that the capitalist system has encouraged, the main changes in the past 100 years have been a matter of degree: an intensification of the horrors of high-tech war from the machine gun to the laser gun; from fire bombs to atomic bombs; from dirty and dangerous working conditions that ruined people's lives and poisoned their cities to shiny clean (yet carcinogen filled) working conditions that ruin people's lives and poison their planet. A sense of urgency is upon us: we know that all of the hope promised by capitalism remains trapped beneath the weight of the horrors that a system based exclusively on the drive for profit necessarily promotes. We also know that the horror will not be stopped with technological salvation.

It was in a moment of horror that Percy Shelley's maniac maid "whose name is Hope, but she looks more like despair," threw herself down in front of horses' hooves and sparked the resistance. It was in such a moment of horror when it looked like the entire Jewish population in the Warsaw Ghetto would be sent to the death camps that five members of the Jewish Socialist Party of Poland (the Bund) led an uprising. The ghetto fighters forced the Nazis in 1943 to fight their largest battle on Polish soil since 1939; they inspired Jewish prisoners at Treblinka to rise up and burn the Nazi death camp to the ground in August of 1943.

As we face the horrors of the capitalist world today with the destruction of people's lives, the environment, and possible nuclear annihilation, what looks like cause for despair should not lead us to despair, but to a sense of urgency: we must work to understand and explain the world as it is while being engaged in the struggle to change it. Our job as thoughtful and engaged communication scholars is not only to explain the horror, but to understand the contradictory nature of moments of despair: the role of human agency at such moments is crucial; an understanding of technology as an agent of change will help. The need to understand the world in order to alter it assumes that scholars should be active agents in altering the world, not passive commentators on its horrible condition: the need for activist Marxist scholarship has never been greater; horror surrounds us, yet we as scholars are merely objects rather than subjects of history if in the face of horror we merely describe despair.

At the same time that I argue for activist Marxist scholarship with a strong sense of human agency in understanding and acting in the world around us, I also argued at the beginning of this essay that forms of communication are agents in historical change as well. Activist Marxist scholarship could benefit from a stronger understanding of media ecology and media theory could benefit from a stronger understanding of the theoretical work within the activist Marxist tradition.

Despite problems with the lack of sense of the drive for profit, class, struggle, and inequality in media ecology, the materialist base of media ecology and the use of the dialectic method make it quite compatible with an activist Marxist approach to the study of history. Thus merging media ecology and the activist Marxist tradition is possible, logical, and would be beneficial.

Media ecology is not plagued by an inherent idealism or calls for "radical thought" as is the tradition of academic Western Marxism as advocated by Hardt and Hall. Media ecology is a materialist theory that investigates how the biases of particular media interact with consciousness and culture. Media ecology, like activist Marxist theory, is materialist in the first instance but also recognizes the dialectic nature of materialist influences on consciousness and culture—neither represent crude mechanical materialism.

The Hegelian dialectic, as transformed by Marx and put to use by Trotsky and Luxemburg, allows for an analysis of the interaction between materialist forces that make human beings objects of history and theorizes reactions to those forces that allow for humans to be acting subjects too. Activist Marxists avoid the dual dangers of economic determinism and ideology fetishism while media ecologists avoid the dual dangers of technological horror and cynicism.

While media ecology could be more nuanced and sophisticated, activist Marxist theorists could also better understand the world with a media ecology-informed sense of history. For example, the internet may help us to understand how old monopolies of knowledge may be challenged, or reinforced, or both, by this new space biased medium. At the same time, an activist Marxist investigation of the internet could help us to understand the power and control that exists with the internet and the possibilities for its use as a revolutionary agent of change but only combined with human agents. The two traditions together could help us to understand the deep structures of oppression and how new forms of communication may reinforce or cut against them, without making the mistake that access to information equals change. New forms of communication may alter access to information, and access to information may break monopolies of knowledge, but only active human agents can break monopolies of power.

While media ecology needs activist Marxist theory to help philosophers better understand the world, activist Marxist theorists need media ecology in order to better understand the world so that we can help to change it—not with radical thought alone, but with revolutionary action.

Media Ecology Thus Far: No Sense of Class

In the opening section of this essay I argued that the method employed by media ecologists was a radical and insightful use of dialectical materialism. What would now lead to further insight when fusing the dialectical materialism of media ecology with the dialectical materialism of the activist Marxist tradition would allow for the most complete and accurate analysis of the current social order as well as pointing to the inherent contradictory forces that may lead to change—not in a mechanistic and stages form—but in revolutionary forces that are then shaped by the human beings in society that find themselves suspended within these forces.

In this section I want to demonstrate how the media ecology of Carey, Meyrowitz, and Ong could be enriched with a strong sense of the drive for profit, class, and inequality as forces interacting in the dialectical drive of new communication technologies.

Carey, in keeping Marxism from taking over the theoretical house, makes too much of an explicit plea for a move away from structural Marxism while his own insightful analyses benefit from a clearer notion of power and economics than does the media ecology of either Meyrowitz or McLuhan. Yet unlike Marx, Carey does not take the further step in his analysis. He does not discuss the context of capitalism that interacted with the bias of the telegraph. The importance of the space bias of the telegraph that allowed communication to control the physical movement of things for the first time in human history is clear in Carey's analysis. Yet Carey does not "look to the left" (to use a horizontal metaphor for understanding capitalism's incessant drive for profit) to see that a system based on the drive for profit is interacting with the inherent space bias of the new technology to produce the phenomenon of price speculation based on time and not place. While this point is obvious, it is still important to note that it is needed to round out a medium theory investigation of the telegraph.

Adding a stronger sense of the biases of a system based on the inherent drive for profit would round out Carey's astute observations regarding the space bias of the telegraph and its separation from control of communication by the movement of physical objects to control of the movement of physical objects by communication. Of course the telegraph did not lead to commodity fetishism, but it allowed time to become more important than space and place for price speculation. Within a system based on the drive for increased profit, the telegraph allowed for, even exert-ed pressure toward, the development of price speculation, commodity fetishism, and set the standards for the world stock exchange that we know today due to the inces-sant drive for profit. It is in the combined materialism of medium theory and Marxism that we can more fully investigate the impact of forms of communication on culture due to inherent biases in the forms themselves, and due to inherent bias-es in the drive for profit in developing new technologies and in influencing, but not wholly determining, the uses to which technology is put.

The above analysis highlights how the drive for profit of the larger capitalist-system is too often left out of communication scholarship, as is the case with Carey's medium theory investigation of the telegraph. The dynamic of class strug-gle and living conditions determined (but not static, not set) by class position are also too often left out of communication scholarship. Only a peripheral sense of class is the base of the criticism of Meyrowitz's medium theory discussed below.

Meyrowitz's medium theory may be criticized for not adequately addressing the physical places that most people lived in and the physical conditions that they worked in during the era pre-dating electronic media. The spheres were not so sep-arate as Meyrowitz often suggests. Class position clearly played a significant role in whether a child was raised in the separate spheres or in cramped quarters with adults and children living, eating, and sleeping within view of one another every day (Cowan, 1983). As the Victorian household with its separate rooms separated information access for children and adults and the Victorian concept of education and incremental literacy led to an ideal view of stages in childhood, most children were still living in the merged physical sphere of cramped apartments and one-room dwellings (See Ruth Cowan's 1983 *More Work for Mother* for a detailed historical description of the living conditions of the majority of people in the United States in the early 20th century). Most working class children were not experiencing the isolation from adult behavior and conversation that is the central concern for Meyrowitz.

It is important to keep in mind, however, that the ruling ideas and values of time periods do tend to be those of the ruling class. Therefore, notions of what children should be exposed to and when, while not the actual experience of the majority of children, were the expected experience of children. Thus even though Meyrowitz's argument does not hold up for all in society in actual experience, it is the ideal to which people were encouraged to aspire that was fundamentally challenged for most adults and children with the introduction of television. The actual changes in access to information and social behavior are only experienced by those who had been pre-viously isolated—ruling class families.

Adding a greater sense of class to Meyrowitz's childhood/adulthood analysis is necessary, and adding a sense of class and changes in class living conditions, combined with a stronger sense of human agency, could provide a more nuanced perspective to his merging of masculinity and femininity arguments. In the eighteenth and nineteenth centuries bourgeois women and men and girls and boys were encouraged to, and often operated in, clearly separate physical and, therefore, social spheres. In post-World War II America this previously bourgeois experience, but generalized ideal, starts to be the experience of the newly emerging middle-class women, men, and children. With rural to suburban and urban to suburban migration combined with the largest economic boom in world history, many middle-class Americans do start to emulate the private (women) and public (men) split that they may have admired or aspired to, but did not experience, before World War II.

Meyrowitz's discussion of television blurring formerly private and public spheres could be enriched by emphasizing that contradictory social forces were at work in the 1950s: just as the ruling ideal of separate spheres for women and men experienced mainly by the bourgeoisie started to be experienced by the newly emerging middle class, with television entering the majority of American homes. Thus Meyrowitz could more fully explore the contradictions of the historical period: simultaneous separation of physical spheres for middle-class men and women in the suburbs with the merging of social spheres in the 19-inch neighborhood of television. A stronger sense of class in general, and changes in trends in living conditions based on class position in the 1950s in particular, would enrich Meyrowitz's medium theory analysis of the merging of feminine and masculine information spheres and behavior.

A final critique of Meyrowitz's merging of genders argument concerns a lack of recognition of where progressive change historically has come from. Just as Meyrowitz gives insufficient attention to the nuances of class and contradictory physical and social experiences, he only minimally addresses the role of social struggle and social movements in challenging traditional notions of masculinity and femininity. Meyrowitz generally attributes too much agency to forms of communication and access to information in social change. His discussion of "effect loops" (1985, p. 173) half-way through *No Sense of Place* does get at the idea of human actors pushing for changes, yet it underestimates their role.

Meyrowitz makes valid points concerning the breaking of monopolies of knowledge and the desire for social change that such breaks may encourage. Yet encouraging the desire for change as even Meyrowitz admits in passing (p. 133), is not the same as actually bringing the changes about.

Some observations made by Frederick Douglass after learning to read should help to illustrate this point of critique. In *Narrative of the Life of Frederick Douglass: An American Slave,* Douglass reflects on learning to read and the understanding (the breaking of the slave owner's monopoly of knowledge) brought with it (1845, p. 42):

> The more I read, the more I was led to abhor and detest my enslavers. I could regard them in no other light than a band of successful robbers, who had left their homes, gone to Africa, and stolen us from our homes, and in a strange land reduced us to slavery. I loathed them as being the meanest as well as the most wicked of all men. As I read and contemplated the subject, behold! that very discontentment which Master Hugh had predicted would follow my learning to read had already come, to torment and sting my soul to unutterable anguish. As I writhed under it, I would at times feel that learning to read had been a curse rather than a blessing. It had given me a view of my wretched condition, without the remedy.

Thus altering patterns of access to information (Meyrowitz's language) or the-breaking of monopolies of knowledge (Innis's language) clearly provided an impetus for change. Yet actual changes in social relations do not automatically follow; they must be fought for. Once Frederick Douglass escaped slavery he worked tirelessly with other activists in the abolitionist movement. To wrestle power from the powerful takes much more than knowledge, although knowledge is a key first step.

While there is merit in Meyrowitz's argument that television contributed to the merging of information spheres for bourgeois men and women and did not allow the separation to be experienced by the emerging middle class, his analysis did not make such qualifications. Moreover, Meyrowitz tends to attribute too much agency to television. That electronic media are an important part of, but only a part of, the struggle for change by real human beings living at particular historical moments indicates that access to information alone, just knowledge, does not necessarily lead to change; it could just as easily lead to frustration. It is when the frustration is linked with an actual social movement that dominant power structures are challenged (not just despised) and progressive reforms are won.

The final critique of Meyrowitz's work that I will offer in this essay stems from approaching medium theory from a primarily change-oriented perspective. It has led to a celebratory tendency within Meyrowitz's early formulations of medium theory: because his site of analysis is communication and change, there is an inherent bias making it difficult for current medium theory to fully investigate how new forms of communication may strengthen existing power structures. This idea of how changes due to biases of communication may indeed strengthen existing power structures is discussed in the critique of Ong's work below.

This critique illustrates how Meyrowitz's medium theory would benefit from fusion with an activist Marxist tradition that centers on social class and class domination, but also recognizes that struggle and resistance to domination are carried out by human beings acting as subjects, rather than objects, of history. Merging medium theory with an activist Marxist theoretical tradition will also help it to avoid the mistake of liberal theory that knowledge equals power. All historical struggles suggest that knowledge and access to information are important, but not an isolated cause of the move toward progressive change.

Walter Ong's scholarship could also be extended in interesting directions if it is infused with a stronger sense of class and inequality and how that may have an uneven impact on the consciousness of various groups in a society depending upon access to, and training in, dominant forms of communication. Whether we think of the modern dividing lines of ruling class and working class, white and black, male and female, or the more historical dividing lines of (Marx and Engels, 1848, p. 1) "Freeman and slave, patrician and plebeian, lord and serf, guild-master and journeyman, in a word, oppressor and oppressed," Ong's insights on orality and literacy may be extended to explain how new forms of communication may exert pressure to increase or alter the form of already existing inequalities.

While the distinctions between orality and literacy described by Havelock and Ong in are extremely valuable for understanding the impact of forms of communication on consciousness and culture, both scholars fail to recognize the implications of one crucial point: historically literacy has been introduced into unequal societies. Both Ong and Havelock recognize that cultural consequences of the introduction of literacy varies from culture to culture and over time (Ong, 1982, p. 96). However, both fail to recognize that the impact of the introduction of literacy varies from subculture to subculture *within* a given society.

Literacy was introduced into an *unequal* society in Ancient Greece. The new literate ways of thinking were not distributed evenly throughout society—women and slaves were excluded from entry into the new noetic world described by Ong and Havelock. Once it is recognized that the changes in noetic worlds did not occur symmetrically throughout society in Ancient Greece, for example, we can begin to theorize the form that the oppression of women has taken in the Western world as an interaction between the existing social relations and the new communication technology. Put simply, a combination of Engel's Marxist materialist analysis of the origins of the oppression of women in *The Origins of the State, the Family, and Private Property* with Ong's medium theory analysis of the biases of literacy and the implications for consciousness in *Orality and Literacy* could move Marxist medium theory in a direction of understanding the consequences for consciousness, culture, and the oppression of women when literacy is introduced unequally.

While Ong clearly recognizes that (1982, p. 96) "the amount of credence accorded to written records undoubtedly varied from culture to culture," he fails to recognize that the credence accorded written law also varies within cultures, particularly within the society in which (p. 24) "literacy first clashed head-on with orality," that was saturated with inequality for women and slaves.

An indication that the clash between orality and literacy was intertwined with the clash between the power of men and women in Greek society is apparent in the recurrent theme of women valuing the older religion in Greek drama (Saliou, p. 196):

> women deities are the ancient gods like Erinyes, bound to the clan, or those ancient statues one embraces at a time of peril with a great deal of *emotional* fervor. Opposite these stand the young gods of Olympus who are revered with *measure* and *distance* as befits the citizen.

This discussion by Monique Saliou is strikingly similar to Havelock's assessment that primary oral discourse favors action and is fused with emotion for maximum retention; but literate thought favors reflection with a detached, emotionless analysis. It is clear that throughout the tragedies of the sixth century BC women are most closely associated with the oral noetic realm and men are most closely associated with the literate noetic realm—men other than poets and slaves, that is. This is a realm that could be explored in great detail with a Marxist informed medium theory approach to the study of history.

In "Poetry as Preserved Communication," Havelock argues convincingly that Plato's attacks on the poets in ancient Greece were actually attacks against "the oral state of mind" (Havelock, 1963, pp. 36–49). Because primary oral societies must preserve information in living people, it is stored rhythmically and emotionally: rhythm and emotion serve as the bases of oral technologies. Because of this, Havelock argues that the oral state of mind (p. 39) "constituted the chief obstacle to scientific rationalization in ancient Greece." It is only through the reflexive, detached thought processes enhanced by writing that the scientific revolution was able to occur. Plato did not hate poets: he hated the way that they thought and the way that they taught people to think.

Just as Havelock argued that Plato was really attacking the oral way of thinking when he attacked the poets, it is possible that the intellectual and emotional traits ascribed to women in Ancient Greece and for which they were devalued could be a consequence of women being excluded from the realm of literacy and the implications that has for consciousness.

This is but one of many directions that a Marxist-informed media ecology could go to enhance our understanding of the unintended consequences of communication technologies when introduced into already unequal societies.

Ultimately, the media ecology of Innis, McLuhan, Ong, Carey, and Meyrowitz is not mystical or inaccessible nor is it one dimensional and pessimistic. These scholars represent two generations of well theorized and empirically investigated approaches to media ecology. What current media ecologists have to say is important, and if extended to include a more explicit analysis of the capitalist drive for profit, class, inequality, and social struggle, then their work could be pushed in interesting new directions that could help us to better theorize and understand the impact of new communication technologies for consciousness and culture.

Conclusion

Throughout this essay, I have demonstrated that the method of dialectical materialism is a useful tool for analyzing the role of contradictory forces in pushing societies to change in certain ways. I have also argued that what many Western scholars think as the radical scholarship of critical theorists is actually not really radical scholarship at all and does not employ a dialectical and materialist analysis of society. Thus critical theory is static and conservative and media ecology is fluid and dynamic. Media ecology, not critical theory, has much in common with an activist Marxist tradition. Thus media ecology is radical methodologically and politically while those critical theorists associated with radical critiques of everything are actually methodologically bankrupt and politically conservative, perhaps even reactionary.

References

Bernstein, E. (1993). *The preconditions of socialism and the task of social democracy.* Tudor, H. (Ed. & Trans.). New York: Cambridge University Press. (originally published in 1899)

Carey, J.W. (1989). *Communication as culture: Essays on media and society.* Boston: Unwin Hyman.

Cliff, T. (1993). *Trotsky: The darker the night, the brighter the star.* London: Bookmarks.

Cowan, R.S. (1983). *More work for mother.* New York: Basic.

Douglass, F. (1973). *Narrative of the life of Frederick Douglass.* Garden City, NY: Anchor/Doubleday. (originally published in 1845).

Grosswiler, P. (1998). *Method is the message: Rethinking McLuhan through critical theory.* Montreal: Black Rose Books.

Hall, S. (1985). Signification, Representation, Ideology: Althusser and the Post-Structuralist Debates. *Critical Studies in Mass Communication 2* (2): 91-114.

Hall, S. (1980). Cultural Studies: two paradigms. *Media, Culture and Society* 2: pp. 57-72.

Hardt, H. (1992). *Critical communication studies: Communication, history, and theory in America.* New York: Routledge.

Havelock, E.A. (1963). *Preface to Plato.* Cambridge, MA: Belknap, Harvard.

Horkheimer, M., & Adorno, T. (1972). *Dialectic of enlightenment* (J. Cumming, Trans.). New York: Herder & Herder. (Work originally published in 1947)

Innis, H.A. (1950). *Empire and communications.* New York: Oxford University Press.

Innis, H.A. (1951). *The bias of communication.* Toronto: University of Toronto Press.

Innis, H.A. (1952). *Changing concepts of time.* Toronto: University of Toronto Press.

Innis, H.A. (1954). Concept of monopoly and civilization. In *Explorations,* No. 3.

Kolakowski, L. (1978). *Main currents of Marxism.* P.S. Falla (Trans.). Oxford: Clarendon.

Lenin, V.I. (1969). *What is to be done? Burning questions of our movement.* New York: International Publishers. (originally published in 1903).

Luxemburg, R. (1986). *The mass strike.* New York: Free Press.

Marx, K. and Engels, F. (1978). Manifesto of the Communist Party. *In The Marx-Engels Reader.* Tucker, R. C. (Ed.), pp. 473-500. New York: Norton. (originally published in 1848).

McLuhan, M. (1951) *The mechanical bride: The folklore of industrial man.* New York: Vanguard.

McLuhan, M. (1962). *The Gutenberg galaxy: The making of typographic man.* Toronto: University of Toronto Press.

McLuhan, M. (c1988). *Laws of media: the new science.* Toronto: University of Toronto Press.

McLuhan, M. (1964). *Understanding media: The extensions of man.* New York: McGraw-Hill.

Meyrowitz, J. (1985). *No sense of place: The impact of electronic media on social behavior.* New York: Oxford University.

Meyrowitz, J. (1993). Images of media: Hidden ferment—and harmony—in the field. *Journal of Communication, 43,* (3). pp. 55–66.

Novack, G. (Ed.), (1983). *Their morals and ours: Marxist vs. liberal views on morality: Leon Trotsky/ John Dewey/ George Novak.* New York: Pathfinder.

Ong, W. (1982). *Orality to literacy: The technologizing of the word.* London: Methuen.

Pipes, R. (1963). *Social democracy and the St Petersburg labor movement 1885-1897.* Cambridge, MA: Harvard University.

Rees, J. (1990). Trotsky and the dialectic of history. *International Socialism,* 47: 113-135.

Saliou, M. (1986). Subordination in primitive and archaic Greece. In *Women's work, men's property: The origins of gender and class.* Coontz, S. & Henderson, P. (Eds.), pp. 169-206. London: Verso.

Stamps, J. (1995) *Unthinking modernity.* Montreal & Kingston: McGill-Queen's University Press.

Veblen, T. (1979). *The theory of the leisure class.* Middlesex, UK: Penguin.

CHAPTER SIX

McLuhan and Marxisms Past and Present

PAUL GROSSWILER

Introduction

Two broadly drawn, conflicting Marshall McLuhans can be found in interpreting his work–the conservative, technological determinist and the radical technological humanist (Genosko, 1999). McLuhan can be approached as a cheerleader for technology and capitalism. By contrast, he may be viewed as a technological skeptic who seeks ways to increase human autonomy and control the technological extensions of humans. It is the second McLuhan, the humanistic, skeptical critic of technology who advances the possibility of human intervention and agency in technological society, who is most useful for critical media studies.

Pursuing this second McLuhan, my work has attempted to draw together his and other media ecologists theories with the dialectical methods and social theories of Marxism, the Frankfurt School, cultural studies and postmodernism (Grosswiler, 1991, 1996, 1997, 1998a, 2005b).

To extend this line of interpretation, this chapter will explore the compatibility of Marxism and its offshoots with the media and culture theories of McLuhan in light of my previous work juxtaposing McLuhan's thinking with Marx's Communist Manifesto (1998b); Jurgen Habermas's bourgeois public sphere (2005a, 1998c); Immanuel Wallerstein's black period (2001, 2000a, 1998d); and Jacques Ellul's dialectic of freedom and determinism through anarchy and Christianity (2003, 2000b).

As a proposed graduate program at New York University in the early 1970s, media ecology centered on the work of McLuhan. Media ecology was conceived as the interaction of people, messages and message systems within the overarching context of how media affect perception, understanding and values (Postman and Weingartner, 1971, p. 139). Ecology implies the study of environmental structures, content and impact, defining environment as a "complex message system which regulates ways of feeling and behaving" that "structures what we can see and say and, therefore, do" (ibid.). Media environments pose invisible and unspecified impacts, which are hidden in part because of the erroneous assumption that technology itself is benign. Media ecology strives to raise these hidden effects to awareness and discover the ways that media structure experience in the study of communication technologies as environments (ibid.).

1. McLuhan and Marx

Parallels between McLuhan and Marx can be found by going back 150 years to Marx's *Communist Manifesto*, following a post-Eastern communist interpretation by political theorist Marshall Berman (1998), in juxtaposition to McLuhan's *The Gutenberg Galaxy: The Making of Typographic Man* (1962). Berman's "ground level" reading of Marx compared with McLuhan's *Gutenberg Galaxy* suggests that McLuhan and Marx shared a vision of an expansive and hopeful technological humanism.

Common ground emerges in this comparison between McLuhan and Marx in four themes: Extravagant praise for capitalism; admiration of capitalism's global horizon and a vision of the first-ever world culture; a critique and an indictment of capitalism on humanistic grounds; and identification of an immense working class, a global community waiting for the promise of a revolution.

Marx and the *Manifesto*

Berman first separated Marx from Soviet communism: What happened to Marx from 1917 until 1989 was a disaster. The so-called fall of communism should be welcomed as a chance to read Marx at ground level. The first thing Berman finds looking anew at the *Manifesto* is extravagant praise and awe for capitalism, along with its material and spiritual dynamism. Marx's contemporary radicals charged that Marx betrayed their cause with this celebration. Marx both hated capitalism and recognized its amazing benefits, which he wanted to see shared rather than monopolized.

The second aspect of capitalism Marx most admired was its globalism. Capitalism must spread everywhere, Marx wrote, destroying old industries for new ones whose products are consumed globally and creating a world in its own image. Not that this was capitalism's goal. The narrowly focused yet incessant quest for profits wrought profound transformations, tearing apart all societies, Berman believes. Yet capitalism's globalism was an incredible feat that was a foundation for socialism. A critical component of global capitalism was the first world culture, which Marx called "world literature" at a time when the mass media were in their infancy. The world culture, as Berman calls it, expands human needs and desires—in food, clothes, religion, and music, for example. This world culture also becomes common property, slipping through the control of the owners so that everyone, including the poor, can possess culture. Through world culture, people everywhere can imagine everyone sharing the world's resources. This rarely discussed vision of culture is "one of the most expansive and hopeful things Marx ever wrote," Berman suggests, and today, movies, television and computers have created a "global visual language that brings the idea of world culture closer to home than ever" (p. 15).

Marx's indictment of capitalism was not about exploiting workers or class conflict. It was about destroying people's feelings for each other and reducing the complexity of human relations to self-interest, "cash payment," and "egotistical calculation" (p. 15). Both the capitalists themselves who succeed in this brutal system and the immense group that Marx called the "modern working class" are affected by this change in human relations. The crucial factor of what Marx predicted to be a growing majority of the modern working class was "the need to sell your labor to capital in order to live, the need to carve up your personality for sale," Berman argues (p. 16). Many people in the working class don't know it: well-dressed, well-educated, well-off (for now) office workers, for one, and intellectuals, such as physicians, lawyers, poets, scientists, for another.

Marx saw the working class as an "immense worldwide community waiting to happen," Berman writes, in anticipation of people discovering who they are and fulfilling themselves through involvement with others (ibid.)—through a revolution. The moral vision underlying the *Manifesto* is communism as a way to make people happy, by creating "an association in which the free development of each is the condition of the free development of all" (ibid.). Marx offered a revolution from capitalism's market demand and the resulting deformed development. Marx believed that modernization made the self's free development possible for everyone, but that capitalism's worst qualities stunted its potential, Berman argues. The end of the twentieth century reveals a "dynamic global society ever more unified by downsizing, de-skilling and dread—just like the old man said" (p. 16).

McLuhan and Capitalism

It is important to acknowledge the link in McLuhan's writing between print culture and capitalism. As a self-described footnote to Harold Innis, *Gutenberg Galaxy* cites Innis's explanation that print caused nationalism, price systems and markets that could not exist without print (p. 50). Print introduced Europe's first consumer phase because print as a consumer medium and commodity taught people how to organize all other activities in a systematic, lineal basis; for example, how to create markets, national unity and power (p. 138). The penetrative power of the price system swept aside feudalism based on oral culture and translated its structures into a nationalist-mercantilist one (p. 162). Walter Ong also agreed that the book was the first mass-produced item that provided the basis for commodity culture in the 16th and 17th centuries (p. 163). Print translated discourse into a commodity, creating markets and a price system inseparable from literacy and industry (p. 164). Print was *the* commodity that showed people how to tap all kinds of resources, including human beings (ibid.).

McLuhan cites political economist Karl Polanyi for his analysis of how the capitalist economic system was absorbed into the social system. This, in McLuhan's view, was parallel to the situation of literature and the arts (p. 270). This process, it should be emphasized, is centuries long. In *Gutenberg Galaxy*, the transformation of the mechanization of crafts proceeded slowly in the 16th and 17th centuries (ibid.). This process accommodated literature, industry and economics—and anyone who questioned this was simply denying the facts of science (p. 271). The market economy could only exist in a market society, which requires centuries of transformation of perception and sense ratios by print. In the arts, the novel was one of the "most radical" literary inventions of market society in the 18th century. The author abandoned the patron and offered a homogeneous body of knowledge to the public (p. 273). Literature became a consumer commodity (p. 275). As a result, the same means that created mass production also created an assured basis for the highest levels of art (ibid.).

Capitalism's Creation of a Global Culture

Marx's vision of capitalism's creation of a global culture that everyone can possess is a prototypic expression of McLuhan's "global village." Yet, it implies more than the interconnectedness of humanity through electronic technology. If capitalism is a print culture product, and if the global village undoes print culture, it must in some way undo or weaken capitalism, too. This seems to be a key to McLuhan's radical message, particularly if we focus not on every twist and turn of electronic media, but keep the 500-year focal distance and consider ourselves to be 150 years into a changing social structure of, say, the Morse Millennium, or some other equivalent to the Gutenberg Galaxy.

McLuhan says electronic media have created a "simultaneous field in all human affairs" so that the "human family" exists under the conditions of a global village (p. 31). People can now live in many cultures and worlds at once, but be uncommitted to any single culture (ibid.). McLuhan also introduces what turns into his critique of print culture, and, by extension, capitalism. Even in its early stages in the 18th century, the first violent revulsion against print culture arose (ibid.). Today, print culture has encountered the organic mode of electronic culture, and, as print's extreme mechanization is interpenetrated by the electronic, the resulting reversal makes the electronic age "connatural" with non-literate cultures (p. 46). This occurs after the hot print culture collides with a world for thousands of years served by the cool script culture (p. 138).

Rather than specialism and private enterprise, electronic media create the condition and need for dialogue and participation . Today's electronic culture comprises a "painful but fruitful" frontier, between five centuries of print and the new electronics (p. 141). This is painful because the global village is reversing the key characteristics of print, including individualism. If people decided to modify print by the electronic, "individualism also will be modified" (p. 158). The dramatic struggle, McLuhan wrote, is both rich and terrible, as the electric age already has penetrated deeply within the Gutenberg Galaxy in a collision bringing trauma, tension, grotesquery, menace and malignancy (p. 279).

What Marx envisioned as potential 150 years ago, McLuhan asserted as a fait accompli 35 years ago: That a communism, or a common culture, has already been realized as an effect of technology. The rich and poor consumed the same goods and lived the same lives (McLuhan, *Understanding Media*, 1964, pp. 198–199). The service environment of the 19th century had provided everyone with communal services (McLuhan, *War and Peace in the Global Village*, 1968, pp. 4–5). Electronic media have deepened the consumer service environment of travel, information and education, creating a tribal communism on a scale previously unknown in history (McLuhan, *Letters of Marshall McLuhan*, 1987, p. 373). As McLuhan wrote: "What are we fighting Communism for? We are the most Communist people in world history" (ibid.).

Critique of Capitalism

As with Marx, McLuhan finds print culture's primary casualty is the human. The creation of applied knowledge led to the segmentation of all processes, as well as human beings. McLuhan writes that one observes the individual to see what "makes him tick." "You reduce him to a machine, you isolate his ruling passion . . . .Then you have him" (McLuhan, *Gutenberg Galaxy*, p. 174). People were reduced to things by the segmented, itemized methods of the new print culture. As much as the book is a thing, so is speech reified, and capitalists "hypostasize" expression in order to sell it (ibid.). Print for centuries destroyed oral culture and created the uniformly processed individual of commercial society that by the 18th century had refined, homogenized and visualized the culture to the point of self-alienation from "natural man" (p. 212).

The 18th century industrial economy was imbedded in a self-regulating system of land, labor and capital. Adam Smith translated Newton's laws of mechanics to govern the laws of production and consumption. Smith also declared these mechanical economic laws applicable to intellectual production—and thinking became a business for a few who provided all thought sold in a commercial market to those who labor (pp. 268–269). Eighteenth century people were locked into this closed, enveloping system of a self-regulating economy, and they proceeded "robocentred" to carry out its commands (p. 271).

McLuhan borrowed from Innis to argue that improved communication in newspapers, movies and radio created increased difficulties of understanding and classes of audiences with little communication between them (p. 216). This capitalist print system, while powerful, required a countervailing system from which to break the spell. Now, it is possible to "meditate on the dilemmas of the self-regulating economy and the hedonistic calculus with light hearts and clear heads" (p. 271).

Global Community and Revolution

The key for Marx and McLuhan to this rich and terrible world created by capitalism is the immense global community waiting to realize a world in which the deformed development of capitalism and print culture is transformed. In Marx's terms, it will be transformed into the free development of each and all. In McLuhan's terms, it will be transformed into in-depth participation and dialogue in his version of tribal communism. It is a global village that lives in many cultures at once. It is a diverse, polymorphous, heterogeneous community with a universal common culture and communal services. It is propertyless and workless—an idea in itself that should strike fear in the hearts of capitalists everywhere (p. 275).

2. Jurgen Habermas as Media Ecologist

Similarities between the work of McLuhan and late Frankfurt School philosopher Jurgen Habermas suggest that Habermas should be included in the pantheon of media ecology thinkers. Like Habermas's concepts of the bourgeois public sphere of print culture and the manipulated public sphere of electronic culture, media ecology's concepts of print and electronic media cultures study the effects of technologies of communication on culture and history. Comparing McLuhan and media ecology with Habermas's *The Structural Transformation of the Bourgeois Public Sphere* (1989) suggests:

First, that media ecology's notion of print culture is comparable to Habermas's idea of the bourgeois public sphere—although the translation into English of Habermas's most celebrated phrase is an unfortunate choice from a media ecology perspective.

Second, that media ecology's concept of electronic culture is similar to Habermas's notion of the manipulated or manufactured public sphere.

Third, that media ecology's concept of retribalization, or secondary orality, and Habermas's notion of refeudalization are comparable.

Fourth, media ecology's notion of synaesthesia bears similarities with Habermas's theory of communicative action and the ideal speech situation.

Bourgeois Public Sphere/Print Culture

Habermas's bourgeois public sphere is primarily "private people come together as a public" who claimed the public sphere "regulated from above against the public authorities themselves" (Habermas, 1989, p. 27). Connecting the private realm to public authority, the three parts of the public sphere in the eighteenth century included the public sphere in the "world of letters," composed of clubs and the press, "through which the vehicle of public opinion it [the public sphere] put the state in touch with the needs of society" (pp. 30–31). The institutions of the public sphere, after coffee houses and salons, included art and cultural criticism journals (p. 41), and "moral weeklies," which expanded the circle of the coffee houses (p. 42). Their "dialogue form" attested to their closeness to the spoken word and thereby the "public held a mirror up to itself" (pp. 42–43).

In England, the end of licensing in 1695 allowed the "influx of rational-critical arguments into the press" and made the press into an "instrument" to bring political decisions before the public (p. 58). Throughout the 1700s, the public sphere's development was measured by the degree of confrontation between the government and the press, as the latter was "raised to the status of an institution" (p. 60). The press uncovered accusations against public authorities in the 1760s—1770s that were brought forth "in a manner that ever since has been exemplary of a critical press" (pp. 60–61).

Habermas documented the shift in the growth of the public sphere in the "transformation of the public sphere's preeminent institution, the press" (p. 181). Habermas traces the early press's emergence as a "small handicraft business" that followed the tenets of early capitalism (ibid.). Evolving from "pure news reporting" to include literary journalism, the press became political as well as economic. With scholarly journals, moral weeklies and political journals, this literary journalism put commercial needs in the background in pursuit of critical-rational reflections (p. 182). Publisher-printers dominated, yielding in the 1800s to independent editorships (p. 183).

In media ecology, literate and print culture favors the linear, detached, abstract, rational and individual, while print culture, by extension, encourages individualism, nationalism, and democracy. All of these qualities are encompassed in Habermas's bourgeois public sphere, which is created primarily by the press and which furthers critical-rational debate within the newly media-created space of civil society.

Manipulated Public Sphere/Electronic Culture

In Habermas's analysis, even as the bourgeois literary public sphere was forming, it was also beginning to collapse, due in part to the type of privacy that evolved in the 1700s to create the literary public sphere. The world of letters' public sphere and its rational-critical debate gave way to the "pseudo-public or sham-private world of culture consumption" (Habermas, 1989, p. 160). Habermas centers this collapse on the broadening of the reading public to include almost everyone, thereby creating the "mass public of culture consumers" (pp. 167–168). Reflecting this change in the early 1800s was the rise of the penny press throughout Europe and America–beginning in 1816 in Germany. The penny press depoliticized content to maximize sales. This trend intensified in the latter 1800s through the yellow press and the human-interest story, the weekend press and illustrated magazines, all part of what he calls the "'American' form of mass press" (pp. 167–169).

As the mass press, which was based on commercialization of the public sphere, offered the masses access to the public sphere, this expanded public sphere lost its political character. This "consumption of culture" was fostered as picture and sound-based media—still visible in the daily press—replaced the literary press and critical debate disappeared (p. 169).

Thus, the mass-mediated world is a public sphere only in appearance, according to Habermas, as is the private sphere the media promise to consumers (p. 171). He called the product of mass media culture one of "integration" of information with critical debate, journalistic formats with novel forms, and advice shaped by human interest. The "culture of integration" also assimilates advertising as a "kind of super slogan" and is a means of political and economic propaganda while becoming unpolitical and "pseudo-privatized" (p. 175).

In the 1830s in Europe and America, the press began the transition from an ideological press to a press that was primarily a business (p. 184). Throughout the 1800s, editor-publisher relations changed, the major newspaper chains emerged and technological advancements made economic growth possible (pp. 185–187). The degree of concentration was modest by comparison to that of film, radio and television, which in Europe were initiated by government and were turned from "private institutions of a public formed of private people into public corporations" (p. 187). This has reversed the original basis of the press in the public sphere as institutions that were protected from government by being in the hands of private people; with their commercialization and economic concentration, the media have become "complexes of societal power" that threaten the critical role of the press (p. 188).

Media ecology similarly marks the beginning of electronic culture with the penny press in the 1830s and the introduction of the telegraph in 1844, as McLuhan argues. This electronic media culture only intensifies with the sound and images of film, radio and television. The effect of electronic media culture is a reversal of the cultural effects of print culture, the loss of rationality, detachment, linearity, nationalism and individualism. The new values are involvement, simultaneity, globalism and the collective, and the retreat of rationality, detachment, individualism, and the nation.

Refeudalizaton/Retribalizaton

Habermas describes the process by which the manipulated public sphere of consumption resembles the process found in a medieval feudal system. He called this "refeudalization." The "flooding" of the public sphere with advertising arose as economic concentration increased in order to assure market stability and share (Habermas, 1989, p. 189). Economic advertising became political with the development of public relations and "public opinion management" invading public opinion by creating and exploiting events (p. 193). The result is the "engineering of consent" with features of a "staged public opinion" (p. 194). A consensus created by "sophisticated opinion-molding" lacks the criteria of rationality of a consensus reached by "the time-consuming process of mutual enlightenment." Shaped by public relations, the public sphere takes on "feudal features" as the public is presented a "showy pomp" that it is ready to follow. It is feudal in that it imitates the "aura" of "personal prestige and supernatural authority" given to the publicity of feudal courts (p. 195). In short, refeudalization. Within the "decayed form of the bourgeois public sphere" (p. 215), and the "manipulated public sphere" and "manufactured public sphere," the media both represent political ideology and are ineffectual in political communication except as advertising (p. 217). In *Structural transformation of the public sphere*, Habermas offers no emancipatory alternative.

Media ecology's broad historical sweep moves from an initial stage of oral culture and tribalism to a second stage of print culture and nationalism, then into a third stage of electronic culture and retribalization characterized by the creation of the "global village." In part, retribalization recovers the orality of pre-print culture. Medieval culture, although a thousand years into scribal culture, is described by media ecology as oral culture. Orality, to McLuhan and Innis and Ong, represents a balanced stage of dialogue and the interplay of the human senses. In part, retribalization is the recovery of synaesthesia through the electronic media that overcomes the fragmented, visual sensory system created by print media. Electronic and oral cultures integrate thought, feeling and action and erode national identities in favor of the global village.

Ideal Speech Situation/Synaesthesia

Although communication clearly was a significant element in *The structural transformation of the public sphere* with the notion of rational-critical debate, Habermas moved beyond the Frankfurt School with the later theory of "communicative action." Rational discourse is free of domination, and oriented toward consensus and understanding, which is seen as the most appropriate type of activity for the public sphere (Holub, 1991, p. 8). Communicative rationality is the basis for critical social theory and has an analytical as well as utopian aspect. It is able to criticize distorted communication by basing the theory on the validity claims of normal speech. At the same time, it provides as an end the "never-realizable . . . state in which unconstrained, perfectly free communication occurs. With the theory of communicative action, Habermas has come full circle and arrived back at his starting point in the public sphere." But, instead of a historical structure that has collapsed, Habermas projects "a state of affairs whose realization lies in the future" (p. 15).

His system offers two types of action. Rational-purposive action involves technical knowledge that includes manipulation in order to achieve social goals, while communicative action is related to praxis and the realization of human potential (Hallin, 1986, pp. 122–123). Underlying Habermas's communication theory is the concept of dialogue, in that all forms of communication, regardless of how unequal, derive from dialogue between human subjects, and must be evaluated on that basis (p. 142).

Habermas moved from a bleak critique of modernity in *The structural transformation of the public sphere*, to communication theories based on emancipatory potential. Habermas offered a utopian model of rational-critical debate through communicative action with a model of oral communication culture. Even as he criticizes the "refeudalization" of the media, Habermas returns to an oral mode of communication for his ideal speech situation, an oral mode that last existed in the feudal era.

Media ecologists, too, have a tendency toward idealism and utopianism centered on communication. Ong's study of orality and literacy (1982, p. 2, pp. 5–15) rehabilitates orality as integral to human communication. Innis clearly prefers the balanced dialogue of oral culture in his plea for time (1951, pp. 41, 68, 105–106, 190). McLuhan's transformation of print culture's alienation by electronic media culture's integration of the senses through synaesthesia also is based on a privileging of the oral, of dialogue and conversation. McLuhan described synaesthesia as the unified sensory and imaginative experience that is the crowning effect of electronic media culture as television provides an all-enveloping extension of the central nervous system (McLuhan, 1964, pp. 274–275). Even Postman, in his championing of typographic culture attends to the orality of dialogue and debate, and the rationality that print culture makes possible (1985, pp. 44–48).

In Habermas's early writing, media ecologists may find another founding philosopher who examines the impact of media environments on culture and history, and who offers a media ecological approach for communication as a liberating activity.

3. The Morse Millennium: McLuhan, Wallerstein, and Innis

Innis, McLuhan, and Wallerstein would agree that we are witnessing the end of the "longue duree" of the capitalist world-economy and print culture in a historical rupture that has been and will be a time of intense and painful political and cultural struggle. The way through in part involves a reinvention and recommitment to values that are being discarded in the cultural shift from modernity. In Wallerstein's case it is a recommitment to the modernity of liberation during a half century or more of a "Black Period" (Wallerstein, 1998). In McLuhan's thought it is print culture's ability to be detached and "think things out before we put them out" as we move from the Gutenberg Galaxy to the Global Village, which I suggest calling the Morse Millennium (McLuhan, 1964, p. 57). For Innis, new communication media spur the rise and fall of monopolies of knowledge (Innis, 1964). Together, Wallerstein's "utopistics," McLuhan's "laws of media" and Innis's notion of monopolies of knowledge provide a means of navigating through the transition to a new historical system.

Wallerstein and McLuhan provide complementary visions, existing in creative tension with each other, of the past and the future. According to Wallerstein, the modern world system has coopted major challenges during the last half millennium by, for example, incorporating popular sovereignty and citizenship after the French Revolution (1998, pp. 15–16); allowing the rise of universal suffrage and the welfare state after the World Revolution of 1848 (p. 17); and to achieving globalized liberalism after the Russian Revolution (p. 25). According to McLuhan, visual culture's modern world of individualism, nationalism, industrialism and capitalism was created over a period of centuries, absorbing opposition movements such as Marxism and communism (1964). Wallerstein's concept of a modernity of technology also fits easily within McLuhan's concept of print culture in the modern world. Wallerstein's technological modernism offers a view of endless progress and innovation, a concept consistent with McLuhan's concept of print culture's approach to technology, beginning with the alphabet, as embodiments of linearity, continuity, consistency and uniformity (p. 157).

Wallerstein and McLuhan both bear witness to the decline of the world capitalist economy and print culture, and the rise of a new world system, with key shifts occurring in the 1960s. For Wallerstein, it was the "world revolution" of 1968 and the collapse of the Berlin Wall, and along with it liberalism, in 1989. The effect of the "world revolution" of 1968 was to dethrone liberalism as the underpinning of the world-system geoculture and to revive the anti-statist, laissez-faire political right (Wallerstein, 1998, pp. 28–29). For McLuhan it was the rise of electronic media, beginning with the telegraph, but becoming a decisive change with the advent of television and its saturation of culture in the 1960s.

Wallerstein's Black Period

With the fall of liberalism, Wallerstein predicts that three forces will cause systemic eruptions accompanying the crisis of the world system, all three challenging Eurocentric ways of thinking and living. The first relates to a rejection of liberalism's ideology of progress, for example, by religious fundamentalists, including

Christians, and the rise of anti-statism (pp. 58–59). The second relates to immigrants from the Third World, largely, to rich First World states (p. 61). The democratizing of weapons in ways that proffer repeats of the conflict between the United States and Iraq is the third force suggesting scenarios of "great disorder and personal insecurity" of this systemic crisis (pp. 60–63).

Enter the "Black Period." Wallerstein foresees a limited time frame of roughly fifty years, predicting the period's unpredictability as well as its "terrible political struggle" from which chaos will produce order (p. 64). The historical choice he outlines is between defenders of the current system who tout its material wealth, liberal political structures, and a longer life span; and detractors of the system, who criticize its inequality and conflict, its low level of real political participation, and its degraded quality of life (pp. 65–66). This "Black Period" will entail a period of "Hell on Earth," of struggle at a life and death level, as it lays the basis for the historical system for the next five hundred years (pp. 82–85). The privileged will struggle to preserve their interests through historically proven methods of repression and concession. Working in their favor, the vastly improved means of world communication serve them with more intelligent reflection and the opportunity for conscious decisions. They will try the principle of seeming to change everything so that nothing changes, although it seems to, through the co-optation of rhetoric and the creation of new institutions. He maintains that the privileged groups of the feudal world system were able to invent ways to continue to ensure privilege to the same strata of people. Some ways of protecting privilege in the transition to a new world system in the twenty-first century will be adopting the terms of the discontented, such as ecology, multiculturalism, and feminism. The oppressed will respond, Wallerstein predicts, with a variety of means, from violence to electoral challenge, theoretical development in institutions of knowledge, and public appeals. And he suggests the only viable option is a rainbow coalition demanding that the privileged live up to liberal rhetoric (pp. 87–88).

To pursue the democratic and egalitarian alternative to continued privilege, Wallerstein suggests retaining Enlightenment ideals, including Jeremy Bentham's utilitarian concept of maximized public good and Mill's value of individual liberty, by changing ideas about money and work to substitute autonomy for pay (p. 71), and to eliminate "the endless accumulation of capital" with non-profit and non-state structures that are decentralized and managed by some regulations and collective worker interests (pp. 74–75). To democratize political institutions, he urges organizing the new media technologies outside of the financial system to garner widespread participation (p. 80).

McLuhan's Morse Millennium

For McLuhan, the decline of typographic culture is accompanied and fueled by forces of change that may be said to center on the emergence of a "global village" that challenges the Western biases of the existing world system, although the catalyst for McLuhan is technology. A surprising amount of McLuhan's work in the 1960s focuses on international communication issues. The telegraph, which ushered in the Age of Communication, offers a route to synaesthesia, or unified sensory experience, as it decentralized communication and recreated social awareness on a village scale (McLuhan, 1964, pp. 219–225). As the electronic media "retribalize" Western culture, they also open that Western way of thinking to the "uniqueness and diversity" of women and people of color (pp. 275–276). This element of the "global village" is often misinterpreted as a universally homogeneous monolith—which is actually more of a print culture application than an electronic culture vision of multiculturalism. Meanwhile, in McLuhan's analysis, the rising mechanization and literate technology among non-literate cultures are unleashing "explosive and aggressive energies" that are then shared via electronic media on a global scale (ibid.).

Throughout McLuhan's writing, the transition from a print to an electronic culture, a transition now a hundred years in the making but still just beginning, is rife with pain and trauma as he suggests adaptations and controls of the new media environment and the culture it is imposing. In contrast to readings of McLuhan as a technotopian who forecasts a predetermined end of history within a "single consciousness" (McLuhan, 1964, p. 67) or a "Pentecostal unity" (p. 84), these occasional excesses are contrasted with abundant evidence of the pain and trauma of this systemic transition. With electronic media extending the central nervous system into space, the emergence of this media culture is greeted with numbness (p. 19). The "retribalization" is traumatic (p. 30), as the common result of technological transformation is mental breakdown (p. 31). The responses to electronic media move from alarm to resistance to exhaustion (p. 39), although this breakdown in McLuhan's thinking also is an opportunity for "breakthrough." Yet the violence and pain of this process is impossible to miss. McLuhan alludes, for example, to the "desperate and suicidal auto-amputation" of the central nervous system (p. 53), the "civil war in . . . psyches" engendered by the interplay of media (p. 57); the "fate . . . more terrible" (p. 59); and "collective surgery . . . with complete disregard for antiseptics" (p. 70).

McLuhan focuses only occasionally on the struggle between the privileged defenders of the status quo and ordinary people. He remarks consistently but infrequently that media owners are not concerned about media content, but with the media as such (p. 60). With a more radical bent, he also consistently but infrequently comments on the problems posed by corporate media interests, saying, for example, that giving control of the media to corporations strips us of our rights (p. 73). It is in the interest of most people to reclaim these rights and to counteract the control of media owners who are not interested in electronic media effects.

McLuhan offers suggestions, too, about the choices to be made in this traumatic transition between media cultures, and it often focuses, too, on defenders vs. critics of print culture. For McLuhan there is no going back, as electronic culture is "within the gates" and destroying the Gutenberg technology on which Western existence is based (p. 33). Despite the inevitability of systemic change, the forces of print culture approach electronic media culture with "somnambulism" (p. 26), promoting values of a print-based, and thus incomplete, rationality that is literate, visual, uniform, continuous, and sequential. Opposing the effects of print culture, McLuhan suggests values of participation and involvement, wholeness, empathy and depth (p. 20) must replace those of detachment and non-involvement, which are the most significant results of centuries of print culture (p. 157), along with fragmentation and specialization (p. 34). McLuhan suggests that shifting experiences of identity, family and community are creating new demands (McLuhan, 1967). He urges educational institutions to reinvent themselves on a model other than that of the factory (p. 18). He recognizes that fragmented job patterns need to be reformulated to meet the demand for roles (p. 20), a move that would undermine the underpinnings of capitalist self-interest and the demand for accumulation of capital. He also advocates the mass audience as a creative, participating force in a new politics in which the living room is a voting booth (p. 22). Ironically, though it is the ability to understand and clarify issues that is at the heart of increasing human autonomy for McLuhan (1964, p. 59), and the basis for his "laws of media."

But, ultimately, given McLuhan's focus on the long duree, it may still be premature to make claims about the Morse Millennium. Having selected Johannes Gutenberg—an obscure German printer who devised movable types in 1440, leading eventually to the rise of the Gutenberg Galaxy—McLuhan might as easily have chosen Samuel Morse, whose innovation of the telegraph in 1840 led eventually to the rise of the global village and electronic media culture. If the analogy holds, in the year 2000 we are roughly in the Morse Millennium where Europe was in the year 1600 in the Gutenberg Galaxy—its own period of intense political and cultural struggle. But it is our position relatively early in the transition to a new world system that prevents us from understanding it well. It is alienation from print culture that deepens understanding of both the print and electronic revolutions. Those most deeply immersed in a revolution are least likely to be aware of its dynamics. It is usually wrongly assumed the future will be an extension of that past. In 1960, McLuhan thought it was futile to discuss the electronic media revolution, although he thought it would be easy to describe it by today. For a "previously opaque" age to become clear requires that culture moves first to another age to reflect the preceding one clearly (1962, p. 275). If Morse is to the electronic culture as Gutenberg was to print culture, then McLuhan is roughly the Shakespeare of our time. The full definition of the post-print, post-capitalist electric age could be several centuries in the making.

"Utopistics"/Laws of Media

Wallerstein's method for assessing the alternative historical systems that are possible successors to the modern capitalist world-system is called "utopistics." McLuhan's earlier implicit method for assessing changes in cultural and communication systems he later named the "laws of media."

Facing an uncertain future, Wallerstein proposes "utopistics" as a way to engage in the serious assessment of historical alternatives in the moment of "transformational TimeSpace" (Wallerstein, 1998, p. 3). The security that Wallerstein finds in this period of change is that within a system in crisis small changes have great effects, in contrast to periods of stability, within which large changes have minimal effect (p. 63). He also finds encouragement in the structure of systems, which are born, live long lives, come into crisis, and transform themselves into a new form during an unpredictable transition that is heightened by an increase of free will as a factor (p. 88).

McLuhan would agree with the notion that periods of systemic crisis offer the greatest opportunities for human intervention. The transition from typographic to electronic media systems offers a "break boundary" much like the alphabet and printing (McLuhan, 1964, pp. 49–50). The cross-fertilization or hybridization of media releases "great force" (p. 57) and offers a "furious release of energy" (p. 58). By understanding and clarifying issues, McLuhan hopes to increase human autonomy (p. 59). He suggests that the artist—a group that comprises any one in the sciences and humanities—can provide a "history of the future" and provide immunity to the electronic media environment (p. 70). A key step is to separate action and reaction and stand aside from media forms (p. 69) so that we can "think things out before we put them out" (p. 57). Toward this end he published (McLuhan, 1988) the laws of the media, a diachronic and synchronic model based on his earlier hybrid media model that looked at each technology in terms of what it extends, obsolesces, retrieves, and reverses into. If taken at a systemic rather than individual medium level, this tool becomes a powerful means of experiencing and predicting significant historical changes.

Innis's Monopolies of Knowledge

Innis directly implicates new forms of communication media in the process of establishing, "checking," destroying, and creating monopolies of knowledge. He argues that the bias of modern civilization based on radio and television, from which we can extrapolate new media, will presume a perspective of civilizations dominated by other media. We can do little more than be alert to the implications of this bias and hope that the implications of other media to other civilizations may enable us to see more clearly the bias of our own. We can assume that the use of a medium of communication over a long period of time will to some extent determine the character of knowledge and will eventually create a civilization in which life will be difficult to maintain and the advantages of a new medium will lead to the emergence of a new civilization (Innis, 1964, p. 34).

Innis traced the implications of the media of communication for the nature of knowledge from the beginnings of civilization in Mesopotamia. He suggests that a monopoly of knowledge is built up to a point that equilibrium is disturbed. Inventions in communication compel realignments in the monopoly of knowledge (pp. 3–4). The demands of the new media are imposed on the older media (p. 82) and these sudden extensions of communication are reflected in cultural disturbances (p. 31).

Looking back to the beginning of civilization, it would be hard to defend the priestly organizations against trade, small nations and new languages. But that is exactly what we risk doing today with the mainstream media. Innis's advice is in part an answer to the question why we should not defend the old media today. If we are indeed between civilizations, the dying of print culture capitalism and the emergence through a Black Period of a Morse Millennium, Innis's cautionary advice may go far in helping us chart the transition:

Our civilization, like all civilizations, believes in its uniqueness and superiority. Print ushered in a new and superior civilization of democracy, education, progress, and individualism. "At this point," Innis warns, "the water becomes swift and we are in grave danger of being swept off our feet by the phenomenon we are describing. . . . Civilizations have their sacred cows. Some burn their heretics; the modern age threatens them with atom bombs" (p. 139).

4. Ellul and Media Anti-Environments

In media ecology, media anti-environments provide what French sociologist and theologian Jacques Ellul (1981) calls "the positivity of negativity" as the only way to induce change in any system. Media anti-environments consciously express "contradiction, contestation, and negativity" (p. 296) to the media environment dominated by neoliberal—or corporate controlled—global, propagandistic, totalized and belligerent formal structures.

Ellul argued that if a positive remains alone, such as in an uncontested society, it remains "shut up in the indefinite repetition of its own image" (p. 295). As the only agent of possible change, "negativity has a wholly positive side. If there is transition from one state to another, we can thank negativity alone." The individual's duty is to say "no" (p. 297). Ellul wrote: "When we shake the edifice, we produce a crack, a gap in the structure, in which a human being can briefly find freedom, which is always threatened" (1988, p. 174). He goes on to say that to create this crack, however, requires "radical, total refusal. Any concession to power enables the totality of power to rush into the small space we have opened."

In media ecology, it is the media anti-environment that creates the "positivity of negativity" as the only means to bring the hidden ground of media environments to awareness. Without media anti-environments, the media environment remains invisible and we remain somnambulant. McLuhan introduced the idea of media anti-environments in *Understanding Media*. Technology, McLuhan believed, reaches beneath consciousness and alters perception without human awareness or resistance. Because the media are auto-amputated human extensions, we respond to the media environment like somnambulists, with a sort of shock and awe. Only the media anti-environment of the artist or new media can counter these hidden technological effects. Only media anti-environments make it possible to change the media and increase human freedom. "If we understood our older media, such as roads and written word, and if we valued their human effects sufficiently, we could reduce or even eliminate the electronic factor from our lives," McLuhan wrote (1964, p. 93).

Ellul's work on the social impact of technology is usually described as pessimistic, fatalistic, and deterministic. Rarely do scholars describe his approach to technological society as centered on individual freedom or anarchy. His later works, particularly *Jesus and Marx* (1988) and *Anarchy and Christianity* (1991) argue that anarchism is an effective, if not perhaps the only, response to challenge and seek to change the deterministic power of technological society.

Ellul's dual scholarly career as a sociologist and theologian created a dialectical body of work that he sought for decades to keep apart, according to his own comments (Ellul, 1981). Yet he merged these separate spheres in the last few years of his life, primarily in *Jesus and Marx* (1988) and *Anarchy and Christianity* (1991). The union of the analytical, more deterministic sociological works and the more dialectically open and activist theological works, however, followed on decades of separation in scholarly criticism of the two disciplines.

Through anarchism and Christianity, Ellul pursues creating cracks in the walls of technological society in order to fill the spaces with human freedom. *Jesus and Marx* and *Anarchy and Christianity* provide the link between the dialectic of freedom and determinism, the possibilities created by anarchy and faith for authentic human existence.

Ellul has been grouped with Lewis Mumford, Neil Postman and others as social critics, beginning with Ellul's *Technological Society* (1964), who have "sounded the alarms about the stress to the human mind" of constant technological innovation and the "potentially dehumanizing effects of out-of-control technology," and who view technology as a system in which society is trapped (Nardi and O'Day, 1999, pp. 26–27). Ellul is seen as presenting a "sweeping vision of technology" based on the cultural mindset of technique, in which efficiency is the sole criterion. Technological efficiency becomes the standard for measuring everything, even people. Reading Ellul is "not to be undertaken by the faint of heart" (p. 34) because Ellul's, Postman's and Winner's systemic view creates a sense of the "inexorability of technological change" (p. 35). At his "bleakest," Ellul's view is "deeply pessimistic, claustrophobic" and comprises "no-holds-barred laments" (p. 63).

For his part, Ellul has been disputing charges of pessimism, determinism, fatalism, and freedom of action in his work since *Technological Society* first appeared in English. In his foreword, he compares himself to a physician in an epidemic. Although he may seek objectivity, there is a "profound tension of the whole being" because he is involved in technological society and its history is his history. Because he does not exceed description, he writes, readers may get the impression that he is pessimistic. He responds: "I am neither by nature, nor doctrinally, a pessimist, nor have I pessimistic prejudices" (p. xxvii).

Anarchy in a Technological Society

In his essay on dialectics, Ellul (1981) approached his subject both as a social and historical force, and as it affects his own work. The heart of dialectics in history is made clear in his adoption of Hegel's notion of "the positivity of negativity." If a positive remains alone, such as in an uncontested society or a church without heretics, it remains unchanged, "shut up in the indefinite repetition of its own image" (p. 295). The only way to change the positive is "contradiction, contestation, the appearance of the negative, negativity," which bring about transformation. For Ellul, someone must consciously express the contradiction to induce innovation in order to change history. In this way, "negativity has a wholly positive side. If there is transition from one state to another, we can thank negativity alone." Although unwilling to give a

Hegelian or Marxist spin to this process and imply that it leads to progress, negativity retains a positive value because it is the only chance for change (p. 296). In negativity, the individual's duty is to say "no" (p. 297). This dialectical process suggests an anarchistic core, the resistance to and negation of power.

It is also a dialectical approach that introduces a "double element" in his positions. For example, he considers that people are powerless to change technological society, but that they should do all they can to change it. For another example, society, as a system of determinisms, must always be attacked, but society must also be maintained, so the attacks must not be destructive (p. 307). These contradictory positions may be read as confusion by critics, but these explanations appear lucidly put. If the technological system is a total system, it is no longer dialectical. But if dialectics is thought to be essential to life and history, the negativity must come from outside the technological system. That, Ellul argues, which exists outside the system, must be the transcendent. The transcendent is "the necessary condition for the continuation of life, the unfolding of history, simply the existence of man as man" (p. 308).

Nowhere can be found a more cogent expression of this linking of the sociological and theological dialectic than in the last chapter of *Jesus and Marx* and in *Anarchy and Christianity*. In 1974, Ellul wrote that he had long thought anarchy was the "only acceptable stance in the modern world," although he strongly believed an anarchist society was not possible, in true dialectical fashion (*Jesus and Marx*, 1988, p. 156). Anarchism also is the only "anti-political political position in harmony with Christian thought" (p. 157). He sides with anarchist criticisms of God, the church, and religion, "as long as we clarify that they criticize God as modified by . . . bourgeois theology, and the Church as the power it had become. . . . The anarchists (and Marx) erred in believing they had come face to face with Christianity itself" (p. 161). They were attacking a "deviation" rather than the "reality" of Christianity, Ellul argues (p. 162).

In his biblical analysis of the Old Testament, Ellul interprets a number of events to argue that political power has no value in itself. The Old Testament "radically repudiates, challenges, and condemns it whenever it claims to exist as political power rather than as a sign." The New Testament, he argues, has a tendency of being "hostile to power" (p. 166). Jesus had a radically negative stance toward power, holding it up to ridicule and refusing to exercise it himself (p. 167). Any power exercised on earth is "evil, should be obliterated, denied," Jesus contends. He represents a fundamental attack on power rather than a spiritual or apolitical attitude (p. 168). Ellul offers multiple evidences of a "consistent biblical series of negations of political power, of witnesses to its lack of validity and legitimacy." Among the "Christians of the first generation" he finds a "rejection of the authorities" (p. 169). And these are the only Christians whom Ellul finds worthy of the name.

Christian anarchists have to offer their "conscious, well-founded refusal" to the political world, as the only way to "challenge and occasionally impede the unlimited growth of power." As anarchists, Christians can offer anarchism a corrective to the "illusion" that power can be abolished; the Christian, on the other hand, insists on trying to abolish power because human action is always limited (p. 173). An anarchist society will fail, he thinks, because of the nature of power, but anarchism remains the only option. "Freedom exists today, or not at all," he writes. "When we shake the edifice, we produce a crack, a gap in the structure, in which a human being can briefly find his freedom, which is always threatened". To create this crack, however, requires "radical, total refusal. Any concession to power enables the totality of power to rush into the small space we have opened" (p. 174).

Ellul sets as a first principle the "absolute rejection of violence" (p. 11). He offers a variety of reasons, including society's ability to resist and react; violence's expression of despair and loss of hope; the effectiveness of non-violent movements; and the Christian way of love (pp. 12–13). What remains after removing violence is:

> pacifist, antinationalist, anticapitalist, moral, anti-[bourgeois] democratic anarchism
> . . . . There remains the anarchism which acts by means of persuasion, by the creation
> of small groups and networks, denouncing falsehood and oppression, aiming at a true
> overturning of authorities of all kinds as people at the bottom speak and organize them-
> selves (pp. 13–14).

Ellul advises that anarchists should not vote as part of conscientious objection to "everything that constitutes our capitalist (or degenerate socialist) and imperialistic society (whether it be bourgeois, communist, white, yellow, or black)" (p. 15). This conscientious objection would be to military service, taxes, vaccinations, compulsory schooling and all "demands and obligations imposed by society" (ibid.). To confront the enemy of "omnipotence and omnipresence of administration," he urges filing objections to everything (p. 16) in an organized fashion. If one taxpayer objects, there is no effect, but if thousands object, and the media are brought in, the state must respond. He also offers the example of parents organizing an alternative school (p. 17). Beyond marginal actions that object to authority, Ellul recommends the dissemination of anarchist thinking and the drawing of support from existing resistance groups, such as ecologists (p. 18).

Ellul reiterates his lack of faith in the possibility of an anarchist society (p. 19), although he does grant it possible to create new grass-roots institutions to replace the powers that must be destroyed and to begin afresh (p. 21). The opportunity today is heightened by the existence of "empty political institutions" in which people have lost confidence and the "almost infinite growth of power, authority, and social control" that renders democracies authoritarian as the result of technique. Ellul regards anarchy as the "only serious challenge," "the only means of achieving awareness," "the first active step" (p. 22). Power may not be prevented, but it can be struggled against and denounced by anarchists organizing on the fringe (p. 23). Even as power grows, anarchy becomes more important as the individual's last defense. "It has a bright future before it. That is why I adopt it" (ibid.).

Conclusion

Comparing similarities between McLuhan and media ecology, and this broad range of Marxist-related critical thinkers, from Marx to Habermas, Wallerstein and Ellul, has attempted to strengthen the interpretation of McLuhan as oppositional and radical.

Marx's *Communist Manifesto* and McLuhan's *The Gutenberg Galaxy: The Making of Typographic Man* suggest that McLuhan and Marx shared a vision of an expansive and hopeful technological humanism. Extravagant praise for capitalism; admiration of capitalism's global horizon and a vision of the first-ever world culture; a critique and an indictment of capitalism on humanistic grounds; and identification of an immense working class, a global community waiting for the promise of a revolution link Marx and McLuhan thematically.

An examination of Habermas's *The Structural Transformation of the Bourgeois Public Sphere* reveals similarities in several key concepts of Habermas with McLuhan and media ecology. Comparing McLuhan's and media ecology's notions of print culture, electronic culture, retribalization and synaesthesia with Habermas's ideas of the bourgeois public sphere, the manipulated public sphere, refeudalization and the ideal speech situation draws many parallels between their media and culture theories.

Wallerstein's and McLuhan's respective analyses of the decline of the capitalist world-economy and print culture unite these two thinkers in heralding a historic shift to a long transitional period of political and cultural struggle between the old and new. Wallerstein seeks a recommitment to the modernity of liberation to endure the Black Period; McLuhan values print culture's ability to be detached and "think things out before we put them out" as we move from the Gutenberg Galaxy to what I suggest calling the Morse Millennium. Wallerstein's "utopistics," McLuhan's "laws of media" and Innis's notion of monopolies of knowledge provide a means of navigating through the transition.

McLuhan's and media ecology's central notion of media anti-environments share with Jacques Ellul the "positivity of negativity" the distinction of being the sole means of change in any social and media system. The media anti-environment is the "crack" in the structure that allows a small, single hope of change in a highly deterministic technological society, bringing the hidden ground of media environments to awareness. Only media anti-environments make it possible to change the media, increase human freedom, and, as McLuhan wrote, "reduce or eliminate the electronic factor from our lives." Regaining human control of technological systems is what McLuhan and these four critical thinkers have most in common.

Regaining human control of technological systems is what McLuhan and these four critical thinkers have most in common.

References

Berman, Marshall. (1998). "Unchained Melody." *The Nation* , 266 (17), 11–16.

Ellul, Jacques. (1964). *The Technological Society*. New York: Knopf.

Ellul, Jacques. (1981). "Epilogue: On Dialectic." In C.G. Christians & J.M. Van Hook (Eds.), *Jacques Ellul: Interpretive Essays* (pp. 291–308). Urbana, IL: University of Illinois Press.

Ellul, Jacques. (1988). *Jesus and Marx: From Gospel to Ideology*. Grand Rapids, Mich.: Eerdmans.

Ellul, Jacques. (1991). *Anarchy and Christianity*. Grand Rapids, MI: Eerdmans.

Genosko, Gary. (1999). *McLuhan and Baudrillard: The Masters of Implosion*. London: Routledge.

Grosswiler, Paul. (1991). "A Dialectical Synthesis of Marshall McLuhan and Critical Theory." Paper presented to the philosophy of communication division of the International Communication Association, Chicago, Illinois.

Grosswiler, Paul. (1996). "The Dialectical Methods of Marshall McLuhan, Marxism, and Critical Theory. *Canadian Journal of Communication*, 21(1): 95–124.

Grosswiler, Paul. (1997). "A Q-methodology Study of Media and Ideology Orientations: Exploring Medium Theory, Critical Theory and Cultural Studies." *Canadian Journal of Communication*, 22 (2): 261–287.

Grosswiler, Paul. (1998a). *The Method Is the Message: Rethinking McLuhan Through Critical Theory*. Montréal: Black Rose Books.

Grosswiler, Paul. (1998b). "The Marriage of McLuhan and Marx: Hold the Wedding, or the Odd Couple?" A paper presented to the Many Dimensions: Extensions of Marshall McLuhan conference. McLuhan Program in Culture and Technology, University of Toronto, Ontario, Canada.

Grosswiler, Paul. (1998c). "McLuhan, Habermas, and the Mediated Shape of the Public Sphere." A paper presented to the Canadian Communication Association, Congress of the Social Sciences and Humanities, University of Ottawa.

Grosswiler, Paul. (1998d). "Connecting Medium Theory and World-Systems Theory: Marshall McLuhan Meets Immanuel Wallerstein." A paper presented to the New York State Communication Association's 56th annual convention, Monticello, New York.

Grosswiler, Paul. (2000a). "The Hated and the Cherished: Technology and Print Culture Concepts of Free Speech." *The Maine Scholar*, 13: 139–160.

Grosswiler, Paul. (2000b). "Anarchy in a Technological Society: An Ellulian Perspective." *New Dimensions in Communication*, 13: 29–45.

Grosswiler, Paul. (2001). "The Black Period, the Morse Millennium and the New Phoenicians." Presented to the New York State Communication Association Annual Convention, Monticello, New York.

Grosswiler, Paul. (2003). "Understanding Media Anti-environments." Presented to the Media Ecology Association 4th Annual Convention, Hofstra University, New York.

Grosswiler, Paul. (2005a). "Jurgen Habermas: Media Ecologist?" *Media Ecology Association 2001 Proceedings.*

Grosswiler, Paul. (2005b). "Retrieving McLuhan for Cultural Studies and Postmodernism." In Strate, Lance, and Wachtel, Edward (Eds.) *Legacy of McLuhan.* Cresskill, NJ: Hampton Press, pp. 245–258.

Habermas, Jurgen. (1989) *The Structural Transformation of the Public Sphere: An Inquiry into a Category of Bourgeois Society.* Translated by Thomas Burger. Cambridge, MA: MIT Press.

Hallin, Daniel C. (1986). "The American News Media: A Critical Theory Perspective." In John Forester, *Critical Theory and Public Life.* (Ed.) Cambridge, MA: MIT Press.

Holub, Robert C.(1991). *Jurgen Habermas: Critic in the Public Sphere.* London: Routledge.

Innis, Harold A. (1964). *The Bias of Communication.* Toronto: University of Toronto Press.

McLuhan, Marshall. (1962). *The Gutenberg Galaxy: The Making of Typographic Man.* Toronto: University of Toronto Press.

McLuhan, Marshall. (1964). *Understanding Media: The Extensions of Man.* New York: Mentor.

McLuhan, Marshall, with Fiore, Quentin, & Agel, Jerome. (1968). *War and Peace in the Global Village.* New York: Bantam.

McLuhan, Marshall. (1987). *Letters of Marshall McLuhan.* Matie Molinaro, Corinne McLuhan, & William Toye (Eds.) Toronto: Oxford University Press.

McLuhan, Marshall, with Eric McLuhan. (1988). *Laws of Media: The New Science.* Toronto: University of Toronto Press.

Nardi, B.A. & O'Day, V.L. (1999). *Information Ecologies: Using Technology with Heart.* Cambridge, MA: MIT Press.

Ong, Walter. (1982). *Orality and Literacy: The Technologizing of the Word.* New York: Methuen.

Postman, Neil, and Weingartner, Charles. (1971). *The Soft Revolution.* New York. Dell.

Postman, Neil. (1985). *Amusing Ourselves to Death: Public Discourse in the Age of Show Business.* New York: Penguin.

Wallerstein, Immanuel. (1998). *Utopistics: Or, Historical Choices of the Twenty-first Century.* New York: New Press.

Section Three: McLuhan and Postmodernism

CHAPTER SEVEN

Specters of McLuhan:
Derrida, Media, and Materiality

RICHARD CAVELL

A spectre is both visible and invisible, both phenomenal and nonphenomenal: a trace that marks the present with its absence in advance. The spectral logic is de facto a deconstructive logic. It is in the element of haunting that deconstruction finds the place most hospitable to it, at the heart of the living present, in the quickest heartbeat of the philosophical.
—Jacques Derrida, *Echographies of Television* (2002, p. 117)

Kant and Hegel simply flipped out of Hume's visual determinism into acoustic subjectivism. All of their followers are still under the illusion that the acoustic world is spiritual and unlike the outer visual world, whereas, in fact, the acoustic is just as material as the visual.
—Marshall McLuhan, *Letters* (Molinaro et al. 1987, p. 489)

The final phase of Jacques Derrida's philosophical career was marked by an extended inquiry into electronic media, or "teletechnologies," a phase in which he increasingly encountered the specter of Marshall McLuhan, whose ghost he had sought to lay to rest as long ago as 1971 in his landmark essay "Signature Event Context." While the importance assigned to this essay in the Derridean canon is considerable, and would suggest that the anxiety of Derrida's relationship to McLuhan was much more significant than this single reference would warrant, Derrida studiously avoided discussing McLuhan in the intervening decades, a silence all the more remarkable in that Derrida's writings on electric technologies echo in many places those of the Thulean ghost whose presence Derrida had already invoked *Of Grammatology* (1978).

In the years following "Signature Event Context," Derrida made only two additional references to McLuhan. The first was in a 1982 interview which he gave to Paul Brennan (1983, p. 42). Brennan comments: "You've suggested we should stop thinking about various media—speech and writing—that we should stop thinking about them ethically and that the two media of language are beyond good and evil. This obviously puts you at variation with someone like Marshall McLuhan who talks about the medium in very ethical terms—'the microphone created Hitler' and so on." Derrida replies: "Mm . . . I think that there is an ideology in McLuhan's discourse that I don't agree with, because he's an optimist as to the possibility of restoring an oral community which would get rid of the writing machines and so on. I think that's a very traditional myth which goes back to . . . let's say Plato, Rousseau. . . . And instead of thinking that we are living at the end of writing, I think that in another sense we are living in an extension—the overwhelming extension—of writing. At least in the new sense. . . . I don't mean the alphabetic writing down, but in the new sense of those writing machines that we're using now (e.g., the tape recorder). And this is writing too." The second reference was in a footnote to *On Touching, Jean-Luc Nancy* (2005), where Derrida notes that "Marshall McLuhan said about the sense of touch that it is the sense of the electronic age" (p. 354, n. 22) in the context of a discussion of touch and its prohibition.

Nick Couldry has written that "the post-structuralist subtlety of . . . Derrida provides few clues to interpreting a television talk show or a televised state funeral" (2003, p. xi); as the present essay seeks to demonstrate, this comment is at once true and false. More productive is the paradigm suggested by Patricia Ticineto Clough (2000b), who argues that the "later" Derrida is haunted by his earlier encounter with Freud. Clough proposes that the ontological elements within poststructuralist thought have been profoundly influenced by "teletechnology or telecommunications" (p. 383), which "drew Derrida's writings to the deconstruction of the opposition of nature and technology, the human and the machine, the virtual and the real, the living and the inert" (p. 383). Clough (2000a, 2000b) traces this development in Derrida's thought through a reading of his encounters with Freudian texts; of particular importance to her argument is Derrida's return in *Archive Fever* (1996) to his 1978 essay, "Freud and the Scene of Writing" and its discussion of a "writing machine" (the memory pad) as a metaphor of the unconscious. Clough attributes the shift in Derrida's argument over the course of the 20-year hiatus between the two works to the notion that in the interim Derrida had had a "tele-vision" (2000b, p. 387). I do not dispute this reading, but seek to add to it by identifying its larger context, specifically positing McLuhan as the specter that haunts Derrida, given that McLuhan was the founder of a certain discourse around "teletechnologies." My argument is supported by the emphasis Clough places on "Signature Event Context"

(p. 392 ff), the one place in the Derridean *oeuvre* where McLuhan is specifically named and the point in Derrida's *oeuvre* where the shift Clough is delineating first becomes evident. "It would seem," she writes, "that a machine other than Freud's mystic writing-pad is offering itself as metaphor for the psychic apparatus of unconscious memory. It would seem that Derrida is having a tele-vision" (p. 392). My argument, in effect, is that McLuhan looms large in that vision.

Derrida's reticence about McLuhan, it must be admitted, is isomorphic with the waning of interest in McLuhan's work beginning in the 1970s. "Signature Event Context" coincided with a point in the reception of McLuhan's work when it was being read narrowly within the domain of communications studies and according to the strictures of both technological determinism and technological utopianism, and Derrida was an unexceptional reader in this regard. The 1970s, in McLuhan criticism, were marked, tellingly, by the publication of Raymond Williams' *Television* (1974), whose charge against McLuhan of technological determinism is repeated to this day, despite, or perhaps because of, McLuhan's scathing review of the book (McLuhan 1978, pp. 259–61). Williams also accused McLuhan of "formalism," that is, of neglecting the material aspects of media, which was a major bone of contention within Marxist critiques of media (as discussed by K. Ludwig Pfeiffer in "The Materiality of Communication" [1994]). One gauge of the anxieties around the materiality of media was the exhibition on "new" media held in 1985 at the Pompidou Centre which was given the title "Modernes, et après?: Les Immatériaux." Pfeiffer clearly locates the exhibition within a post-Marxist anxiety about materiality (cf. Lecourt 2001, pp. 72–73), and it is significant that both McLuhan (who is cited) and Derrida hovered spectrally over the exhibition (cf. Krapp 1996, pp. 159–173).

While the significant resurgence of interest in McLuhan's media theories, beginning in the 1990s, has sought to frame those theories in other and more nuanced terms, McLuhan's rehabilitation in terms of critical theory has been slow. One sign of that resurgence is the inclusion of a text on McLuhan in the *Postmodern Encounters* series in contemporary theoretical discourse, inaugurated in the year 2000 by Icon Books (UK) / Totem Books (USA). The series was meant to approach major theorists and philosophers in a way that would be at once conspectival and interventionist, providing an overview, in other words, from a particular theoretical position. Works in the series include *Nietzsche and Postmodernism* (Dave Robinson), *Foucault and Queer Theory* (Tamsin Spargo), *Derrida and the End of History* (Stuart Sim), and *Marshall McLuhan and Virtuality* (Christopher Horrocks).

Another sign of the re-evaluation of McLuhan's media theory is the increasingly interdisciplinary interest it is engaging. Deconstructivist architectural theory, for example, has sought to bring McLuhan back into the orbit of the *maître penseurs* who first limned the theoretical matrices in which the critical / theoretical / philosophical implications of electric technologies continue to be articulated, and this connection between mediation and spatialisation is crucial to positioning McLuhan within critical theory (as I have argued elsewhere; see Cavell 2002). Thus, Mark Wigley (2001, p. 84) asks, "What if much of our net talk is just an echo? An echo of an echo?" in the context of a discussion of McLuhan's work and that of Buckminster Fuller, and their connections to the Ekistics movement founded by Constantinos Doxiadis. Fuller's and McLuhan's "mark is everywhere. They voiced so much of what is said today. They wrote a lot of our script," remarks Wigley (p. 84). At the first Ekistics meeting, McLuhan's "argument [was] that electronics is actually biological, an organic system with particular effects. The evolution of technology is the evolution of the human body. Networks of communication, like any technology, are prosthetic extensions of the body. They are new body parts and constitute a new organism, a new spatial system, a new architecture" (p. 86). The remainder of this first meeting (held, like the following ones, on a cruise ship) was organized "in response to McLuhan's first statements" (p. 100) that "electronics presents new challenges to planners because this latest prosthetic extension of the body defines an entirely new form of space" (p. 97). "McLuhan's initial image of prosthetic growth was elaborated in more and more detail as the annual boat trips gradually embraced the centrality of electronics" (p. 101). "It took decades to forget such experiments so that a new generation could present itself as the first to engage seriously with the architecture of electronics. Much of what we hear today is an echo— but so delayed that it sounds fresh. It is as if the discourse forgets its own history precisely because it is too afraid to leave those earlier positions behind" (p. 111).

Wigley's comments are cautionary; the enormous barrier to a general critical reappraisal of McLuhan, in fact, has been "McLuhanism": figured as 1960s mediolatry, it plays much the same role in McLuhan's critical legacy as "marxism" does in the contemporary reception of Marx (Rockmore, 2002). This essay thus begins with a brief critique of McLuhanism before going on to examine McLuhan's media theories as they impinged on Derrida as his work moved toward a (re)consideration of media and especially toward the philosophical questions raised by "virtuality" and concomitant issues of materiality.

McLuhanism has made of McLuhan a media triumphalist; a utopian philosopher of social remediation through television; a crypto-Catholic prophet of a return to "orality" and the "full presence" of communication; a naive proponent of globalisation; and, ultimately, a techno-determinist. In the epigraphs to Horrocks' *Marshall McLuhan and Virtuality* (2000), we meet two of these aspects of "McLuhanism": McLuhan the prophet, and McLuhan the crypto-Catholic. The first epigraph, from sometime collaborator Robert Logan (a physicist at the University of Toronto who has written a number of books on media), needs little comment: "He *was* the

Internet in the sixties. The world's just finally caught up to him" (p. 3). The second quotes from an interview given by McLuhan to G.E. Stearn (1967) in which McLuhan states, "the Christian concept of the mystical body—all men as members of the body of Christ—this becomes technologically a fact under electronic conditions." The next sentence, not quoted by Horrocks, reads: "However, I would not try to theologize on the basis of my understanding of technology. I don't have a background in scholastic thought, never having been raised in any Catholic institution. Indeed, I have been bitterly reproached by my Catholic confrères for my lack of scholastic terminology and concepts" (Stearn, p. 267). The point is that McLuhan ascribes a *secular* fulfilment to divine prophecy (if that is what it is), *and* that this prophecy is *dystopian*, rather than utopian: "TV, in a highly visual culture, drives us inward in depth into a totally non-visual universe of involvement. It is destroying our entire political, educational, social, institutional life. TV will dissolve the entire fabric of society in a short time" (p. 301).

Why, in an otherwise acute essay on McLuhan, does McLuhanism of this sort persist? There are, in fact, a number of pragmatic barriers that continue to hamper McLuhan's critical reception: (1) McLuhan was a non-linear thinker who developed his thoughts not in a single place but through an interdisciplinary range of books (circa 25), articles (hundreds) and thousands of letters and difficult-to-classify works such as the *Dew Line Newsletters*, not to mention audiotapes, records, videos and films; (2) most of his books are out of print (although Gingko Press of California is in the process of re-issuing some of them, plus unpublished material); (3) there is no complete bibliography of the remaining materials; (4) not all of the letters are in print; the *Newsletters* are difficult to access (and each was unique in format); and the other materials are scarce.

Furthermore, McLuhan's notion of "the media" (a terminology he coined in its contemporary usage) was idiosyncratic. Although the term most often refers to the media of communications (and especially electronic media), it was applied much more broadly by McLuhan—roads, clothing, housing, money, clocks, comics, photographs, automobiles, typewriters, telephones and weapons all have chapters devoted to them in *Understanding Media* (1964). Furthermore, as McLuhan argued, a medium is comprised by the totality of its environment—although I may think of my cell phone as a medium, McLuhan argued that the medium was in fact comprised of the network of communications which the phone brings into being, and hence the spatial dimension of his theory. "Communication" was, in addition, a problematical term for McLuhan; he argued that communication did not take place in the sense of transporting a message from a sender to a receiver. As he wrote, "There is a kind of illusion in the world we live in that communication is something that happens all the time, that it's normal. . . . In the sense of a mere point-to-point correspondence between what is said, done, and thought and felt between people—this is the rarest thing in the world. . . . Most people have the idea of communication as something matching between what is said and what is understood. In actual fact, communication is *making*" (Stearn, p. 292). Media, in McLuhan's formulation, transform what they communicate, much in the way that rhetoric does, and, like rhetoric, they are "determinist" in this manner. As Nicholas Garnham has written:

> many scholars have cogently argued that the book as a form enabled the development of individual, private, and domestic appropriation, which itself helped to develop both the Kantian Enlightenment view of humans as intellectually autonomous and the revaluation of the relation between the private and domestic and the public, between fiction and the feminine on the one hand and male and the political on the other. It is this view that forms of consumption are in complex ways embodied in different forms and institutions, and that they in turn reinforce certain personal and social character traits, that is the rational core of McLuhan's theories, which in their turn derive from studies of the ways in which the development of printing and reading and the shift from orality changed society and the individuals within it. If so much is granted then we also know that the production and distribution of cultural commodities, what is made available for consumption and to whom, is structured—in specific, determinate ways. If the connection to individual and group identity formation is granted, then how that power of structuring works and with what effects becomes a matter of legitimate interest. This is what [J.] Thompson has called 'the double-bind of mediated dependency.' 'While the availability of media products serves to enrich and accentuate the reflexive organisation of the self, at the same time it renders this reflexive organisation of the self increasingly dependent on systems over which the individual has relatively little control' (Garnham, 2000, p. 135, quoting Thompson, 1995, p. 214).

Another charge brought against McLuhan was that of techno-utopianism, a legacy he inherited largely through his coining of the phrase "the global village." This phrase has suggested to McLuhan's critics—and especially to Derrida—that he understood globalisation as a benign force which would inevitably inculcate communitarian values. But McLuhan did not write about "globalisation"; rather, he sought to theorize a dynamic process whereby the experience of the local is altered relationally through its place within a global network of intermediation. And, as the tensions within the phrase imply, the relationship it expressed was often bellicose and not meant to be synonymous with a bland communitarianism (McLuhan, 1968). As McKenzie Wark has remarked, "Under no illusions about Ancient Greek tribal life, he saw the village as riven by war and conflict, not peace and harmony" (Wark, 2000, p. 94).

If the process of displacement denoted by the phrase promised enhanced communicational possibilities by creating broad new configurations, it also promised to place such possibilities in crisis through an intensification of local "dialects" (Cavell, 2002, pp. 139–41). McLuhan held to this notion consistently, and did not suddenly begin in the late 1970s to argue that the utopia "promised" by the media was an illusion, as Guy Debord, among others, has had him doing (Horrocks, pp. 7–8; Cavell, 2002, pp. 187–89); he had written at the end of *The Gutenberg Galaxy* (1962) of the "terror" that would be unleashed by the interface of the literate and the orally empathic electronic, and stated emphatically in 1967 that "It never occurred to me that uniformity and tranquillity were the properties of the global village" (Stearn, 1967, p. 279). It is important to note, furthermore, that in addition to critiquing electronic media throughout his career, McLuhan also critiqued print culture, thus unmooring his position vis-à-vis electronic media from the certainties that literacy might have afforded him as a cultural critic. As part of this critique of literature culture, he refused, after a certain point, to write "academic" books, preferring a "mosaic" structure to the linear processes of print (and this played a large role in the decline of his reputation within academia in the 1970s and 80s). McLuhan likewise adopted strategies, or tactics, of critique, such as irony, which made his writing difficult to recuperate within the canon of contemporary cultural theory, where critical positions were more apt to be identified through their association with a specific theoretical school, such as marxism or structuralism or deconstruction. Indeed, his rejection of marxist theory set him apart from a large segment of the theoretical practice of the time. Nor was he writing within the Saussurean paradigm that informed many of these theories; language, he argued, is a medium, and as a medium it must be understood within a much broader spectrum of mediation than the linguistic model would allow (*pace* Gordon, 2003, pp. 441–448).

McLuhan's most important insights have to do with the spatialising tendencies (or biases) of the mass media (though McLuhan understood "mass" as at once spatial and temporal). McLuhan associated the spacetime phenomena of mass media with acoustic space (rather than "orality"), which is simultaneous in character and tends to call into play all of the senses rather than just the visual sense. Acoustic space in his articulation is the disruption of enclosed, static, Euclidean space–the space of literacy and the single point of view; it is, in the Lefebvrian sense, a social space, and Lefebvre, in fact, twice acknowledges McLuhan as one of his spatialist predecessors (1991, p. 261, 286). Rather than writing about an uninflected "orality" to which electronic media were "returning" us, then, McLuhan theorized the production of a space that was profoundly different from the visual space which was the prime product of print culture.

Of crucial significance in McLuhan's theorisation of acoustic space was his insistence that it is *material*. It has been proposed that McLuhan was rejected by the Left (at least in Germany) "because his focus on bodies and media, extensions, narcosis and self-amputation was *more* materialist than Marxism had ever been" (Winthrop-Young and Wutz, 1999, pp. 267–68). McLuhan had written in a 1953 article about

Harold Innis that "Media are staples" (p. 385), suggesting that media had taken on the role in information culture that raw materials had had in mechanical culture. Innis was a Canadian political economist who wrote a number of important works on Canadian staples–the cod fisheries, fur trade, and so on. He developed the notion that media exhibited spatial or temporal bias in later two books, Empire and Communications (1950), and The Bias of Communication (1951). The critical dimension of McLuhan's work proceeds from this materialist understanding of media, which is particularly significant in the case of acoustic space, since its materiality is not exclusively within the regime of the visual but extends to the domain of the virtual. It is important to note that McLuhan writes about acoustic *space*, a space which does not conform to the linear, sequential paradigm of visual *space*, even though it may contain visual elements. A screen of hypertext, for example, would be acoustic in McLuhan's understanding of the way it functioned. Acoustic space, in short, is not exclusively comprised of phonemes, which is another reason why Saussure did not particularly attract McLuhan's interest.

The "realness" of the virtual, or the materiality of the non-material, constitutes a paradox that is crucial to the importance ascribed to media in contemporary theoretical debate (and in social discourse generally): are media merely epiphenomenal or are they fundamental to the way we know the world today as well as to our "being" in it? McLuhan's rehabilitation within contemporary theoretical discourse (as opposed to the more delimited confines of a resurgent media theory which seeks to confront the relatively new phenomenon of the internet through the McLuhanesque rearview mirror) must be addressed precisely in these terms. At the same time, his insistence on rethinking traditional categories of theoretical inquiry must also be given its due.

McLuhan was a counter-intuitive thinker, and he was perhaps most contrarian in not theorizing a stable subject position; as Horrocks puts it, "For McLuhan, immersion in electronic media . . . has a psychological and sensory impact that profoundly affects the ontological security of the individual" (p. 66), an impact that McLuhan referred to as "discarnation" (McLuhan, 1989, pp. 196–200). "[W]hen you are 'on the telephone,' or 'on the air,' you do not have a physical body. In these media, the sender is sent, and is instantaneously present everywhere. The disembodied user extends to all those who are recipients of electronic information. It is these people who constitute the *mass* audience, because mass is a factor of speed rather than quantity" (p. 197). If the medium is the message, then, in any communication, the system of communication "speaks" and not (just) the subject. This position has been taken up by such theorists as Luhmann, for whom (in the words of Bruce R. Smith), "a society is made up, not of individual subjects, not of the actions those subjects perform, but of systems of communication" (Smith, 1999, p. 19). As McLuhan put it, all *utterance* is at the same time *outerance*, at once private *and* public, at once

personal and rhetorical; as he had learned through his study of Renaissance literature in his dissertation at Cambridge on Thomas Nashe, rhetoric profoundly
unmoors the speaking self from "presence."

In the era of electronic communication, this tendency is exacerbated because
communication takes place at a level removed from the individual subject. This is
so even in the era of the "new" media (such as the Internet), which Lev Manovich
has theorised (2001) as more involving than the previous generation of communication devices, such as television. The notion of participation and intervention
does not mean that these media no longer operate at the level of the mass, however; rather, the element of participation is a concomitant of the mass media, which
operate by heightening individual experience (me in my room listening to a CD I
burned by downloading songs from the net) within the context of mass communications (the CD, the net, the electronic media that made the downloads possible).
While the media may be new, the questions they raise are old, insofar as media technologies increasingly ask us to consider their ontological and epistemological implications. Electronic communication, in McLuhan's understanding of it, particularly
of television, tends to be ritualised and tribal, rather than "original" and "individual" (attributes which were the effects of written communication). It is with observations such as these that we begin to enter into the ontology of the "virtual."

But this inversion of private and public, inner and outer, is itself part of a much
larger one in which technology has superseded nature (and mediation has replaced
presence), such that our very being has been turned inside-out—extended and
amputated (Cheah, 1996)—and extruded into an environment which is at once ourselves and utterly "other," a prosthetic environment which appears foreign to us—
even though it is us—because it is now outside us. As Bruce R. Smith notes, an oral
utterance is "an *environmental* gesture" in that, in speaking, "I extend my person into
'the about me.' Both the Italian and the German equivalents of 'environment' carry,
perhaps, a stronger sense of this unmarked spatiality than the English word now
does: *ambiente* waves a hand toward the air around the speaker, while *Umgebung*
invokes the 'givens' that surround the speaker" (1999, p. 14). McLuhan employed
the term "environment" to argue that there was no longer a "natural" environment,
but only the one that we ourselves had created and which encompassed us totally.
What was once the "natural" environment had become an artifact that we tend. We
have, in this sense, been *incorporated*.

These paradoxical notions are brilliantly captured in the *Alien* movies (and particularly *Alien 4*), movies which represent in the most visceral way possible this sense
of the *prosthetic* (another notion that has come to dominate Derrida's thought), of
the way in which living within a totally technologized environment (the spaceship)
has as its concomitant aspect the inescapable prostheticization of our selves. At the
end of *Alien 4*, the protagonist, Ripley, has been cloned and is thus completely "out-

side" herself; as she approaches earth and prepares for re-entry we see, through the window "screen," the globe hovering in space, a purely esthetic object—"It's beautiful,'" remarks one of the characters. A shipmate, also a clone, asks Ripley what it's like on earth, to which she replies with the harrowing line "'I don't know; I'm a stranger there myself.'" Here the very materiality of the earth—*terra firma*—has itself become an exercise in virtuality, while the "human" has collapsed into the "other." McLuhan had argued consistently, throughout his career, that it is our technologies that *make* us human. "In the sense that these media are extensions of ourselves . . . then my interest in them is utterly humanistic," McLuhan states (Stearn, 1967, p. 294). Similarly: "all technologies are completely humanist in the sense of belonging entirely to the human organism." (Bornstein interview, 1966, p. 67). Timothy Clark's assertion that "McLuhan . . . remain[s] as committed as [his] unacknowledged precursors to a presupposed understanding of what is properly human and hence—beneath [his] stance of technological determinism—to a metaphysical disavowal of the place of the technical in the constitution of humanity" (Clark, 1999, p. 58) demonstrates thus, how the polarities of McLuhanism often find themselves in uneasy conjunction.

John Hunter has remarked that knowledge, for Plato, was the recollection of immaterial forms that took knowledge out of the material world, as well as out of the human world (Hunter, 2002, p. 201). McLuhan's media theories took the classic philosophical concern with immateriality and applied it to electronic media, seeking, in a sense, to return philosophical inquiry to the material world (as he suggests in the epigraph to this essay) and to re-discover our humanity there in the form of technology. He was writing, however, in a context in which media were largely considered to be peripheral to philosophies of knowledge and of being; only recently, with a renewed interest in the philosophical implications of virtuality, have media been factored into these traditional realms of philosophical discourse. As Bernard Stiegler has put it, "It is in the inheritance of this conflict—in which the philosophical *episteme* is pitched against the sophistic *tekhné*, whereby all technical knowledge is devalued—that the essence of technical entities in general is conceived" (Stiegler, 1998, 1). As Horrocks notes, there is in fact a longstanding interest in the "virtual" within philosophical discourse, starting with Plato's notion of the "shadow" world of sensory phenomena as developed in the parable of the cave. Horrocks associates McLuhan's elaboration of "virtuality" with the "weak" version of this concept, whereby the term is broadly applicable to Automatic Teller Machines and email, for example, as opposed to the "strong" version, with its links to applied science (2000, pp. 33–5). The "weak" version of virtuality is related to "cool" media, as defined by McLuhan; these are media, such as television, which invite involvement through low definition, as opposed to media such as print, which are high in definition. Horrocks draws on Richard Coyne's *Technoromanticism* (1999), a classic exercise in McLuhanism, to argue that McLuhan's notion of "virtuality" posits space ("cyberspace") as a transcendent realm of unity and oneness (Horrocks, 2000, p. 39) that is "premised on a 'myth of return,' via technology, to a pre-literate social reality" (p. 40).

Rather than theorising a transcendent realm of cyberspace, however, McLuhan posited a *material* acoustic space which he theorised to be *dynamic*: that acoustic space retrieved, *from within literacy* (and is thus post- rather than pre-literate), residual aspects of orality *as historically constructed*, thus interfacing orality and literacy. Indeed, McLuhan theorised that *all* media were intermediated, insofar as the "content" of a medium was the previously dominant one, media being profoundly "spectral" in this sense. And the materiality of acoustic space meant that "[t]he new media are not ways of relating us to the old 'real' world; they are the real world" (McLuhan, 1995, p. 272). As Horrocks comments, "This particularly 'weak' or loose definition of virtuality makes sense when the real is construed as socially and culturally constructed" (2000, p. 46). And because, for McLuhan, this socially and culturally constructed environment was a prosthetic extension of ourselves, it was fully involving. As Horrocks writes, the "ideology of involvement cuts to the core of virtuality, and *the user becomes the medium* through which the Internet operates" (p. 58; emphasis added); as I have indicated above, this notion is inherent in McLuhan's formulation that the *medium* is the message and that "in all media the user is the content" (McLuhan, 1995, p. 276). Both the medium and the user have the status of content in these formulations; this derives from the notion that media are extensions of our selves.

It is worth emphasizing that McLuhan did not use the word, or the concept, of virtuality; rather, he theorised the acoustic. His notion of acoustic space is not the "ineffable" of Coyne (1999); nor is it the "simulacral" of Jean Baudrillard (1983); as he indicates in the epigraph to this essay, his concern was with the *materiality* of the acoustic. Nor was acoustic space meant to be understood through a "myth of return"; rather than "return," McLuhan used the term "retrieval," which implies coexistence and confrontation and is itself part of a quadripartite set of laws—the "Laws of Media" (McLuhan & McLuhan, 1988)—which operate simultaneously in terms of enhancement, obsolescence and retrieval, and are interrelated through the fundamental principle of reversal.

The paradoxical materiality of the virtual thus poses an especially compelling area of inquiry, particularly in the post-marxist era, in which these issues have been raised anew. I approach these issues in the remainder of this essay by considering some work produced by Derrida at the end of his career, work which, in addressing questions of virtuality, materiality, and the media, invokes—spectrally—his earlier engagements with McLuhan.

Derrida considers the problematics of materiality in his contribution to a recent volume, *Material Events* (Derrida, 2001), focusing on the late writings of Paul de Man (1996), "Phenomenality and Materiality in Kant" (pp. 70–90) and "Kant's Materialism" (pp. 119–128). In the first essay, de Man argues that the "critique of the aesthetic ends up, in Kant, in a formal materialism that runs counter to all values and characteristics associated with aesthetic experience, including the aesthetic experience of the beautiful and of the sublime as described by Kant and Hegel themselves. The tradition of their interpretation, as it appears from near contemporaries such as Schiller on, has seen only this one, figural, and, if you will, 'romantic' aspect of their theories of the imagination, and has entirely overlooked what we call the material aspect. Neither has it understood the place of formalization in this intricate process" (p. 83; materiality here, in keeping with Kant's discussion, belongs very much to the realm of the ocular). In the second essay, de Man is likewise concerned with the relationship between the material and the aesthetic: "Kant's critique of representation is . . . said to engender a new tension between the transcendental order of negative cognition, in which a degree of formalization is necessary, and the singularity of the empirical world, which demands formalization in order to be known but refuses it because this singularity is the very element that made the critique of the classical models of cognition necessary" (p. 120). What de Man seeks to tease out of Kant's third *Critique* is whether "one [can] speak of a Kantian idealism without taking into account the simultaneous activity, in his text, of a materialism much more radical than what can be conveyed by such terms as 'realism' or 'empiricism'?" (p. 121). He answers: "the radical formalism that animates aesthetic judgment in the dynamics of the sublime is what is called materialism. Theoreticians of literature who fear they may have deserted or betrayed the world by being too formalistic are worrying about the wrong thing: in the spirit of Kant's third *Critique*, they were not nearly formalistic enough" (p. 128).

As Tom Cohen, J. Hillis Miller, and Barbara Cohen write in *Material Events*, "What if any claim might a project [such as de Man's] so linked to a 'theory' that seems out of fashion—that is, rightly or not, to literary preoccupations and close reading—have in an era, say, moving beyond 'cultural studies' to a reworking of technology, of technicity, of concerted political imaginaries and revived notions of materiality?" (Cohen, Miller and Cohen, 2001, p. vii). The problematics of that question are announced in the Derridean title of the introduction, "A 'Materiality without Matter'?" The editors argue that de Man's writings (and especially his later ones, collected in *Aesthetic Ideology* [1996]), propose "a treatment of 'materiality' that compels a rethinking of technicity and the 'sensorium' on the basis of inscription. Among other things it would be an approach, given the 'materiality of inscription,' to the notion of the 'virtual' and toward a rendering virtual—and hence, toward alternative histories to those programmed by inherited regimes of definition and perception" (p. viii).

The reference to the "sensorium" is noteworthy in this context, in that it reinvokes arguments about speaking and writing made by Derrida in his 1972 essay "Signature Event Context" (Derrida, 1988), which is the locus of his emblematic encounter with McLuhan, and which occasioned the controversy documented in Derrida's *Limited Inc.* What is so extraordinary about this invocation of the sensuous aspect of language is that McLuhan's use of the concept in his own theoretical formulations has remained a major impediment to his recuperation within contemporary theory, and especially by deconstructionists, who, following Derrida's 1968 essay "Différance," are leery of the sensuous domain as leading to arguments about presence (Derrida, 1986, pp. 396–420).

As Horrocks (2000) remarks, "the foundational concept on which McLuhan builds his technological humanism . . . is the principle of sensory harmony" (p. 41); this, he argues, negates any claims that might be made for aligning McLuhan with postmodern or post-structural thought because it implies that "[w]hen media deliver the requisite means to enable senses to work in accord, communication becomes inherently transparent, direct, full and immediate" (p. 41), notions which are utterly contradicted within postmodernist thought. What McLuhan theorised, however, was that electronic media addressed all of the senses (as opposed to print media, which addressed the eye primarily). As Michael Geisler (1999) notes, "the virtual realities created by the new media play their songs directly on our bare senses" (p. 82). Rather than a formulation about transparent communication, McLuhan's theory of the sensorium seeks to articulate the effects of mediation on the senses within historical context.

McLuhan's understanding that mediation had material effects raises the question of how those effects can be measured, a question which is exacerbated by the assumption that materiality must belong to the visual domain—how can one measure that which one cannot see? This problem is the classic one of quantum mechanics, as Arkady Plotnitsky (2001) notes in his article in *Material Events*, and, in a philosophical vein, it opens up a vast discourse on regimes of visuality within the history of philosophy. McLuhan addressed this issue through his theory of acoustic space, which constituted itself as a critique of the visual regime (Levin, 1997, pp. 1–67), the assumptions of which persist in *Material Events*. J. Hillis Miller (2001, pp. 183–204), for example, seeks to address the paradox by adducing arguments from performativity. However, his arguments merely reproduce the paradox on another level, insofar as performativity is presented as an *oral* mediation but without an accompanying argument for the *materiality* of the acoustic. Miller thus concludes that de Man's work ultimately "becomes a performative utterance . . . by the route of the materiality of the letter, and once more in a way that is counterintuitive, since it is another materiality that is nonphenomenal, unable to be seen" (p. 197), a comment which is highly indicative of his supposition that the non-visible is nonphenomenal. As Miller goes on to note, the opposition of materialist and idealist elements is often traced to "vulgar understandings of marxism" (p. 186); Rockmore comments, however, that "If we understand 'idealism' as referring to the idea that the subject in some sense produces its world and itself, then Marx is clearly an idealist. There is no evidence that Marx's position depends on any specific claim about matter" (p. 70).

The casting of these (and other) arguments about the material and the virtual in terms of speaking and writing returns us to McLuhan's concerns and, inevitably (in this context) to Derrida's response to them. As Horrocks remarks, McLuhan's apparent insistence on the primacy of speech over writing is contradicted by Derrida's insistence that writing always precedes speech, insofar as communication is formulaic and dependent upon a set of prior assumptions. Yet McLuhan begins *The Gutenberg Galaxy* (1962) with a meditation on the formulaic, and thus "written," quality of oral cultures precisely as a way of indicating the intermediated status of communicational phenomena which is the subject of his book (pp. 1–9); subsequently, he writes of scribal culture as intermediating oral and literate norms; of print culture and its attempt to reproduce the scribal; and of electronic culture's subservience to the form of the printed page. Nor is his formulation of *electronic* "speech" one that invokes the *primacy* of the speaking subject; rather, McLuhan argues that such media effect a degree of ontological uncertainty, in that they render the speaker "discarnate."

The importance of the orality / literacy debate to these questions of virtuality and materiality is signalled by the fact that Derrida reinvokes it in his contribution to the *Material Events* volume, "Typewriter Ribbon: Limited Ink (2) ('within such limits')" (2001, pp. 277–360). This essay repeatedly refers to the earlier essay on performativity, (1988, pp. 1–23), in which Derrida sought to deconstruct McLuhan's notions of orality and literacy. Derrida's title ("Limited Ink") for his *Material Events* essay, as well as his use of the phrase "signature, event, context" (p. 281) in it, direct us to the earlier essay as well. Delivered by Derrida at a 1971 conference (held in Montréal) on "Communication," that paper begins by questioning the very idea of communication: "Is it certain that to the word *communication* corresponds a concept that is unique, univocal, rigorously controllable, and transmittable: in a word, communicable?" (1988, p. 1). Polysemy, in other words, always complicates the notion that communication is transparent, and, as Derrida goes on to suggest, polysemy cannot be made determinate through context, even though the idea that writing achieves its effects through spatial and temporal "*extension*" (p. 3; the italicized word recalls the subtitle of *Understanding Media: The Extensions of Man*) assumes "a sort of *homogeneous* space of communication." Indeed, the medium itself, in such communications, "remains fundamentally continuous and self-identical, a homogeneous element through which the unity and wholeness of meaning would not be effected in its essence." These are the assumptions of the transference or transportation model of communication which Derrida particularly critiques in Condillac's assumption that "writing will never have the slightest effect on either the structure or the contents of the meaning (the ideas) that it is supposed to transmit [*véhiculer*]" (p. 4; Derrida is summarising Condillac's *Essay on the Origin of Human Knowledge*). Condillac's theory, in other words, argues the transparency of written communication in which the "presence" of the spoken communication remains unaltered in the written one. Derrida refers to this theory as "ideological" (p. 6) because it reflects the position of "the French 'ideologues'" who argued that "communication is that which circulates a representation as an ideal content."

At this point in his analysis, Derrida introduces the notion of absence: there is a fundamental contradiction in Condillac's theory of language, he argues, since the "presence" of the spoken communication must function "in the absence of the receiver" (p. 7) as well as the sender (p. 8), which is to say that it must be fundamentally repeatable, citable, or "iterable." This, however, would undermine the notion of originality which is Condillac's point of departure; indeed, the notion of iterability demands that all utterance—spoken or written—be coded, and, to this extent, iterability also undermines context as a determinant of meaning. As a test of this analysis, Derrida moves to a consideration of the linguistic notion of the "performative" (p. 13), which argues that certain forms of speech are able to perform an action. Such acts would obviously be original, transparent in meaning, and context bound, performed in "the conscious presence of the intention of the speaking subject in the totality of his speech act" (p. 14). Yet, as Derrida is able to demonstrate, such acts must admit the possibility of iterability and with this admission their claim to transparency evaporates, even in the "presence" of a signature, which achieves its effect of "originality" precisely through the necessity that it be *repeated* in the *same* way in each of its occurrences.

Bruce R. Smith (1999) has made a major critique of Derrida's attempt to "decenter voice"; this argument is most convincing when understood in the context of rhetoric. As Smith remarks, "Whatever Aristotle may have said about the direct transformation of ideas into sounds, Renaissance rhetorical training was designed to make the student self-conscious about his own voice. . . . With due respect (in all senses of the word) to Derrida, the O-factor [orality, writ large] accepts the logic of deconstruction, but it refuses the supposed transparency—or rather the supposed transitivity—of voice deconstruction needs in order to assert its own *différance*" (p. 12). One could also adduce the notion of the pun, which is likewise multivocal and unwriteable, except hypertextually, which again leads one to believe that what Derrida was theorizing all along was a form of *electric* writing, which is the point at which Derrida encounters the ghostly presence of McLuhan.

Derrida expresses that encounter in "Signature Event Context" as follows: "We are witnessing not an end of writing that would restore, in accord with McLuhan's ideological representation, a transparency or an immediacy to social relations; but rather the increasingly powerful historical expansion of a general writing, of which the system of speech, consciousness, meaning, presence, truth, etc., would be only an effect, and should be analyzed as such" (p. 20). Derrida's assumptions here are, first of all, that McLuhan employed a "transference" model of communication, whereas he repeatedly critiqued this model (which he referred to as a "transportation" model). As Derrick de Kerckhove has remarked, "[c]ontrary to the Shannon-Weaver model of communication devised in the late forties for application to information theory and machines, McLuhan's interpretation was that in communication there is no transportation of information (concepts or 'content') from a source to a target, but a transformation of the source and target simultaneously" (de Kerckhove, 1981, p. 33).

Secondly, Derrida assumes that McLuhan is ideologically representing the "end of writing," whereas his concerns were consistently with media as rhetorical forms, iterative in their mechanical applications (such as printing) and resonant in their electronic guises. (Unlike Derrida, he did not conflate mechanical and electronic media.) Third, Derrida assumes that McLuhan's analyses posit essentialisms of "speech, consciousness, meaning, presence, truth," whereas McLuhan insisted these notions were mediated. Finally, Derrida suggests that McLuhan's argumentation is made in the service of prophesying that the acoustic era will bring transparency of communication and with it a form of social amelioration (with the idea of the "global village" understood as underpinning this comment), notions which, as we have seen, were refuted by him. What is excluded from Derrida's analysis, however, is any reference to McLuhan's theories of electronic media, since Derrida seeks to *generalize* the effect of writing within telecommunications, rather than argue a special case for electronic media.

Richard Dienst's analysis of this passage in "Signature Event Context" is that it seeks to cancel, "at different points, McLuhan's dictum 'the medium is the message': (1) 'the medium' cannot be a transparent and homogeneous operation outside of effects of writing, for all media are writings; (2) 'is,' the copula indicating identity, can do no more than graft one term onto another without enforcing an equality or transparency; (3) 'the message' cannot remain a singular, ideal entity, for there is never just one message" (Dienst, 1994, p. 133). In McLuhan's understanding, the medium had an epistemic function as the epistemic locus of power which shaped the discourse of specific historic periods. As for the copula, it identifies a metaphor, and all metaphors operate according to the principle of non-identity ("My love is a red, red rose"). Thus, the "message" was never represented by McLuhan as identical with itself; it appears in his work as the "mess age," the "massage," and the "mass age."

Thirty years after he wrote "Signature Event Context," the question of electronic media came back to haunt Derrida's thought. In the mid-1990s we find him writing that "the organizations of the media . . . deserve an almost infinite analysis" along with the "technology of the tele-technological simulacrum, the synthetic image, virtual space" and so on (Derrida, 1994a, p. 38). Perhaps it was this sense of urgency that led him to begin the *Material Events* chapter in the apocalyptic mode: "there will be no future," he writes, except on the condition that we are prepared "to think *both* the event *and* the machine as two compatible or even indissociable concepts, although today they appear to us to be antinomic" (Derrida, 2001, p. 277); by "machine," Derrida means the process of iterability. "Machinery" is "the installation of a certain 'technology,' *through iterability*, within our mental operations" (Derrida, 2000, p. 415). Like Miller, Derrida invokes at the outset an acoustic metaphor ("somewhat like musicians who listen to their instruments and tune them before beginning to play" [2001, p. 279]), though complicatedly ("in front of our eyes"), in order to introduce a reference to the performative speech act, noting that, for its theorists, such an act could never be mechanical because it relies on "the presence of a living being, and of a living being speaking one time only, in its own name, in the first person" (p. 279). We are once again on the terrain first mapped out in "Signature Event Context," but now "technicity" has been factored much more overtly into the communicational framework. Derrida argues that the theorists of performativity must exclude technicity from their equations. But of course, by deconstructive logic, no such performance is free of "repetition, calculability" (p. 279) and so on. The notion of "iterability," thus, has now been made to include the notion of technicity and, indeed, the entire range of mediation beyond that of print culture *per se*. Derrida thus formulates his critical task, accordingly, as that of "a thinking of machinistic materiality without materialism and even perhaps without matter" (p. 281). In the performance of this task, Derrida uses the McLuhanesque tropes of amputation (p. 318) and "prosthesis" (p. 333), of the "*non-sensuous sensuous*" (p. 7), and of "disincarnation" (p. 41), noting that de Man's idea of materiality is predicated on "figures of . . . 'material disarticulation'" (p. 319) which run the risk of "becoming a simulacrum or a virtuality without consistency" (p. 335)—in short, a "spectral machine" (p. 359).

Derrida developed this notion of the "spectral" in what might initially appear to be an odd context: his first extended study of Marx. *Specters of Marx* (1994b) is especially important for the present discussion in that it specifically invokes a discourse around the role of electronic media in "today's most *phenomenal culture*:

what one hears, reads, and sees, what is most *mediatized* in Western capitals" (p. 15). Interestingly, Derrida plays on the trope of return at the beginning of the book: "everything begins in the imminence of a *re*-apparition, but a reapparition of the specter as apparition *for the first time in the play*" (p. 4). Derrida invokes Hamlet, here, though the ghost of the Commendatore in *Don Giovanni* would also be relevant to his discussion (cf. the reference to the "Commandatore" [*sic*] p. 135).

Drawing on an analogy with *Hamlet* (that work in which "being" is questioned iteratively), Derrida puts into play the tropes of seeing and hearing that, post-McLuhan, have governed this discourse of the spectral, of the virtual ("the virtual space of spectrality" [p. 11]): "The Thing [the ghost of Hamlet's father] is still invisible, it is *nothing* visible . . . at the moment one speaks of it and in order to ask oneself if it has reappeared. It is still nothing that can be seen when one speaks of it" (p. 6). Derrida notes that, "[a]s theoreticians or witnesses, spectators, observers, and intellectuals, scholars believe that looking is sufficient. Therefore, they are not always in the most competent position to do what is necessary: speak to the specter" (p. 11; there is no concomitant theorisation in *Specters* of the acoustic, however). Derrida summarizes this position in the last of the book's chapters:

> The production of the ghost [in Marx's *The German Ideology*], the constitution of the *ghost* effect is not simply a spiritualization or even an autonomization of spirit, idea, or thought, as happens *par excellence* in Hegelian idealism. No, once this autonomization is effected, with the corresponding expropriation or alienation, and only then, the ghostly moment *comes upon* it, adds to it a supplementary dimension, once more simulacrum, alienation, or expropriation. Namely, a body! In the flesh (*Lieb*)! For there is no ghost, there is never any becoming-specter of the spirit without at least an appearance of flesh, in a space of invisible visibility, like the dis-appearing of an apparition. For there to be a ghost, there must be a return to the body, but to a body that is more abstract than ever. The spectrogenic process corresponds therefore to a paradoxical *incorporation*. (p. 126)

The terms of this passage have a powerful resonance with McLuhan's theorization of how electronic media produce acoustic space (space that is "invisible" in that it is constructed according to canons other than those of visual space) through the extension (spacing) and amputation (absence) of our bodies, such that our bodies expand to fill the universe (in mass, or corporate, culture; compare Derrida's pun on "*incorporation*") with the paradoxical result that we are *outside* those bodies (and thus amputated from them), bodies which we have extruded through our technologies. Derrida in fact refers to this body as 'an *a-physical* body that could be called, if one could rely on these oppositions, a technical body or an institutional body' (p. 127). There is no *authentic* body, in other words, to which this technologized body defers; the technological body is our body. As Derrida puts it, "this egological body . . . is the ghost of all ghosts!" (p. 129). As Derrida puts it In the *Echographies* volume (2002), "what is changing, with all these technical mutations we have been discussing, . . . is really . . . the body. This relation to technics is not something to which a given body must yield, adjust, etc. It is more than anything something which transforms the body" (p. 96). Hence Marx's critique of "all those who want to defend the property and integrity of their home [*chez soi*]: the body proper, the proper name, nation, blood, territory, and the 'rights' that are founded upon thereon" (1994b, p. 145). And, one might add, hence his critique of those who would deny to the material realm precisely that quality which has, for so long, animated philosophy—the ideal.

These paradoxes (in both Derrida and McLuhan) point toward a "haunting" of the discourse of "originality"; Derrida refers to this as a "*hauntology*" (p. 10) that inevitably raises the question "what is the mode of presence of a specter?" (p. 38). Pursuing this question through a consideration of Marx's writings about money, Derrida writes that "Marx always described money, and more precisely the monetary sign, in the figure of appearance or simulacrum" (p. 45). McLuhan makes a similar analysis of money in *Understanding Media* (1964), emphasizing its transformative powers and its analogy with writing: "[It]is . . . a specialist technology like writing; and as writing intensifies the visual aspect of speech and order, and as the clock visually separates time from space, so money separates work from the other social functions" (p. 136). Within electronic culture, however, the role of money changes: "Today, as the new vortices of power are shaped by the instant electronic interdependence of all men on this planet, the visual factor in social organization and in personal experience recedes, and money begins to be less and less a means of storing or exchanging work and skill. Automation, which is electronic, does not represent physical work so much as programmed knowledge. As work is replaced by the sheer movement of information, money as a store of work merges with the informational forms of credit and credit card" (p. 137).

Derrida likewise extends his account of the spectral in Marx to the media. Arguing that performativity displaces public and private acts (because as a private act of utterance it is nevertheless facilitated by a vast social structuration), Derrida notes that the mediated nature of utterance is at the core of this displacement: "if this important frontier [that between public and private] is being displaced, it is because the medium in which it is instituted, namely, the medium of the media themselves (news, the press, tele-communications, techno-tele-discursivity, techno-tele-iconicity, that which in general assures and determines the *spacing* of public space, the very possibility of the *res publica* and the phenomenality of the political), this element itself is neither living nor dead, present nor absent: it spectralizes" (50–51). The connections here between displacement, electronic media, and the production of (acoustic) space, are crucial linkages between Derrida's argument and that made by McLuhan forty years earlier. What would separate these arguments, in Derrida's reading, is McLuhan's apparent insistence on the element of "presence" in utterances. Indeed, it is Derrida's prime criticism of Marx (to whom he otherwise refers as "one of the first thinkers of technics, or even, by far and from afar, of the tele-technology that it will always have been") that Marx "continues to want to ground his critique . . . in an ontology . . . of presence as actual reality and as objectivity" (170).

McLuhan's assessment of Marx (1972) is significant in this context. McLuhan states that "Marx saw money as the magical transformer of all things whatever to money prices" (p. 62), which is to say that Marx saw money as a medium. "As the eighteenth century had hit upon the principle of mass production via *exactly repeated* acts of human labor, so the nineteenth century intensified and extended the process of uniformity and repetition of commensurable prices and commodities. The process of wealth making thus moved steadily from 'hardware' to 'software'" (p. 62). Marx's error, according to McLuhan, was to fail to acknowledge the immense importance of this shift, a shift which necessitated a reconceptualization of the "material": "Marx ignored the hidden environmental effects of the fantastic speed-up of work via steam, which had transformed during the period of his historical studies all the components or situations that he analyzed" (p. 63). In other words, the "'message' of steam as a new 'medium' was not the products, but the acceleration of all the functions in the social surround" (p. 63). Marx failed, thus, to understand the invisible effects of the new media as having material significance. Today, this "specter that was 'haunting Europe' . . . has become our familiar bedfellow" (p. 75), writes McLuhan, making reference here to the Cold War context in which he was writing. McLuhan appropriates the opening of *The Communist Manifesto* to suggest that mediation has become the properly *material* locus of analysis as we enter into an increasingly spectral environment. "Marx went all the way to the boundaries of scientific classification seeking an outlet into a 'field theory' via Hegelian dialectic. He was certain that 'everything is *interconnected.*' He was unprepared for *interplay,* the resonant interval" (1972, pp. 75–6).

Derrida states at the outset of *Echographies of Television* that the philosophical crux of virtuality—"virtual image, virtual space, and so virtual event" (p. 6)—is that it "can doubtless no longer be opposed, in perfect philosophical serenity, to actual [*actuelle*] reality in the way that philosophers used to distinguish between power and act, *dynamis* and *energeia*, the potentiality of a material and the defining form of a *telos*, and therefore also of a *progress*" (p. 6). One might restate this by saying that the mediation of the event must be thought of as forming part of that event, which is to say that the non-material must now be thought of as having entered the material domain. This is at once consistent with Derrida's earlier positions and differs from those positions because of its categorical nature—if telemediation is simply "writing," why the need, now, to differentiate it? This need to make a distinction between writing and "teletechnologies, television, radio, e-mail . . . the Internet" (p. 33) emerges, in fact, as a major point in the dialogues Derrida has with Bernard Stiegler in the *Echographies* volume. Stiegler states that "It is possible to read you [Derrida] and to understand that writing—any form of writing—is already a kind of teletechnology. The power to address a letter is a sending away from oneself which already breaks the circle of any proximity, of any immediacy, and you have indeed shown that there is in fact never any immediate proximity, there is always already something like a writing and therefore like a teletechnology. *What, then, would be the specificity of what you have recently given this name 'teletechnology'?*" (pp. 36–7; emphasis added). Derrida replies that "this specificity, whatever it may be, does not all of a sudden substitute the prosthesis, teletechnology, etc., for immediate or natural speech" (p. 38), which is to affirm his consistent position that speech is neither transparent nor natural but a form of writing (insofar as speech functions through iterability). However, he adds that (a) the "live" quality of teletechnologies marks a specificity, its endlessly repeatable "nowness" (as in the recorded voices of "singers . . . writers, storytellers, orators, politicians, etc." [p. 39]), and that (b) the spatial "polarity" of these teletechnologies marks another specificity—"The greatest intensity of 'live' life is captured from as close as possible in order to be borne as far as possible away. If there is a specificity, it stems from the measure of this distance, it stems from this polarity which holds together the closest and the farthest away" (p. 39); "[a]ll the problems we have been talking about we have been talking about with reference to a technology that *displaces places*: the border is no longer the border" (p. 57). This notion brings together elements similar to those which McLuhan posited in the "global village" phenomenon, and, in Derrida's formulation, these elements have a significant "communitarian" emphasis—an emphasis, as we have seen, often attributed to McLuhan: "I believe that this technical transformation—of the telephone, of the fax machine, of television, e-mail and the Internet—will have done more for what is called 'democratization,' even in countries in the East, than all the discourses on behalf of human rights, more than all the presentations of models in whose name democratization was able to get started" (2002, p. 71). It should be noted that McLuhan did not formulate the local / global elements as a set of polarities but as an interface, such that the global and the local are collapsed into one another. Derrida's notion is less dynamic: "[T]hese problems are at the very heart of an actuality that has been what is called 'globalized' in terms of the circulation of televisual commodities from one country to another, from one nation-state to another, from one cultural or political zone . . . or from one linguistic zone . . . to another" (p. 43).

Stiegler questions Derrida further on the issue of the specificity of teletechnologies by bringing up the culture of the book. "[I]sn't there a need," he asks, "to think a cultural politics that would face, precisely, the new teletechnological horizon, which is no longer simply the horizon of the book, which has remained, until now, despite attempts of sorts to change things, the reference for cultural and educational development?" (p. 46). Derrida replies that the "distinction between formal frame and 'content' is obviously highly problematic. . . . It is all too clear that this distinction has never stood up to analysis. It is less credible than ever today, in the cases and with the teletechnological powers were are talking about" (p. 52). Later in the discussion, Derrida remarks that, while the book and teletechnology both derive from techniques of iterability, they are, nevertheless, "two experiences of repetition . . . that are very far apart, if not heterogeneous" (p. 90). We have come, suggests Derrida, to "the limit of phonetic writing. Now more than ever, the latter has been exceeded. It is not originary, in a sense it is finished, it has been exceeded by the image experiment we are conducting now" (p. 104).

In *Of Grammatology* it was "The End of the Book and the Beginning of Writing" that preoccupied Derrida, and arguably at a moment when the specter of McLuhan loomed over him most powerfully. "The End of the Book and the Beginning of Writing" is the title of the first chapter in part one of the book. In 1967, when the French edition was published, McLuhan had achieved international fame—"Le macluhanisme" [sic] entered the French language at this time—in part by making statements about the fate of the book and the history of writing. Derrida remarks at the beginning of the *Grammatology* that "the development of the *practical methods* of information retrieval extends the possibilities of 'the message' [a loaded term in the McLuhanesque context] vastly, to the point where it is no longer the 'written' translation of a language, the transporting of a signified which could remain spoken in its integrity. It goes hand in hand with an extension [again a significant word in the context I am developing, as it appears in the subtitle to *Understanding Media*] of phonography and of all the means of conserving the spoken language, of making it function *without the presence of the speaking subject* [this emphasis added]. This development, coupled with that of anthropology and of the history of writing, teaches us that phonetic writing, the medium of the great metaphysical, scientific, technical, and economic adventure of the West, is limited in space and time and limits itself *even as it is in the process of imposing its laws upon the cultural areas that had escaped it* [this emphasis added]. But this nonfortuitous conjunction of cybernetics and the 'human sciences' of writing leads to a more profound reversal" (p. 10). That reversal is characterized by the *prior* claim of "writing," which is the theme of Derrida's book.

In the work of both Derrida and McLuhan, the end of the book meant an end to a "centred" way of thinking and the beginning of another which would be characterized by displacement. McLuhan associated this new horizon with electronic technologies; Derrida termed it "writing." Yet these technologies, for McLuhan, could not be reduced to a linguistic model; the acoustic space of electronic mediation was not (only) phonemic, and Derrida's writing did not exclude speaking. As Derrida remarks in an interview titled "Word Processing," "In one respect, it [the computer] seems to restore a quasi-immediacy of the text, a desubstantialized substance, more fluid, lighter, thus closer to speech, or even to so-called interior speech" (Derrida, 1999, p. 7). Gayatri Spivak had cautioned in the introduction to her translation of *Of Grammatology* (Spivak, 1976) that "the name 'writing' is given here [by Derrida] to an entire structure of investigation, not merely to 'writing in the narrow sense,' graphic notation on tangible material. Thus, *Of Grammatology* is not a simple valorization of writing over speech, a simple reversal of the hierarchy, a sort of anti-McLuhan" (p. lxix). The comment is important because it demonstrates that, a decade after its publication in France, *Of Grammatology* continued to be read in a McLuhanesque context, and because its caution bears reiterating. Derrida is not an "anti-McLuhan" because his position is much closer to McLuhan's than polarizing generalities about speaking and writing would allow, and because McLuhan's position is much more ontologically complex than McLuhanism has suggested thus far. As Richard Dienst states at the outset of *Still Life in Real Time: Theory After Television* (1994), "this study begins by assuming that seeing and saying are fundamentally intertwined and unavoidably textual processes" (p. ix).

Reading Derrida and McLuhan together reminds us that *The Gutenberg Galaxy* is very much about the intimate interconnections of speaking and writing throughout their intertwined histories, and that *Of Grammatology* is consistently oriented toward the powerful role that the notion of speech has played in the Western philosophical tradition. Yet the haunting of Derrida by "telecommunications" and "teletechnologies" suggests that the particular historical moment that saw him produce both *Of Grammatology* and "Signature Event Context" was crucial to the formulation of a notion of "writing" which is most powerfully borne out—as his last works argue—by electronic media, specifically, the computer (Bennington, 1993, pp. 313–4), a form of "visible speech," as McLuhan once put it (Cavell, 2002, pp. 136–169). It is important to recall that for theorists of McLuhan's generation, it was precisely "electrical engineering" (as one of McLuhan's sources puts it in *The Gutenberg Galaxy* [2]) that had retrieved oral culture for the poets and scholars of that period, allowing (as McLuhan suggests in the same place) orality to *co-exist* with writing (as opposed to being its residual ground) for the first time since manuscript culture. What separated Derrida's thought from McLuhan's at this point was

Derrida's reluctance to theorize the role of teletechnologies in his formulation of the concept of writing.

It is through McLuhan, in other words—agonistically, and with a powerful anxiety of influence—that Derrida gave writing its philosophical mode of thought: a *hauntology*. It is a mode of thought that acknowledges the role of absence in the production of signification, the spacing (extension, *tele-*) which, neither spoken nor written, calls both into being. That spacing, that absence, is technics itself, the "resonant interval" or "ECO-sounding" (McLuhan and Nevitt, 1972, p. 1) as McLuhan called it; it is the gap in and of signification. Because technology, as McLuhan remarked, is co-terminous with the human it thus provides the basis for rethinking traditional issues of Western philosophy. It allows signification to be understood as a form of free play brought into being through disconnection, as in the dots on a television screen, which produce what might be called a *fröhliche Wissenschaft*. Hence the wittily astute characterization of McLuhan as "Marshall McNietzsche" by Winthrop-Young and Wutz in their preface to Kittler (1999, p. xxvii). What McLuhan sought to theorize was a technics of being; as McKenzie Wark has written, "[a]ll human interaction is mediated"(2000, p. 92). Hence McLuhan's powerful notion of technology is subject to a libidinal economy: "Man becomes, as it were, the sex organs of the machine world, as the bee of the plant world, enabling it to fecundate and to evolve ever new forms" (1964, p. 46). In this formulation, technology is the *pre-condition* of being. This understanding allowed McLuhan to make the counter-intuitive statements that became a hallmark of his writing, suggesting, for example, that television was inherent in the *pointillisme* of Seurat.

McLuhan's view of history as *ricorso*—in which recursiveness is transformation—is Viconian, and it is Derrida in *Of Grammatology* who remarks that Vico, uniquely among Enlightenment thinkers, posited the birth of writing as *co-existent* with speaking. "Vico is one of the rare believers, if not the only believer, in the contemporaneity of origin between writing and speech," Derrida noted (p. 335, n. 5). "Echographies" puts these paradoxes very well: a "sounding" (as in "sonography" but also "ultrasound") that is at the same time a kind of writing, there and not there, material and yet virtual. Again and again in *Specters of Marx*, Derrida will in fact invoke the dimension of speech, of the acoustic, in this hauntological way: "in order to inhabit even there where one is not, . . . to be *atopic* (mad and non-localizable), not only is it necessary . . . to see without being seen . . . it is also necessary to speak. And to hear voices. The spectral rumor now resonates" (135). It resonates with a specter.

References

Baudrillard, J. (1983). *Simulations* (P. Foss, P. Patton & P. Beitchman, Trans.). New York: Semiotext(e).

Bennington, G. (1993). *Jacques Derrida*. Chicago: University of Chicago Press.

Bornstein, E. (1966). An interview with Marshall McLuhan. *The Structurist, 6*, 61–68.

Brennan, P. (1983). Excuse me, but I never said exactly so. *On the Beach, 1*, 42

Cavell, R. (2002). *McLuhan in space: A cultural geography*. Toronto: University of Toronto Press.

Cheah, P. (1996). Mattering. *Diacritics, 26*(1), 108–139.

Clark, T. (1999). Technology inside: Enlightenment and Romantic assumptions of the orality/literacy school. *Oxford Literary Review, 21*, 57–72.

Clough, P. T. (2000a). *Autoaffection: Unconscious thought in the age of teletechnology*. Minneapolis: University of Minnesota.

Clough, P. T. (2000b). The technical substrates of unconscious memory: Rereading Derrida's *Freud* in the age of teletechnology. *Sociological Theory, 18*(3), 383–398.

Cohen, T., Miller, J. H., & Cohen, B. (2001). A "materiality without matter"? In T. Cohen, B. Cohen, J. H. Miller, & A. Warminski (Eds.), *Material events: Paul de Man and the afterlife of theory* (pp. vii–xxv). Minneapolis: University of Minnesota Press.

Couldry, N. (2003). *Media rituals: A critical approach*. New York: Routledge.

Coyne, R. (1999). *Technoromanticism: Digital narrative, holism, and the romance of the real*. Cambridge, MA: MIT Press.

De Kerckhove, D. (1981). Understanding McLuhan. *Canadian Forum, 51*, 8–9; 33.

Derrida, J. (2005). *On Touching, Jean-Luc Nancy*. Stanford: Stanford University Press.

Derrida, J. (2001). Typewriter ribbon: Limited ink (2) ("within such limits"). In T. Cohen, B. Cohen, & J. H. Miller (Eds.), *Material events: Paul de Man and the afterlife of theory* (pp. 277–360). Minneapolis: University of Minnesota Press.

Derrida, J. (2000). Derrida's response to Mulhall. *Ratio, 13*(4), 415–418.

Derrida, J. (1996). *Archive fever: A Freudian impression*. Chicago: University of Chicago Press.

Derrida, J. (1994a). The deconstruction of actuality: An interview with Jacques Derrida. *Radical Philosophy, 8*, 28–41.

Derrida, J. (1994b). *Specters of Marx: The state of debt, the work of mourning, and the new International* (P. Kamuf, Trans.). London: Routledge.

Derrida, J. (1988). Signature event context. In *Limited Inc.* (S. Weber & J. Mehlman, Trans.), (pp. 1–23). Chicago: Northwestern University Press.

Derrida, J. (1986). Differance. In M. C. Taylor (Ed.), *Deconstruction in context: Literature and philosophy* (pp. 396–420). Chicago: University of Chicago Press.

Derrida, J. (1976). *Of grammatology* (G. C. Spivak, Trans.). Baltimore, MD: Johns Hopkins University Press.

Derrida, J., & Stiegler, B. (2002). *Echographies of Television* (J. Bajorek, Trans.). Cambridge: Polity.

Derrida, J. (1999). Word Processing. *Oxford Literary Review* 21: 3–17

Dienst, R. (1994). *Still life in real time: Theory after television*. Durham, NC: Duke University Press.

Garnham, N. (2000). *Emancipation, the media, and modernity: Arguments about the media and social theory.* Oxford: Oxford University Press.

Geisler, M. (1999). From building blocks to radical construction: West German media theory since 1984. *New German Critique, 78* (Fall), 75–108.

Gordon, W. T. (2003). McLuhan and Saussure. In E. McLuhan, W. Kuhns, & M. Cohen (Eds.), *The book of probes* (pp. 441–448). Corte Madera, CA: Gingko.

Horrocks, C. (2000). *Marshall McLuhan and virtuality.* Cambridge, UK: Icon Books.

Hunter, J. (2002). Minds, archives and the domestication of knowledge. In R. Comay (Ed.), *Lost in the archives* (pp. 199–215). Toronto: Alphabet City.

Innis, H A. (1951). *The bias of communication.* Toronto: University of Toronto Press.

Innis, H A. (1950). *Empire and communications.* Toronto: University of Toronto Press.

Lecourt, D. (2001). *The mediocracy: French philosophy since 1968* (G. Elliott, Trans.). London: Verso.

Lefebvre, H. (1991). *The production of space* (D. Nicholson-Smith, Trans.). Oxford: Blackwell.

Levin, D. M. (1997). Introduction. In D. M. Levin (Ed.), *Sites of Vision* (pp. 1–67). Cambridge, MA: MIT Press.

Krapp, P. (1996). Derrida online. *Oxford Literary Review, 18,* 159–173.

Man, P. de (1996). *Aesthetic ideology.* Minneapolis: University of Minnesota Press.

Manovich, L. (2001). *The language of new media.* Cambridge, MA: MIT Press.

McLuhan, M. (1995). A McLuhan sourcebook. In E. McLuhan & F. Zingrone (Eds.), *Essential McLuhan* (pp. 270–297). Toronto: Anansi.

McLuhan, M. (1989). A last look at the tube. In G. Sanderson & F. Macdonald (Eds.), *Marshall McLuhan: The man and his message* (pp. 196–200). Golden, CO: Fulcrum Press.

McLuhan, M. (1978). Review of Williams' *Television. Technology and Culture, 19*(2), 259–261.

McLuhan, M. (1968). *War and peace in the global village.* New York: McGraw-Hill.

McLuhan, M. (1964). *Understanding media: The extensions of man.* New York: McGraw-Hill.

McLuhan, M. (1962). *The Gutenberg galaxy: The making of typographic man.* Toronto: University of Toronto Press.

McLuhan, M. (1953). The later Innis. *Queen's Quarterly, 60,* 385–394.

McLuhan, M., & McLuhan, E. (1988). *Laws of media: The new science* (P. Foss, Trans.). Toronto: University of Toronto Press.

McLuhan, M., & Nevitt, B. (1972). *Take today: The executive as dropout.* Toronto: Longman.

Miller, J. H. (2001). Paul de Man as allergen. In T. Cohen, B. Cohen, J. H. Miller, & A. Warminski (Eds.), *Material events: Paul de Man and the afterlife of theory* (pp. 183–204). Minneapolis: University of Minnesota Press.

Molinaro, M., McLuhan, C., & Toye, W. (Eds.) (1987). *Letters of Marshall McLuhan.* Toronto: Oxford.

Pfeiffer, K. L. (1994). The materiality of communication. In H. U. Gumbrecht & K. L. Pfeiffer (Eds.), *Materialities of communication* (pp. 1–12). Stanford, CA: Stanford University Press.

Plotnitsky, A. (2001). Alegebra and allegory: Nonclassical epistemology, quantum theory, and the work of Paul de Man. In T. Cohen, B. Cohen, J. H. Miller, & A. Warminski (Eds.), *Material events: Paul de Man and the afterlife of theory* (pp. 49–92). Minneapolis, MN: University of Minnesota Press.

Rockmore, T. (2002). *Marx after Marxism: The philosophy of Karl Marx.* Oxford: Blackwell.

Smith, B. R. (1999). *The acoustic world of early modern England: Attending to the O-factor.* Chicago: University of Chicago Press.

Spivak, G. C. (1976). Translator's preface. In J. Derrida, *Of grammatology* (pp. ix–lxxxvii). Baltimore: Johns Hopkins University Press.

Stearn, G. E. (1967). A dialogue with Gerald E. Stearn. In G. E. Stearn (Ed.), *McLuhan: Hot and Cool, a critical symposium* (pp. 266–302). New York: Dial.

Stiegler, B. (1998). *Technics and time, 1: The fault of Epimetheus* (R. Beardsworth & G. Collins, Trans.). Stanford, CA: Stanford University Press.

Thompson, J. B. (1995). *The media and modernity: A social theory of the media.* Stanford: Stanford University Press.

Wark, M. (2000). Watcha' doin', Marshall McLuhan? *Media International Australia, 94,* 89–96.

Wigley, M. (2001). Network fever. *Grey Room, 4,* 83–122.

Williams, R. (1974). *Television: Technology and cultural form.* London: Fontana.

Winthrop-Young, G., & Wutz, M. (1999). Translators' introduction. In F. Kittler, *Gramophone, film, typewriter* (pp. xi–xxxvii). Stanford, CA: Stanford University Press.

CHAPTER EIGHT

McLuhan, Crash Theory, and the Invasion of the Nanobots

PATRICK BRANTLINGER

"... the truth of contemporary science is not so much the extent of progress achieved as the scale of technical catastrophes occasioned."

—Paul Virilio, *The Information Bomb.*

Recent work on new technologies and the emergence of "the information society" suggests that Marshall McLuhan is in a sort of academic purgatory, even though many of his ideas—or the ideas that he expressed, at any rate—are everywhere. Many scholars do not bother to cite him. In *Theories of the Information Society*, for example, Frank Webster does not mention McLuhan, while Darin Barney cites only his "famous aphorism . . . 'the medium is the message'" in *Prometheus Wired* (56). So, too, in *The Informational City*, the most important sociological analysis to date of the paradigm shift to the information age, Manuel Castells ignores McLuhan. This is not to say that he, Webster, Barney, or other recent scholars should necessarily do otherwise; after all, McLuhan published *The Gutenberg Galaxy* and *Understanding Media* four decades ago.

Nevertheless, as Christopher May notes, McLuhan's "discussion of the transformative potential of new communications technologies and practices remains influential, inasmuch as many of his ideas find their way into current discussions, albeit unacknowledged" (May 8). Certainly McLuhan was asking important questions, even if his answers were often inadequate or weakly supported. If that judgment is true from the vantage point of the information age, it is also true concerning his ideas about earlier historical moments. Thus, in *The Printing Revolution in Early Modern Europe*, Elizabeth Eisenstein notes: "By making us more alert to the possibility that the advent of printing had social and psychological consequences, McLuhan performed . . . a valuable service. But he also glossed over multiple interactions that occurred under widely varying circumstances . . ." (92). Perhaps, then, Donald Theall's claim that we should view McLuhan as a "modernist artist" rather than as a historian, philosopher, or social scientist is the fairest way to judge him (15). Theall writes that "McLuhan has frequently been misunderstood by heavy, sombre academics, since he played games, he used wit and satire, and he employed a strategy of decentering and fragmentation" (17); all this is true, although it also explains why "heavy, sombre academics" will continue to ignore him.

Theall makes some intriguing points, however, about similarities between McLuhan's ideas and the emergence of French poststructuralist theory also starting in the 1960s (Theall 125,137). Theall cites John Fekete writing in 1982: "Derrida takes up again and again, without reference to McLuhan, the same themes . . . : logocentrism, phonocentrism, the eye, the ear . . . the impact of the phonetic alphabet, abstraction, writing, linearity as the repression of pluri-dimensional thought, simultaneity, synaesthesia, etc." (qtd. in Theall 131). For other French theorists, including Roland Barthes and Jean Baudrillard, there was an acknowledged interest in "McLuhanism" in the 1960s and '70s. In both *Anti-Oedipus* and *A Thousand Plateaus*, Gilles Deleuze and Felix Guattari drew on McLuhan for the idea that the modern world is moving in "two directions: worldwide ecumenical machines, but also a neoprimitivism, a new tribal society . . ." (360). In the earlier volume, with *The Gutenberg Galaxy* in mind, they claimed that "the significance of McLuhan's analyses [is] to have shown what a language of decoded flows is, as opposed to a signifier that strangles and overcodes the flows" (240). This "language of decoded flows" supported their concepts of the "mechanosphere," "nomadism," "deterritorialization," "machinic assemblages," "bodies without organs," and humans as "desiring machines."

As I shall argue here, McLuhan continues to be important to a radical branch of postmodernist, posthumanist cultural theory in France and elsewhere. This branch merits the title "crash theory," a phrase that comes from Arthur Kroker and Michael Weinstein's *Data Trash*. An apocalyptic version of postmodernism, crash theory treats technology as inexorably pushing humanity toward annihilation, or at least toward the "implosion" of reality into something like its opposite. Besides Kroker and Weinstein, the main crash theorists I will consider are Paul Virilio and Jean Baudrillard, both of whom acknowledge at least some influence from McLuhan. I will also consider several recent computer and robotics scientists who pay little if any attention either to McLuhan or to the crash theorists, but whose ideas about the consequences of technological innovation are clearly versions of crash theory. The crash theorists represent one line of speculation about "the postmodern condition," a line indebted both to McLuhan and to poststructuralism.

The scientists engaged in current debates about GRAIN, or the "megamerger of [the] supersciences" of genetics, robotics, artificial intelligence, and nanotechnology (Mulhall 30), though expressing a McLuhan-like ambivalence toward the technological innovations they are simultaneously promoting and deploring, go beyond even the crash theorists with some of their doomsday scenarios. McLuhan may have been prescient in regard to some of the social and psychological effects of new communications media, but he did not fully foresee the impact of cybernetics and the computer revolution, and did not at all foresee the apocalyptic prospects that are dawning through GRAIN, even though the first annunciations of these new sciences and technologies occurred during his lifetime. McLuhan emphasized communications media, but GRAIN technologies are not easily distinguishable from such media. On the contrary, artificial intelligence, codes such as DNA, and communication between the parts of systems, whether organic or inorganic (or hybrid) are fundamental to the emergent GRAIN technologies that promise and threaten to change the world forever.

1.

At least implicit in McLuhan, crash theory is in part the logical outcome of the technological determinism that McLuhan occasionally disowned but that, in my view, is central to his thinking. All versions of technological determinism are inherently dystopian, because they always transfer agency from humans to machines—they are always expressions of alienation. Paul Grosswiler has argued that "McLuhan's method, like the early Marx's radical dialectical method, was not a mechanistic, technological determinism" (Grosswiler 5). That view depends, however, on just how much weight one gives to McLuhan's disclaimers about techno-determinism, and conversely how much stress one puts on some of his best-known formulations, such as "the medium is the message." McLuhan did on occasion protest that he was not a technodeterminist. Thus, in a 1967 interview he declared: "My entire concern is to overcome the determinism that results from the determination of people to ignore what is going on. Far from regarding technological change as inevitable, I insist that if we understand its components we can turn it off any time we choose. Short of turning it off, there are lots of moderate controls conceivable" (qtd. in Rosenthal 19). But McLuhan was never really interested in figuring out how "we can turn it off," much less conceiving of "moderate controls" to temper the social or psychological effects of new media. The cavalier language here (or is it merely naive?)—"we can turn it off any time we choose"—contradicts his typical mode of argumentation, which entails giving agency to technology and reifying humans.

In *The Dilemma of Determinism,* William James long ago distinguished between "hard" and "soft" versions of determinism (Marx and Smith, *Introduction* xii). Taken in isolation (or perhaps, out of context), many of McLuhan's assertions about the historical impacts of new technologies are clearly "hard"; but he backtracks often enough to make a reasonable case that he is only a "soft" determinist. And as Bruce Bimber argues, "a so-called soft determinism cannot be called determinism at all" (81)—thus, it is possible to maintain that McLuhan was not a techno-determinist. However, my reading of McLuhan's most important texts—*The Gutenberg Galaxy* and *Understanding Media*—suggests otherwise. McLuhan's typical formulations put the cart before the horse, the machine before the human. He regularly makes the key move that defines technodeterminism: he personifies or gives historical agency to new machines and media; in doing so, he also reifies or erases human agency from the historical narratives that he constructs. Although they do not point to McLuhan as an example, the editors of *Does Technology Drive History?* note that "popular narratives" convey a vivid sense of the efficacy of technology as a driving force of history: a technical innovation suddenly appears and causes important things to happen. It is noteworthy that these mini-fables direct attention to the consequences rather than the genesis of inventions. (Marx and Smith, *Introduction* x)

McLuhan's most familiar claims about history take this form: the printing press causes the Reformation and the rise of modern nationalisms; now the electronic media are reversing the linear, centralizing tendency of modernity and producing the retribalizing "global village."

Grosswiler, Judith Stamps, Neil Postman, and I myself have discussed similarities between McLuhan's theories and Marx's, as well as those that have emerged from various marxisms, including the Frankfurt School and the cultural studies movement. Grosswiler acknowledges that "McLuhan consistently attacked or dismissed Marx" (3), but he nonetheless offers a thorough "rethinking" of McLuhan through marxist "critical theory." Stamps likewise offers a useful comparison of the ideas of Harold Innis and McLuhan with those of Theodor Adorno and Walter Benjamin. I compare McLuhan to Marx and the Frankfurt School more briefly in *Bread and Circuses* (263–273). In *Technopoly,* Postman notes some of the basic similarities between Marx and McLuhan, though he adds: "By connecting technological conditions to symbolic life and psychic habits, Marx was doing nothing unusual. Before him, scholars found it useful to invent taxonomies of culture based on the technological character of an age" (22). One of those similarities has to do with determinism—or the degree of it, rather—in both McLuhan's and Marx's versions of history. Marx was certainly capable of aphoristic statements that can be interpreted as technodeterminist: "The hand-mill gives you society with the feudal lord, the steam-mill, society with the industrial capitalist" (qtd. in Bimber 90 n. 17). Marx's more general economic determinism—especially the thesis that the "economic mode of production" or "real foundation" gives rise in every society to the ideological "superstructure"—is, however, a version of "soft" determinism—or in other words, is not strictly deterministic. This is partly because of his other most prominent thesis, that the driving force of historical change is class conflict. And class conflict, Marx believed, produced revolution, including the final revolution that would usher in the classless society of the future. Marx clearly thought that the domination of any given mode of production was subject to revolutionary "Aufhebung" through human agency: "Workers of the world unite! You have nothing to lose but your chains."

In contrast to Marx, McLuhan's typical formulations are about the historical and psychological changes to the human "sensorium" caused by the abrupt (and mysterious or unexplained, at least by McLuhan) appearance of some new machine or medium of communication. He rarely considers how new machines come to be invented, distributed, and used, except in the most abstract sense, though invention, distribution, and uses—plural—would put human agency back into the picture. His stress on the general, totalizing (that is, undifferentiated) effect of a new machine or medium willy-nilly (whether intentionally or otherwise) gives massive historical agency to machines and subtracts it from humans, whether inventors or owners and users.

For McLuhan, new media are both major historical events and mundane miracles (it is no accident that he was a faithful Catholic), though they can be demonic as well as angelic. And indeed, because he saw new media as potent forces, intervening in human history in unpredictable ways, McLuhan remains influential, at least among the crash theorists. Nevertheless, claims that he was a prophet or even just prescient about the era of computers and the Internet strike me as forms of special pleading. Thus, according to Paul Levinson: "The handwriting for coming to terms with our digital age was on the wall of McLuhan's books" (2). Perhaps so, although given television and, for that matter, early computers, "our digital age" was easy enough to predict in the 1960s. Norbert Wiener was attempting to introduce (and simultaneously apologize for) a cybernetic, technologized concept of (post)human identity as early as 1950. See, for instance, Wiener's *The Human Use of Human Beings: Cybernetics and Society*. McLuhan writes: . . . by means of electric media, we set up a dynamic by which all previous technologies that are mere extensions of hands and feet and teeth and bodily heat-controls—all such extensions of our bodies, including cities—will be translated into information systems. (*Understanding Media* 57) In the 1960s, however, that statement would have been more accurate—and sounded less prophetic—if McLuhan had used the present instead of the future tense. Further, McLuhan derived his main ideas about the electronic media from television, not from computers. And there were other technologies which were on the horizon during his lifetime that he paid little or no attention to: besides computers, which he did pay some attention to, these include robotics, genetic engineering, nanotechnology—that is, GRAIN.

What was most original about *The Gutenberg Galaxy* and *Understanding Media* was perhaps not McLuhan's ideas, but the way he presented those ideas as paradoxes, startling claims, headlines, seemingly new insights such as "the medium is the message." Besides that striking paradox—which at least in its wording was original—the other most frequently cited McLuhanism is the idea of an emergent "global village," caused mainly by the rapidly "glocalizing" effects of the electronic mass media. Notions of a shrinking, wired world, however, go back to responses to telegraphy and the first transatlantic cable hook-up in the nineteenth century (see Standage 74–104). McLuhan's additional claims that the electronic global village is both "imploding" and undergoing "retribalization" are more original, especially in light of the recent balkanization, warfare, and genocides in eastern Europe, Russia, the Middle East, and much of Africa. In *Globalization: The Human Consequences,* sociologist Zygmunt Bauman sums up a great deal of recent commentary on this topic, cites McLuhan not once, and yet writes: "Neo-tribal and fundamentalist tendencies, which reflect and articulate the experience of people on the receiving end of globalization, are as much legitimate offspring of globalization as the widely acclaimed 'hybridization' of top [elite] culture" (3). McLuhan couldn't have said it better himself.

In any case, Levinson's claim that McLuhan's stance toward new media is that of a prophet is at least accurate in regard to his rhetoric. McLuhan may have been a Joycean trickster-artist and witty "poseur," as Theall makes him out to be, but he also wrapped himself in the mantle of the seer of new media. He was never sure enough of any of his ideas to issue straightforward jeremiads against technological innovations and new media; but neither was he sure enough to welcome them as ushering in the New Jerusalem. Crash theory is more consistently dystopian than was McLuhan, although there is often an undercurrent of celebration in its assertions of technological doom and anticipations of fulfilled prophecy.

Part of the similarity between crash theory and McLuhan lies in his penchant for making sweeping claims about history, such as these from *The Gutenberg Galaxy:* "A nomadic society cannot experience enclosed space" (64); "The medieval world ended in a frenzy of applied knowledge . . ." (117); and "Heidegger surf-boards along on the electronic wave as triumphantly as Descartes rode the mechanical wave" (248). Imagining Heidegger surfboarding on anything at all is certainly amusing; but one feature that all of these statements share with many of the other headlines (or section headings) in *Galaxy* is their oracular quality. These are more than just aphorisms, and more than just headlines; they are pronouncements on vast, complicated historical transformations or social conditions that imply that their author is close to omniscient or at least has some kind of inner (supernatural?) scoop on past, present, and future that ordinary mortals—even Heidegger and Descartes, unwitting surfers—do not have. Along with technological determinism, it is McLuhan's oracular rhetoric that makes him a forerunner of crash theory. The prophetic, apocalyptic aspects of McLuhan's ideas show up again in Kroker, Weinstein, Virilio, and Baudrillard, though with less ambivalence about possible historical outcomes.

2.

The crash theorists tend to be dismissive of McLuhan as a techno-optimist, utopian, or even crypto-theologian, but they also recognize that McLuhan was not always merely a naive cheerleader for technological innovation. In *Data Trash*, Kroker and Weinstein write: "McLuhan's 'global village' with its promise of technology as a religious 'epiphany' has passed" (52). This judgment may be partly correct, but their own brand of apocalyptic postmodernism begs to be read as a continuation of McLuhanism by other means. After all, later in their manifesto about the "virtual" trashing of the human, they write: "Cross McLuhan's nervous system outerized by the media, with Nietzsche's 'last man' . . . and you get crash theory" (143), which is their theory. Kroker and Weinstein try to distance themselves from McLuhan, but Kroker's first book, *Technology and the Canadian Mind: Innis/McLuhan /Grant*, traced the tradition of theorizing about the links between technology and history to which he and Weinstein belong.

Baudrillard, whose theory of "simulation," "hyperreality," and the "implosion" of the mass media into "posthistory" echoes some of the language of *The Gutenberg Galaxy* and *Understanding Media*, is explicit about his indebtedness to McLuhan: "even if I did not share the technological optimism of McLuhan, I always recognized and considered as a gain the true revolution which he brought about in media analysis . . ." (*Masses* 208; see also Kellner 66–76). Adopting McLuhan's "cybernetic concept of implosion," Baudrillard claims that what "implodes" in the postmodern condition is the distinction between simulation and reality. In *In the Shadow of the Silent Majorities*, Baudrillard acknowledges his debt to McLuhan and goes beyond his predecessor by contending: "the medium is the message signifies not only the end of the message, but also the end of the medium" (102). Both meaning and the media disappear into the simulacral maelstrom of "hyperreality" (*Simulations* 54).

In *The Illusion of the End* (1992), Baudrillard both predicts and contradicts the ultimate Big Bang of all history. Capitalism is cannibalizing everything and virtualizing it into simulation, spectacle, image, copy without original. And/or there is the—more real? or more hyperreal?—threat of nuclear or some other even more advanced form of world-military annihilation. There are at any rate no alternatives either to the end of history or to its simulated illusion, whichever is happening: "For hyperreality rules out the very occurrence of the Last Judgement or the Apocalypse or the Revolution. All the ends we have envisaged elude our grasp and history has no chance of bringing them about, since it will, in the interim, have come to an end . . ." (*Illusion* 8). History as farce? For Baudrillard, as for McLuhan, the chief weapons of destruction seem to be television and cinema, though in *The Spirit of Terrorism*, Baudrillard, like Virilio in *Ground Zero*, interprets 9/11 as an all-too-real, apocalyptic globalization of terror through television and the Internet. More than the other crash theorists, Baudrillard shares with McLuhan a quasi-theological investment in end-of-reality, end-of-history rhetoric and simulations. Flaming icons?

Starting in the late 1960s, Paul Virilio has stressed the importance of wartime and war-related research for technological innovation. As James Der Derian, editor of *The Virilio Reader*, says, "There is certainly more than a hint of millenarian doom to Virilio's work . . ." (11). Der Derian also points out how, in *The Insecurity of Territory* (1976), Virilio introduced "the concepts of "deterritorialization," "nomadism," and the "suicidal state," which Deleuze and Guattari pick up and brilliantly elaborate in their most significant work, *A Thousand Plateaus* (10). In any event, Virilio also cites McLuhan, but only to dismiss him as a quasi-religious optimist about the effects of technology (*The Art of the Motor* 9–10). Yet in his section on weapons in *Understanding Media*, McLuhan recognizes the impetus that war has given to technological innovation, though he is less insistent than Virilio that technology in general can be understood as weaponry, or at any rate as in some sense always destructive. According to Virilio, even information becomes, in the age of the Intenet, an "information bomb" (*Ground Zero* 2; *Information Bomb*). In contrast, McLuhan suggests that technological innovation and its unequal distribution cause war, rather than the other way around: "Previous wars can now be regarded as the processing of difficult and resistant materials by the latest technology, the speedy dumping of industrial products on an enemy market to the point of social saturation. War, in fact, can be seen as a process of achieving equilibrium among unequal technologies, a fact that explains [Arnold] Toynbee's puzzled observation that each invention of a new weapon is a disaster for society, and that militarism itself is the most common cause of the breaking of civilization" (*Media* 344).

Virilio's themes of speed and "speed pollution" are directly linked to war, because "speed is the essence of war" (*Reader* 46). The goal of "the suicidal state," implicit in its drive to perfect its weaponry, is "pure war" and the annihilation not just of its enemies but of itself (*Ground Zero* 37). The computer and the postmodern "cult of information," moreover, are outgrowths of the global war machine or what Norbert Wiener, shortly after World War II, called "the military-communications complex" (*Reader* 153). For "the cult of information," see Theodore Roszak. In *The Art of the Motor*, Virilio writes: "Originating in civil and international war as well as in army logistics, the modern information complex cunningly preserves the deadly features of these" (54). He adds that "the media evolve in tandem with the army" (56), and that even when no actual combat is happening between nation-states (though it is always happening somewhere), the media still seek to annihilate distance, real space and real time: "Territorial distance and media proximity make an explosive cocktail" (57).

Virilio's account of the developing "postindustrial 'technosphere'" (*Open Sky* 51) involves what he calls "dromology"—that is, the critical analysis of the effects of speed (and especially, the "light speed" involved in electronic devices including computers)—although this again is a theme in McLuhan: "The stepping-up of speed from the mechanical to the instant electric form reverses explosion into implosion" (*Media* 35). The language of "explosion" and "implosion" that McLuhan uses in relation to media effects is echoed by all the crash theorists. The metaphor of the bomb, as in Virilio's *Information Bomb*, represents the extreme version of technology run amok. According to crash theory, even the seemingly most benign machines—computers, for instance—are hurtling forward toward "escape velocity" and the ultimate smash-up, the Big Bang that will end reality and history altogether. For Virilio, moreover, the bomb isn't just a metaphor: The metaphor of nuclear catastrophe . . . is no longer a stylistic trope, but . . . an accurate enough image of the damage to human "activity" caused by this sudden implosion-explosion of computerized "interactivity" which Albert Einstein predicted in the 1950s would probably constitute a second bomb, after the purpose-built atomic one. (*Open Sky* 86)

For McLuhan, too, "explosion" and "implosion" are real enough: they describe catastrophic historical transformations caused by new technologies. Unlike the postmodern crash theorists, however, he does not use these terms to predict the end of the world. Nevertheless, in *Understanding Media*, McLuhan writes: "We know . . . the kind of energy that is released, as by fission, when literacy explodes the tribal or family unit. What do we know about the social and psychic energies that develop by electric fusion or implosion when literate individuals are suddenly gripped by an electromagnetic field. . . . the fusion of people who have known individualism and nationalism is not the same process as the fission of . . . oral cultures that are just coming to individualism and nationalism. It is the difference between the "A" bomb and the "H" bomb. The latter is more violent, by far." (50)

Even though Virilio doesn't cite him often, and then only critically, it is difficult not to detect the angelic-demonic, utopian-dystopian figure of McLuhan in the wings, so to speak, of Virilio's catastrophic accounts of "the nihilism of Western technology" (*Open Sky* 97). In a passage like this one, Virilio might as well be quoting McLuhan: Like some gigantic implosion, the circulation of the general accident of communication technologies is building up and spreading, forcing all substances to keep moving in order to interact globally, at the risk of being wiped out, being swallowed up completely. (*Open Sky* 81) For Virilio, moreover, "speed" accelerates everything into a fast-forward leading on to the ultimate technological, industrial "accident": "the coming crash of postindustrial production" (73), the "general global accident" which could well have radio-activity as its emblem" (83), the pending "unprecedented accident, representing the end of the road for history" (125–6), the "general" accident which globally undermines all 'presence' and promotes a 'telepresence' without consistency" (131)—this is the "temporal catastrophe" (134) which is about to sweep away, or perhaps has already swept away, history, human freedom, and individual mobility, identity, and sanity. So whether the world ends in nuclear holocaust or not, it is still driving on, accelerator to floorboard, to the terminal Big Bang.

Adopting McLuhan's "cybernetic concept of implosion," Baudrillard claims that what "implodes" in the postmodern era is the distinction between simulation and reality. So, too, Kroker and Weinstein write that "the USA implodes into the dark and dense nebula of its final existence as an aesthetic hologram of science as the American way" (*Panic* 228). This is "crash history" as media event, or rather as "virtualized" computer event, the final end of "the ecstasy of exterminism" (*Data* 2, 105). Kroker and Weinstein echo McLuhan's electronic "outerings" by calling the Internet an "externalization" of the human psyche, but instead of the consummation of consciousness as in some passages in McLuhan, in *Data Trash* the Internet signifies the arrival of a "posthuman" monstrosity. Data trash is specifically the detritus of the human body as it is cannibalistically devoured by the "virtuality" of the "information leviathan" (150). In the "electronic abattoir" of postmodernism, we are all doomed to be flayed alive and re-wired as mere simulations of ourselves. In contrast to the crash theorists, McLuhan in seemingly optimistic mode can write: "The computer . . . promises . . . a Pentecostal condition of understanding and unity" perhaps leading to "a perpetuity of collective harmony and peace" (*Understanding Media* 80). This sounds rosy enough, even "paradisal"—an overcoming of the old divisiveness of the "Tower of Babel"—though the "general cosmic consciousness which might be very like the collective unconscious dreamt of by Bergson" will, it seems, come at the expense of language. The future, global era of "harmony and peace" will also be an era of "speechlessness," whatever that means (80). And just how "cosmic consciousness" meshes with Bergson's "collective "un"conscious" is a puzzle. As is well known, McLuhan borrowed the idea of the "noosphere" or world-brain from Teilhard de Chardin as well as from Bergson. Here, on the terminal "digital beach," the "data-net" hatches as a monstrous new species through "the externalization of the human nervous system (McLuhan)" (*Data* 104).

3.

Perhaps McLuhan intended to be a "soft" determinist—that is, according to Bruce Bimber, not really a determinist at all—but again, many of his boldest assertions express versions of techno-determinism, and there is also McLuhan's stress on the modern (and now postmodern) acceleration of technological innovation. This theme foreshadows Virilio's "dromology" with its twinned emphases on speed and the ultimate accident, and it relates to the idea of "technological momentum" elaborated by, among others, Thomas Hughes in *Does Technology Drive History?* In contrast both to technological determinism and to notions of "social construction," through which technology tends to be viewed optimistically as directly responsive to human designs and wishes, technological momentum "avoids . . . extremism" and still allows for human agency, though it also suggests that time is running out (Hughes 104).

Somewhere between Bimber's notion that "soft" determinism is not strictly deterministic at all and the idea of "hard" determinism, technological momentum suggests that the rate of innovation, which is also the rate at which we are surrounding ourselves with new machines on which we become increasingly dependent, may lead to a version of strict determinism—a historical catastrophe whereby the machines really do take over and start running human affairs. In an attention-grabbing article for *Wired* magazine (April, 2000), whose first issue proclaimed on its masthead that McLuhan was its "patron saint," computer engineer and CEO Bill Joy writes: "The 21st-century technologies—genetics, nanotechnology, and robotics . . . are so powerful that they can spawn whole new classes of accidents and abuses" (242). I am grateful to Ivan Amato for informing me about the article by Bill Joy and about K. Eric Drexler's *Engines of Creation.* Joy claims that "we are on the cusp of the further perfection of extreme evil, an evil whose possibility spreads well beyond that which weapons of mass destruction bequeathed to the nation-states . . . ." (242). This "evil" stems partly from the prospect that the new technologies, or some of them at any rate, will be within the reach of individuals as well as governments, but partly also from the possibility that they will spin out of the control of everyone: . . . robots, engineered organisms, and nanobots share a dangerous amplifying factor: They can self-replicate. A bomb is blown up only once—but one bot can become many, and quickly get out of control. (240)

The inspiration for Joy's distinctly dystopian vision about self-amplifying technologies running amok came partly from Ray Kurzweil, also a computer scientist and inventor, who in his 1999 bestseller, *The Age of Spiritual Machines: When Computers Exceed Human Intelligence,* predicted that in just a few decades computers would be capable of replicating all aspects of human intelligence and, following Moore's Law, would leave us in the dust. (An important indicator of technological momentum, Moore's law states that computer power has been doubling and will continue to do so every eighteen months.) Although Kurzweil is more optimistic than Joy, "destruction of the entire evolutionary process" is a distinct possibility (256).

The key apocalyptic event predicted by Kurzweil, the moment when computers surpass human intelligence, has been dubbed "The Singularity" by another scientist, Vernor Vinge. In a 1993 article entitled "The Coming Technological Singularity: How to Survive in the Post-Human Era," Vinge claims that "within thirty years, we will have the technological means to create superhuman intelligence. Shortly after, the human era will be ended" (1). Vinge cites I. J. Good, who in the 1960s declared that "the first ultraintelligent machine is the "last" invention that man need ever make, provided that the machine is docile enough to tell us how to keep it under control" (2). But the proviso in Good's statement is like the wishful thinking expressed in Isaac Asimov's famous "laws" for robots, whereby they will not harm humans (Kaku 133–4). On Vinge and the concept of "The Singularity," see Mulhall 27–29, and also Edwards. Vinge, Joy, Kurzweil are in varying degrees skeptical about humans' ability to render the super-intelligent computers and robots we are developing "docile" or "harmless" (on "The Singularity," see also Muhall 27–29; Edwards).

So, too, in *Mind Children: The Future of Robot and Human Intelligence* (1988), Hans Moravec, whose main area of expertise is robotics, claims that we are on the verge of the displacement and perhaps even elimination of the entire human species by "intelligent robots." The very machines that Moravec is helping to invent, he declares, will soon be able to "carry on our cultural evolution, including their own construction and increasingly rapid self-improvement, without us, and without the genes that built us. When that happens, our DNA will find itself out of a job, having lost the evolutionary race to a new kind of competition" (2). In this doomsday scenario, machines prove superior to humans both because they become far more intelligent and because they are made of far more durable materials. Worn parts can always be replaced, so if the robots that replace us choose, they can be close to immortal (but never completely so, given entropy and the eventual heat-death of the universe).

Even if one rejects Joy's, Vinge's, Kurzweil's, and Moravec's expert forecasts about computers and robots, there remain the specters of genetic engineering and nanotechnology. Debates over cloning and other aspects of genetic engineering have become routine in the press. But as long ago as 1959, nanotechnology appeared on the horizon in Richard Feynman's talk, "There's Plenty of Room at the Bottom" (Mulhall 31; Kaku 268). The key idea that Feynman broached was the possibility of building anything at all, including new machines, from the level of atoms and molecules upward. In 1974, Japanese scientist Norio Taniguchi coined "nanotechnology" to refer to manipulating molecules into potentially any arrangements which they are capable of forming, or in other words to "machining with tolerances of less than a micron" (Mulhall 32). In *Engines of Creation* (1986), K. Eric Drexler explored these possibilities, including the development of "nanomachines" capable of "assembling" anything at all, but also of "dissembling" or destroying anything and, perhaps, everything. These nanomachines, like Moravec's "intelligent robots" and Kurzweil's "spiritual" computers, will have the power to reproduce themselves. While Drexler's vision in 1986 was more optimistic than otherwise, he also warned of dire prospects if this quite miraculous "molecular" technology gets out of control, or gets into the wrong control.

According to Drexler, "engines of creation" can just as well be "engines of destruction" (171–190). For instance, "Advanced technology will make workers unnecessary and genocide easy" (176). Self-reproducing nanomachines or "replicators can be more potent than nuclear weapons . . . to destroy all life with replicators would require only a single speck made of ordinary elements" (174). Further, "they could spread like blowing pollen, replicate swiftly, and reduce the biosphere to dust in a matter of days" (172). Already by 1986, "this threat" had been named the "gray goo problem" by "the cognoscenti of nanotechnology" (172). And that problem is the theme of Michael Crichton's latest horror science fiction novel, *Prey*. Needless to say, Drexler argues that extreme caution will be necessary to keep the new nano-engines on the side of "creation" rather than "destruction." In their anthology, *Digital Delirium,* Arthur and Marilouise Kroker interview nanotechnologist B. C. Crandall, who says: "the potential for losing our evolutionary purchase on the planet is very real, as is the possibility of boldly carrying DNA to where no man—and no woman—has gone before" (169). Crandall's main idea about how to survive the consequences of nanotechnology seems to be the colonization of other worlds after ours becomes uninhabitable.

What distinguishes Joy, Vinge, Kurzweil, Moravec, and Drexler from the crash theorists (and also from McLuhan) is that they are themselves scientists, working to create the very technologies they warn against. Like Virilio in particular, they are all keenly aware of technological momentum. Kurzweil and Drexler believe that that momentum has not yet foreclosed the possibility of humans retaining control over the new technologies that will both improve and reproduce themselves at an accelerating rate. Joy, Vinge, and Moravec might as well be called crash theorists, because they suggest that machines may already have gotten beyond the control of their inventors—or if not already, then very soon. There is little difference between their dire warnings and Arthur Kroker's digital "exterminism" or Paul Virilio's ultimate Big Bang.

Perhaps because of his Catholicism, McLuhan wavered between utopianism and dystopianism. That wavering may prove to be one aspect of his thinking that will keep his ideas in circulation. While he certainly tended toward technodeterminism in many of his annunications about new media and technologies, he apparently did not understand such determinism itself to be a version of dystopianism. However, his more utopian moments are, as Kroker suggests, also deterministic, in the sense that they approximate "religious epiphanies." But at least McLuhan did not abandon the thought that humans "should" control the technologies we create. Just what forms such control might take he did not venture to speculate—no more than do the crash theorists. Indeed, for Kroker, Weinstein, Virilio, and Baudrillard, no control seems possible: as technology accelerates, the ultimate Big Bang becomes inevitable. The GRAIN scientists also have difficulty imagining how the new technologies they are helping to create can be rendered "docile" or mainly beneficial instead of destructive to "homo sapiens". Drexler includes a thoughtful chapter, "Strategies and Survival," dealing with possible institutional and political ways of controlling the new technologies (191–202), but this is not typical of the other GRAIN scientists.

In GRAIN discourse, the tendency is to imagine technological solutions to the problems posed by technology. There is, for instance, the now common idea that "cyborgization," or the combining of machines and humans as in scenarios of downloading human psyches into computers (and thereby achieving a sort of immortality), will allow the era of the "posthuman" to continue to be at least partly human. But this idea is hardly reassuring, and it does not constitute a "political" vision. New tools will not get "homo sapiens" out of the very dangerous toolbox the species is, it seems, busily locking itself within. I suspect that the absence of a political theory of new technologies, one that would put human consciousness and agency once again in charge of the toolbox, is partly the result of the current hegemony of globalized capitalism or "free market" ideology and its corollary, the current weakness of international institutions and laws. In *Toward a Rational Society*, first published in German in 1968, Jurgen Habermas wrote: "Our problem can then be stated as one of the relation of technology and democracy: how can the power of technical control be brought within the range of the consensus of acting and transacting citizens?" (57). So far as I am aware, neither Habermas nor anyone else has provided any very satisfactory answers to that question. And such answers are certainly not going to come from crash theory and probably not from the GRAIN scientists. What is wanting in McLuhan, in crash theory, and among the GRAIN scientists is the sociological and political imagination (and, indeed, the will) to avert disaster by ensuring that new technologies contribute to social progress—to peace and plenty for all humanity (and nature)—rather than to "exterminism" and the end of the road for history.

Works Cited

Barney, Darin. *Prometheus Wired: The Hope for Democracy in the Age of Network Technology.* Chicago: University of Chicago Press, 2000.

Baudrillard, Jean. *In the Shadow of the Silent Majorities . . . or the End of the Social.* Tr. Paul Foss, Paul Patton, and John Johnson. New York: Semiotext(e), 1983.

_____. The Masses: The Implosion of the Social in the Media. *Jean Baudrillard: Selected Writings.* Ed. Mark Poster. Stanford: Stanford UP, 1988: 207–219.

_____. *Simulations.* Tr. Paul Foss, Paul Patton and Philip Beitchman. New York: Semiotext(e), 1983.

_____. *The Spirit of Terrorism and Requiem for the Twin Towers.* London: Verso, 2002.

Bauman, Zygmunt. *Globalization: The Human Consequences.* New York: Columbia University Press, 1998.

Bimber, Bruce. Three Faces of Technological Determinism. In Smith and Marx, (Eds.) *Does Technology Drive History?:* 79–100.

Brantlinger, Patrick. *Bread and Circuses: Theories of Mass Culture as Social Decay.* Ithaca: Cornell UP, 1983.

Castells, Manuel. *The Informational City.* Oxford: Basil Blackwell, 1989.

Deleuze, Gilles, and Felix Guattari. *Anti-Oedipus: Capitalism and Schizophrenia.* Minneapolis: U of Minnesota P, 1983.

_____. *A Thousand Plateaus.* Minneapolis: U of Minnesota P, 1987.

Der Derian, James. Introduction. *The Virilio Reader:* 1–15.

Drexler, K. Eric. *Engines of Creatio.* Garden City, NY: Anchor Press/Doubleday, 1986.

Edwards, Steve Alan. Surviving the Singularity. www.members.aol.com/salaned/writings/survive.htm [April 27, 2003].

Eisenstein, Elizabeth L. *The Printing Revolution in Early Modern Europe.* Cambridge: Cambridge UP, Canto Edition, 1993.

Grosswiler, Paul. *Method Is the Message: Rethinking McLuhan through Critical Theory.* Montreal: Black Rose Books, 1998.

Habermas, Jurgen. *Toward a Rational Society: Student Protest, Science, and Politics.* Tr. by Jeremy J. Shapiro. Boston: Beacon, 1971.

Hughes, Thomas P. "Technological Momentum." In Smith and Marx (Eds.) *Does Technology Drive History?:* 101–113.

Joy, Bill. "Why the Future Doesn't Need Us." *Wired.* April, 2000: 238–246.

Kaku, Michio. *Visions: How Science Will Revolutionize the 21st Century.* New York: Random House, 1997.

Kellner, Douglas. *Jean Baudrillard: From Marxism to Postmodernism and Beyond.* Stanford: Stanford UP, 1989.

Kroker, Arthur. *Technology and the Canadian Mind: Innis/McLuhan/Grant.* New York: St. Martin's, 1985.

Kroker, Arthur, and Michael A. Weinstein. *Data Trash: The Theory of the Virtual Class.* New York: St. Martin's, 1994.

Kroker, Arthur, and Marilouise Kroker (Eds.) *Digital Delirium.* New York: St. Martin's, 1997.

Kroker, Arthur, Marilouise Kroker, and David Cook, (Eds.) *Panic Encyclopedia: The Definitive Guide to the Postmodern Scene.* New York: St. Martin's, 1989.

Levinson, Paul. *Digital McLuhan: A Guide to the Information Millennium.* New York: Routledge, 1999.

McLuhan, Marshall. *The Gutenberg Galaxy: The Making of Typographic Man.* U of Toronto P, 1962.
_____. *Understanding Media: The Extensions of Man.* New York: McGraw-Hill, 1965.

May, Christopher. *The Information Society: A Sceptical View.* Cambridge: Polity Press, 2002.

Mulhall, Douglas. *Our Molecular Future: How Nanotechnology, Robotics, Genetics, and Artificial Intelligence Will Transform Our World.* Amherst, NY: Prometheus Books, 2002.

Postman, Neil. Technopoly: *The Surrender of Culture to Technology.* New York: Vintage Books, 1993.

Rosenthal, Raymond, (Ed.) *McLuhan: Pro and Con.* Baltimore: Penguin, 1968.

Roszak, Theodore. *The Cult of Information: The Folklore of Information and the True Art of Thinking.* New York: Pantheon, 1996.

Smith, Merritt Roe, and Leo Marx (Eds.) *Does Technology Drive History? The Dilemma of Technological Determinism.* Cambridge, MA: MIT Press, 1994.
_____. Introduction. *Does Technology Drive History?:* 1–35.

Stamps, Judith. *Unthinking Modernity: Innis, McLuhan, and the Frankfurt School.* Montreal: McGill-Queen's UP, 1995.

Standage, Tom. *The Victorian Internet: The Remarkable Story of the Telegraph and the Nineteenth Century's On-Line Pioneers.* New York: Walker, 1998.

Theall, Donald. *The Virtual Marshall McLuhan.* Montreal: McGill-Queen's UP, 2001.

Vinge, Vernor. The Coming Technological Singularity: How to Survive in the Post-Human Era. Paper presented at the VISION-21 Symposium, March 30–31, 1993. Online: www.rohan.sdsu.edu/ faculty/vinge/misc/singularity.html [July 7, 2001].

Virilio, Paul. *The Art of the Motor.* Tr. Julie Rose. Minneapolis: U of Minnesota P, 1995.
_____. *Ground Zero.* Tr. Chris Turner. London: Verso, 2002.
_____. *The Information Bomb.* Tr. Chris Turner. London: Verso, 2000.
_____. *Open Sky.* Tr. Julie Rose. London: Verso, 1997.
_____. *The Virilio Reader.* Ed. James Der Derian. London: Blackwell, 1998.

Webster, Frank. *Theories of the Information Society.* New York: Routledge, 1995.

Wiener, Norbert. *The Human Use of Human Beings: Cybernetics and Society.* 1950. New York: Avon, 1967.

CHAPTER NINE

Reflections on Modernity and Postmodernity in McLuhan and Baudrillard

DOUGLAS KELLNER

In the 1960s, Marshall McLuhan emerged as a guru of the emergent electronic media culture. His book *Understanding Media* (1964) was celebrated as providing key insights into the role of the media in contemporary society and McLuhan became one of the most discussed and debated theorists of the time. During the 1980s, Jean Baudrillard was promoted in certain circles as the new McLuhan, as the most advanced theorist of the media and society in the so-called postmodern era. His analysis of a new, postmodern society rests on a key assumption that the media, simulations, and what he calls "cyberblitz" constitute a new realm of experience and a new stage of history and type of society.

Both McLuhan and Baudrillard provide provocative theses on the role of the media and new technology in constituting the contemporary world. They provide important and influential models of the media as all-powerful and autonomous social forces that produce a wide range of effects. In this study, I first explicate McLuhan's media theory and how it can be deployed to produce analyses of modernity and postmodernity that connect McLuhan's work with Baudrillard. I then explore how McLuhan's media theory shaped Baudrillard's theory and the similarities and differences in their work. I lay out what I consider the important contributions of their work, but am also concerned to delineate the political implications of their media theory and to point to alternative theoretical and political perspectives on the media and the contemporary moment.

McLuhan, Modernity, and Postmodernity

Marshall McLuhan was acclaimed in the 1960s and 1970s as one of the most influential media theorists of our time and is once again becoming widely discussed and debated in the computer era. His 1960s writings dramatized the importance of television and electronic broadcasting and entertainment media on contemporary society (McLuhan, 1964). The eventual decline of influence of McLuhan's work perhaps resulted in part from his exaggeration of the role of television and electronic culture in effecting a break from the print era and producing a new electronic age. Yet McLuhan in retrospect anticipated the rise and importance of computer culture and the dramatic emergence and effects of personal computers and the Internet that provide even more substance to McLuhan's claim that contemporary society is undergoing a fundamental rupture with the past.

Indeed, McLuhan can be read in the light of classical social theory as a major theorist of modernity, with an original and penetrating analysis of the origins, nature, and trajectory of the modern world. Furthermore, he can be read in retrospect as a major anticipator of theories of a postmodern break, of a rupture with modernity, of leaving behind the previous print-industrial-urban-mechanical era and entering a new postmodern society with novel forms of culture and society. McLuhan's work proposes that a major new medium of communication changes the ratio of the senses, the patterns of everyday life, modes of social interaction and communication, and many other aspects of social and individual life that are often not perceived.

"Understanding media," for McLuhan, therefore, requires understanding the form of the media and its structural effects on the psyche, culture, and social life. McLuhan offers an entire vision of culture and history based on analyses of transitions within stages of history unfolding from one dominant medium of communication to another. He describes the move from an oral culture based on the spoken word to print culture generated by the written word to electronic culture produced by electronic media of communication. Oral culture is highly participatory and involves all the senses. It corresponds for McLuhan to "tribal culture" with fixed roles, relatively stable and unchanging values and institutions, and a highly integrated culture and social order. This stage, roughly extending from premodern times to the Renaissance, is followed by print culture that is based on the written word and is codified in the book.

With the development of the printing press and wide-spread dissemination of the book and print media, a whole new "Gutenberg Galaxy" of cultural forms emerged characterized by detached individualism and the values of logic, rationality, and argumentation; linear modes of thought and social organization; the mechanization of labor and assembly lines; centralized social and economic organization; nationalism and a system of competitive nation states; and highly specialized and fragmented culture.

In McLuhan's thematics, print culture is succeeded by electronic culture and technology. For McLuhan, this era exhibits a new tribalism and play of all the senses in a "global village" where individuals all over the world experience the same events and spectacles and come to share a new media and global consciousness and experience. Fragmentation and alienation of the individual is allegedly overcome in the new tribal culture as individuals deeply participate in media forms and events, generating a new sensibility beyond the abstract individualism and rationalism of the earlier era and the nationalism and xenophobias of the modern era.

McLuhan's analyses of print technology, newspapers, books, roads, modern industry and mechanization, war, and other modern technologies and phenomena all illuminate the constitution of the modern world and provide new insights into modernity. His description of specific technologies and how they produced the modern era and anticipation of how new emergent electronic technologies are fashioning a new postmodern era are often highly illuminating. McLuhan, like Baudrillard, Jameson, and other theorists of the postmodern era, presents an ideal type analysis in which modernity is marked by linearity, differentiation, explosion, centralization, homogenization, hierarchy, fragmentation, and individualism. Postmodernity, by contrast, is marked by implosion or dedifferentiation, decentralization, tribalism, synasthesia, and a new media and computer culture that would be called cyberspace and which would be theorized by Baudrillard and other postmodern theorists (Best and Kellner, 1991, 1997, 2001). McLuhan opens *Understanding Media* writing:

> After three thousand years of explosion, by means of fragmentary and mechanical technologies, the Western world is imploding. During the mechanical ages we had extended our bodies in space. Today, after more than a century of electric technology, we have extended our central nervous system itself in a global embrace, abolishing both space and time as far as our planet is concerned. Rapidly, we approach the final phase of the extensions of man—the technological simulation of consciousness, when the creative process of knowing will be collectively and corporately extended to the whole of human society, much as we have already extended our senses and our nerves by the various media (pp. 3–4).

For McLuhan, the modern era is characterized by an "explosion" of technologies, cities, states and empires, cultural forms, specializations, forms of transportation and communication, and, of course, media. The beginning and generating force of the process was produced by the book and technology of the printing press that made possible individualism with individual subjects reading books silently and cultivating their own subjectivity, as opposed to the rote collectivism of medieval education and religious ceremonies. The book gave rise to national cultures and literatures, breaking with the hegemony of Latin, and the new national states used print technology to generate propaganda and ideology, linear modes of accounting and writing, and the rational organization of production bound up with the rise of capitalism.

In *Understanding Media*, McLuhan presents brilliant insights into specific cultural phenomena and particular media, such as his insight that the linear nature of print technology helped bring about a differentiation of poetry, song, rhetoric, prose, and news at the beginning of the modern era that in turn helped generate societal differentiation, specialized jobs, the modern university, and fragmentation and divisions within culture and society (1964, p. 175). McLuhan notes (p. 81ff) that print technology and the written word was the first mass technology, the first teaching machine, and helped generate modern education, culture, and society. Compared to the Chinese ideogram or medieval illustrated handwritten manuscripts, the book and print technology was highly abstract, linear, and homogenized, helping produce distinctive Western and modern modes of thought.

For McLuhan, "printing from movable types was the first mechanization of a complex handicraft and the archetype of all subsequent mechanization" and helped generate the capitalist mode of production (p. 170ff). In addition, "typography ended parochialism and tribalism, psychically and socially, both in space and time" (p. 170), by enabling and exchange of ideas and cosmopolitanism. Typography made possible detachment and non-involvement, producing rational abstraction and critique, but also fragmentation and specialization (p. 173). Further "correct" spelling, behavior, and thought is a result of mechanization and the linear organization of experience, knowledge, and work, producing a need to be clear and precise (p. 175). Religion too shifted from ritual and literary to proclaiming and assimilating the Word with the mass production of the Bible. Supplementing McLuhan, one might note that Descartes reproduces this structural necessity of typography technology in his grounding of philosophy in "clear and distinct ideas," an orderly progression of thought, and abstract and rational concepts, thus giving rise to a distinctive form of modern Western philosophy.

In McLuhan's thematic, the rise of new media is not an addition, or supplement, to previous media and forms of culture, but an explosive force that competes with other media. McLuhan uses the metaphor of war to describe the process through which print replaced the oral tradition of learning and education, displacing rhetoric for the new regime of reading and writing. Yet while McLuhan provides brilliant insights into the role of the media within modernity and how the media function as key constituents of culture and society, it is probably his notion of a rupture with modernity and advent of a new postmodern era, signaled in the passages quoted above (1964, pp. 3–4), that constitute his most important and provocative insight. I suggested that McLuhan is indeed perhaps more important and relevant today as the theorist of a new mode of culture and history in the contemporary era because television could not really bear the burden of constituting a break in the transition to a new historical era that he postulated. TV was obviously a crucially important medium and had tremendous effects, some of which are not yet apparent, but arguably did not create an entire new culture, sensibility, way of seeing, relating, communicating, and so on (although I would imagine that it had much more significant effects than most people were aware).

Hence, McLuhan arguably exaggerated the role of TV and other forms of electronic communication in the 1960s which could not legitimate his claim that we were moving into a new electronic culture, a new stage of history, and a decisive rupture with the past. More harshly, one could argue that McLuhan's categories were not that useful for theorizing the complexity of television and its imbrication in the economy, politics, and social life. McLuhan's claim that TV was an extension of the central nervous system was opaque and vague; his media hot and cool distinction did not always work well and was hotly contested; his disregard for content short-circuited detailed reading and critique of media content; and his failure to theorize the place of television within the corporate economy was a blind spot. Although one could find insights into all of these thematics in McLuhan, his concepts often blocked developing a critical theory of television that theorized its relations to the economy, state, social institutions, and culture.

But reading McLuhan anew in the context of the computer era enables him to be seen as a prophet of the cyberspace and valuable for anticipating the revolutionary effects of the new computer culture, for providing concepts that help us grasp the enormity of the transition, for focusing attention on how important new media can be, and for helping us understand the transformation going on.

In his book *McLuhan and Baudrillard. The Masters of Implosion* (1999), Gary Genosko writes:

"I consider the McLuhan renaissance to be a result of postmodern theory and the enormously influential role played by French social and cultural theory as it has been, and continues to be, translated into English and disseminated across and beyond the disciplines" (p. 3). I would argue instead that it is the force and significance of computer culture and the ways that McLuhan's concepts articulate its significance and effects that account for the renewed interest in McLuhan. There is, moreover, overlap between computer culture and the theorizing of postmodern theory, as Mark Poster (1995) and Sherry Turkle (1995) have noted. Genosko is also off mark when he claims "McLuhan and Baudrillard are the key thinkers to whom postmodernists turn to situate their deviations from them" (p. 3). As Steven Best and I have argued (1991, 2001, 2007), along with Poster and Turkle, there are many competing key postmodern theorists. McLuhan is often neglected in discussions of postmodern theory, and Baudrillard is often considered an extreme and ultranihilist variant. Levinson, (1999) offers a detailed albeit generally uncritical attempt to demonstrate McLuhan's importance for understanding digital culture.

Presaging the transformative impact of digital culture, McLuhan writes:

> Our new electric technology that extends our sense and nerves in a global embrace has large implications for the future of language. Electric technology does not need words any more than the digital computer needs numbers. Electricity points the way to an extension of the process of consciousness itself, on a world scale, and without any verbalization whatever. Such a state of collective awareness may have been the preverbal condition of men. Language as the technology of human extension, whose powers of division and separation we know so well, may have been the 'Tower of Babel' by which men sought to scale the highest heavens. Today computers hold out the promises of a means of instant translation of any code or language into any other code or language. The computer, in short, promises by technology a Pentecostal condition of universal understanding and unity. The next logical step would seem to be, not to translate, but to by-pass languages in favor of a general cosmic consciousness which might be very like the collective unconscious dreamt of by Bergson. The condition of 'weightlessness,' that biologists say promises a physical immortality, may be paralleled by the condition of speechlessness that could confer a perpetuity of collective harmony and peace (1964, p. 80).

This remarkable passage anticipates the revolutionary effects of the digitization of culture and the new languages of computerization. It points to the rise of artificial intelligence and even the fantasies of immortality through virtualization and cloning that Baudrillard would critically engage time and again. It provides an audacious vision of how computer culture might produce new forms of universal consciousness and global understanding and harmony, exaggerated claims that have been rightly polemicized against but which point to the enormous potential as well as current impact of the computerization of the world.

I will suspend further critique of McLuhan until the end of my discussion of Baudrillard. To set up the encounter between the two: McLuhan presents media and technology as major forces of history and no one has provided more penetrating insights into media and technology and their roles in modern Western society and culture and the transition to a new postmodern era. Indeed, McLuhan not only provides brilliant insights into specific media—the printing press, electric lights, cars, airplanes, highways, radio, television, and so on—but has important general insights into the media, Western modernity, and the broad patterns of historical change in the modern era, as well as insight into the force of new information and communication technology in the passage to a new stage of culture and history. Baudrillard would take up McLuhan's emphasis on the form of the media, his insight into the centrality of media in the contemporary era, his vision of stages of history, his analysis of the emergence of electronic media as the constituent force of a new stage of history, and particular concepts like implosion, as well as McLuhan's method of probes, explorations, fragments, and a mosaic shotgun approach that illustrate general theses and specific phenomenon under investigation.

Baudrillard's Postmodern Media Theory

In 1967, Baudrillard wrote a review of Marshall McLuhan's *Understanding Media* in which he claimed that McLuhan's dictum that the "medium is the message" is "the very formula of alienation in a technical society," and he criticized McLuhan for naturalizing that alienation (Baudrillard, 1967). At this time, he shared the neo-Marxian critique of McLuhan as a technological reductionist and determinist. By the 1970s and 1980s, however, McLuhan's formula that "the medium is the message" eventually became the guiding principle of his own thought.

Baudrillard begins developing his theory of the media in an article "Requiem for the Media" in *For a Critique of the Political Economy of the Sign* (1981). The title is somewhat ironic for Baudrillard is really only beginning to develop theoretical perspectives in which the media will play crucial roles in constituting a new postmodernity. Thus Baudrillard is writing a requiem here for a *Marxist theory of the media*, arguing:

> McLuhan has said, with his usual Canadian-Texan brutalness, that Marx, the spiritual contemporary of the steam engine and railroads, was already obsolete in his lifetime with the appearance of the telegraph. In his candid fashion, he is saying that Marx, in his materialist analysis of production, had virtually circumscribed productive forces as a privileged domain from which language, signs and communication in general found themselves excluded (p. 164).

Baudrillard's critique of Marx here begins a radical interrogation of and eventual break with marxism that would culminate in *The Mirror of Production* (1975). Baudrillard begins distancing himself from marxism in "Requiem for the Media," and in particular attacks Marx's alleged economic reductionism, or "productivism," and the alleged inability of the marxian theory to conceptualize language, signs, and communication. Habermas at the time was developing a parallel position within critical theory (Habermas, 1987, Roderick, 1986).

As an example of the failure of marxian categories to provide an adequate theory of the media, Baudrillard criticizes the German activist and writer Hans Magnus Enzensberger's media theory and his attempts to develop a socialist strategy for the media (Enzensberger, 1974). Baudrillard dismisses this effort as a typ-

ical marxian attempt to liberate productive forces from the fetters of productive relations that fails to see that *in their very form* the mass media of communication:

> are anti-mediatory and intransitive. They fabricate non communication—this is what
> characterizes them, if one agrees to define communication as an exchange, as a recip-
> rocal space of a speech and a response, and thus of a *responsibility* (not a psychological
> or moral responsibility, but a personal, mutual correlation in exchange).... *they are what
> always prevents response,* making all processes of exchange impossible (except in the var-
> ious forms of response *simulation,* themselves integrated in the transmission process,
> thus leaving the unilateral nature of the communication intact). This is the real abstrac-
> tion of the media. And the system of social control and power is rooted in it (1981, pp.
> 169–170).

It is curious that Baudrillard, interpreted by many of his followers as an avant-
garde, postmodern media theorist, manifests in this passage both technophobia and
a nostalgia for face-to-face conversation which he privileges (as authentic communication) over degraded and abstract media communication. Such a position creates a binary dichotomy between "good" face-to-face communication and "bad"
media communication, and occludes the fact that interpersonal communication can
be just as manipulative, distorted, reified, and so on, as media communication (as
Ionesco and Habermas, among others, were aware). Denouncing the media *tout court*
in a Baudrillardian fashion rules out in advance the possibility of "responsible" or
"emancipatory" media communication, and indeed Baudrillard frequently argues that
there can be no good use of media.

Thus Baudrillard presents a rather extreme variant of a negative model of the
media that sees mass media and culture simply as instruments of domination,
manipulation, and social control in which radical intervention and radical media or
cultural politics are impossible. He shares a certain theoretical terrain on theories
of the media with The Frankfurt school, many Althusserians and other French radicals, and those who see electronic media, broadcasting, and mass culture simply as
a terrain of pure domination (Kellner, 1989a). Hence, Baudrillard's generally negative and dismissive attitude toward the media could be contrasted with McLuhan's
more "neutral" stance. Yet following McLuhan's analysis of the centrality of television in contemporary culture, Baudrillard noted how the "TV Object" was becoming the center of the household and was serving an essential "proof function" that
the owner was a genuine member of the consumer society (1981, p. 53ff.). The accelerating role of the media in contemporary society becomes for Baudrillard equivalent to THE FALL into the postmodern society of simulations from the modern
universe of production. Modernity for Baudrillard is the era of production characterized by the rise of industrial capitalism and the hegemony of the bourgeoisie while
postmodern society is an era of simulation dominated by signs, codes, and models.

Modernity thus centered on the production of things—commodities and products—while postmodernity in his optic is characterized by radical semiurgy, by a proliferation of signs, spectacle, information, and new media.

Furthermore, following McLuhan, Baudrillard interprets modernity as a process of explosion of commodification, mechanization, technology, and market relations, while postmodern society is the site of an implosion of all boundaries, regions, and distinctions between high and low culture, appearance and reality, and just about every other binary opposition maintained by traditional philosophy and social theory. Furthermore, while modernity could be characterized as a process of increasing differentiation of spheres of life—as Habermas (1987) interprets Max Weber—postmodernity could be interpreted as a process of de-differentiation and attendant implosion.

The rise of the broadcast media, especially television, is an important constituent of postmodernity for Baudrillard, along with the rapid dissemination of signs and simulacra in every realm of social and everyday life. By the late 1970s, Baudrillard interprets the media as key simulation machines which reproduce images, signs, and codes, constituting an autonomous realm of (hyper)reality that plays a key role in everyday life and the obliteration of the social. "Simulation" for Baudrillard denotes a situation in which codes, models, and signs are the organizing forms of a new social order where simulation rules.

In *Simulacra and Simulations*, Baudrillard writes:

> To dissimulate is to feign not to have what one has. To simulate is to feign to have what one hasn't. One implies a presence, the other an absence. But the matter is more complicated, since to simulate is not simply to feign: 'Someone who feigns an illness can simply go to bed and pretend he is ill. Someone who simulates an illness produces in himself some of the symptoms' (Littre). Thus, feigning or dissimulating leaves the reality principle intact: the difference is always clear, it is only masked; whereas simulation threatens the difference between 'true' and 'false,' between 'real' and 'imaginary.' Since the simulator produces 'true' symptoms, is he or she ill or not? The simulator cannot be treated objectively either as ill, or as not ill. (1994, 3).

In the society of simulation, identities are constructed by the appropriation of images, and codes and models determine how individuals perceive themselves and relate to other people. Economics, politics, social life, and culture are all governed by the mode of simulation, whereby codes and models determine how goods are consumed and used, politics unfold, culture is produced and consumed, and everyday life is lived.

In addition, his postmodern universe is one of hyperreality in which entertainment, information, and communication technologies provide experiences more intense and involving than the scenes of banal everyday life, as well as the codes and models that structure social interaction. The realm of the hyperreal (i.e., media simulations of reality, Disneyland and amusement parks, malls and consumer fantasylands, TV sports, and other excursions into ideal worlds) is more real than real, whereby the models, images, and codes of the hyperreal come to control thought and behavior. Yet determination itself is aleatory in a non-linear world where it is impossible to chart causal mechanisms in a situation in which individuals are confronted with an overwhelming flux of images, codes, and models, any of which may shape an individual's thought or behavior.

In this postmodern world, individuals flee from the "desert of the real" for the ecstasies of hyperreality and the new realm of computer, media, and technological experience. Baudrillard's analyses of simulations and hyperreality constitute his major contributions to social theory and media critique. During an era when movie actors and toxic Texans simulate politics and charlatans simulate TV-religion, the category of simulation provides an essential instrument of radical social critique, while the concept of hyperreality is also an extremely useful instrument of social analysis for a media, cybernetic, and information society.

Baudrillard's analyses point to a significant reversal of the relation between representation and reality. Previously, the media were believed to mirror, reflect, or represent reality, whereas now the media are coming to constitute a hyperreality, a new media reality—"more real than real"—where "the real" is subordinate to representation leading to an ultimate dissolving of the real. Interestingly, the concept of reversal is also a major notion in McLuhan's theoretical arsenal that Baudrillard makes his own. For McLuhan, in a discussion of "Reversal of the Overheated Medium," "the stepping-up of speed from the mechanical to the instant electric form reverses explosion into implosion" (1964, p. 35). This is, of course, the very formula that Baudrillard adopts to describe the contemporary situation of the implosion of culture in the media.

In his article "The Implosion of Meaning in the Media," Baudrillard claims that the proliferation of signs and information in the media obliterates meaning through neutralizing and dissolving all content—a process which leads both to a collapse of meaning and the destruction of distinctions between media and reality. In a society supposedly saturated with media messages, information and meaning "implode," collapsing into meaningless "noise," pure effect without content or meaning. Thus, for Baudrillard: "information is directly destructive of meaning and signification, or neutralizes it. The loss of meaning is directly linked to the dissolving and dissuasive action of information, the media, and the mass media. . . . Information devours its own contents; it devours communication and the social. . . . information dissolves meaning and the social into a sort of nebulous state leading not at all to a surfeit of innovation but to the very contrary, to total entropy" (1983a, pp. 96–100).

Baudrillard thus follows McLuhan in making "implosion" a key constituent of contemporary postmodern society, in which social classes, genders, political differences, and once autonomous realms of society and culture collapse into each other, erasing previously defined boundaries and differences. In Baudrillard's society of simulation, the realms of economics, politics, culture, sexuality, and the social all implode into each other. In this implosive mix, economics is fundamentally shaped by culture, politics, and other spheres, while art, once a sphere of potential difference and opposition, is absorbed into the economic and political, while sexuality is everywhere. In this situation, differences between individuals and groups implode in a rapidly mutating dissolution of the social and the previous boundaries and structures upon which social theory had once articulated and critically interpreted.

Like McLuhan's stages of history, Baudrillard offers an analysis of the stages of simulacra. In a study of "Simulacra and Science Fiction," Baudrillard offers a summary of his theory, delineated in detail and with copious examples in *Simulations*:

> Three orders of simulacra: Simulacra that are natural, naturalist, founded on the image, on imitation and counterfeit, that are harmonious, optimistic, and that aim for the restitution or the ideal institution of nature made in God's image;

> Simulacra that are productive, productivist, founded in energy, forces, its materialization by the machine and in the whole system of production—a Promethean aim of a continuous globalization and expansion, of an indefinite liberation of energy (desire belongs to the utopias related to this order of simulacra);

> Simulacra of simulation, founded on information, the model, the cybernetic game— total operationality, hyperreality, aim of total control (1994, p. 121).

Baudrillard's first stage relates to McLuhan's premodern society where words corresponded to things and there was a natural harmony between individuals, culture, and the world. The second stage refers to modernity and the production of a society in which there was a proliferation of commodities, images, and ideas, expanded globally, producing conflicts of ideas and culture, with debates over relations between concepts and the world, theory and reality. In the third stage of simulation, there is an operational order, like McLuhan's global system, that is functional and operational, with a hyperreal computer and media system that seamlessly forms a realm of simulation that models everyday life and eventually absorbs its energy, power, and control. In this stage, the media overpower everyday life and unlike McLuhan's more beneficent vision, create information overload, meaninglessness, and the collapse of distinctions between the virtual and the real.

Baudrillard presents a vision of the media as a black hole of signs and information which absorb all contents into cybernetic noise which no longer communicates meaningful messages in a process of implosion where all content implodes into form. While McLuhan claims to present a "neutral" portrayal of the media in contemporary society, which was read by some as a celebration, Baudrillard has a more neg-ative optic on the media. Yet Baudrillard eventually adopts a key postulate of McLuhan's media theory as his own, claiming that:

> *the medium is the message* signifies not only the end of the message, but also the end of the medium. There are no longer media in the literal sense of the term (I am talking above all about the electronic mass media)—that is to say, a power mediating between one reality and another, between one state of the real and another—neither in content nor in form. Strictly speaking this is what implosion signifies: the absorption of one pole into another, the short-circuit between poles of every differential system of meaning, the effacement of terms and of distinct oppositions, and thus that of the medium and the real. Hence the impossibility of any mediation, of any dialectical intervention between the two or from one to the other, circularity of all media effects. Hence the impossibility of a sense (meaning), in the literal sense of a unilateral vector which leads from one pole to another. This critical—but original—situation must be thought through to the very end; it is the only one we are left with. It is useless to dream of a revolution through content or through form, since the medium and the real are now in a single nebulous state whose truth is undecipherable (1983a, pp. 102–103).

Baudrillard argues that the media and "reality" implode such that it is impos-sible to distinguish between media representations and the "reality" which they sup-posedly represent. He also suggests that the media intensify massification by producing mass audiences and massification of ideas and experience. On the other hand, he claims that the masses absorb all media content, neutralize, or even resist, meaning, and demand and obtain more spectacle and entertainment, thus further eroding the boundary between media and "the real." In this sense, the media implode into the masses to an extent that it is unknowable what effects the media have on the masses and how the masses process the media.

Consequently, on this view, the media pander to the masses, reproducing their taste, their interest in spectacle and entertainment, their fantasies and way of life, producing an implosion between mass consciousness and media phantasmagoria. In this way, Baudrillard short-circuits the manipulation theory that sees media manipulation imposed from above producing mass consciousness, yet he seems to share the contempt for the masses in standard manipulation theory claiming that they want nothing more than spectacle, diversion, entertainment and escape, and are incapable of, or uninterested in, producing meaning.

For Baudrillard, since the media and the masses liquidate meaning, it is mean-ingless to carry out ideological critiques of media messages since the "medium is the message" in the sense that media communication has no significant referents except its own images and noise which ceaselessly refer back and forth to other media images and spectacles. In *On Seduction* (1979), Baudrillard utilizes McLuhan's distinction between "hot" and "cool" media to describe the ways that media devour information and exterminate meaning. According to Baudrillard, the media take "hot" events like sports, wars, political turmoil, catastrophes, and so on and transform them into "cool" media events, which he interprets as altogether another kind of phenomena and experience. Concerning the difference between a televised and attended sports event, Baudrillard writes:

> Do not believe that it is a matter of the same game: one is hot, the other is cool—one is a contest where affect, challenge, mise en scene, and spectacle are present, whereas the other is tactile, modulated (visions in flash-back, replays, close-ups or overhead views, various angles, etc.): a televised sports event is above all a televised event, just as *Holocaust* or the Vietnam war are televised events of which one can hardly make distinctions (1979, p. 217).

For Baudrillard, eventually, all the dominant media become "cool," erasing McLuhan's (problematical) distinction between hot and cool media. That is, for Baudrillard all the media of information and communication neutralize meaning and involve the audience in a flat, one-dimensional media experience which he defines in terms of a passive absorption of images, or a resistance of meaning, rather than the active processing or production of meaning. The electronic media, therefore, on this account have nothing to do with myth, image, history, or the construction of meaning (or ideology). Television is interpreted instead as a media "which suggests nothing, which magnetises, which is only a screen, or is rather a miniaturized terminal which in fact is found immediately in your head—you are the screen and the television is watching you. Television transistorizes all neurons and operates as a magnetic tape—a tape not an image" (1979, p. 220).

Baudrillard, McLuhan and the Ecstasy of Communication

We see here how Baudrillard out-McLuhans McLuhan in interpreting television, and all other media, primarily as machines which produce primarily technological effects in which content and messages, or social uses, are deemed irrelevant and unimportant. We also see how, like McLuhan, he anthropomorphizes the media ("the television is watching you"), a form of technological mysticism (or mystification) as extreme as McLuhan. Like McLuhan, Baudrillard also globalizes media effects making the media demiurges of a new type of society and new type of experience.

Baudrillard practices as well McLuhan's method of probes and mosaic constellations of images and concepts that take on an experimental and provisional nature. Consequently, whereas he sets forth theoretically articulated theses about the media in "Requiem," in his studies of simulations and later writings he tends to cluster images, concepts, and descriptive analyses, within which media often play a key role, rather than systematically articulating a well-defined theoretical position, thus adopting a key McLuhanite literary strategy.

Like McLuhan, Baudrillard's work is implosive, breaking disciplinary boundaries and bringing together material from a variety of disciplines. Over the decades, Baudrillard's style in some ways is more and more McLuhanesque, deploying short essays to provide constellations of ideas, images, stories, quotations, and references to contemporary events to capture the novelty and significance of contemporary events. Like McLuhan, Baudrillard likes to shock and be irrelevant, developing witty puns, paradoxes, and provocations to stir up his readers. Baudrillard sees the "symbolic" as the only refuge of critical thought and only source of alternatives to the operational world of postmodernity, while McLuhan sees artists as the "antennae" of society, with their work constituting "distant early warning" (DEW) systems that provide forecasts of coming events and register changes in society and culture, with art providing counter-environments that provide insight into the contemporary era (1964, p. 65ff).

Yet, in terms of their specific perspectives on the media, we might contrast McLuhan's ecumenical Catholicism with Baudrillard's somewhat puritanical Protestantism (Fekete, 1973, Genosko, 1999, Kroker, 1984). McLuhan fantasized a new type of global community and even a new universal (media) consciousness and experience through the dissemination of a global media system, the global village. McLuhan also believed that the media could overcome alienation produced by the abstract rationality of book culture that was being replaced by a new synaesthesia and harmonizing of the mind and body, the senses and technologies. Baudrillard, by contrast, sees the media as external demigods, or idols of the mind— to continue the Protestant metaphor—, which seduce and fascinate the subject and which enter subjectivity to produce a reified consciousness and privatized and fragmented life-style (Sartre's seriality).

Thus, while McLuhan ascribes a generally benign social destiny to the media, for Baudrillard the function of TV and mass media is to prevent response, to isolate and privatize individuals, and to trap them into a universe of simulacra where it is impossible to distinguish between the spectacle and the real, and where individuals come to prefer spectacle over "reality" (which both loses interest for the masses and its privileged status in philosophy and social theory).

The mass media are instruments for Baudrillard of a "cold seduction" whose narcissistic charm consists of a manipulative self-seduction in which spectators enjoy the play of lights, shadows, dots, and events in our own mind as we change channels or media and plug into the variety of networks—media, computer, information—that surround us and that allow us to become modulators and controllers of an overwhelming panoply of sights, sounds, information, and events. In this sense, all media have a chilling effect (which is why Baudrillard allows McLuhan's "cool" to become downright "cold") that freeze individuals into functioning as terminals of media and communication networks who become involved as part and parcel of the very apparatus of communication. The subject, then, becomes transformed into an object as part of a nexus of information and communication networks.

The interiorization of media transmissions within the screen of our mind obliterates, for Baudrillard, the distinction between public and private, interior and exterior space—both of which are replaced by media space. Here Baudrillard inverts McLuhan's thesis concerning the media as extensions of the human, as exteriorizations of human powers, and argues instead that humans internalize media and thus become terminals within media systems—a new theoretical anti-humanism that might amuse Louis Althusser. The eye and the brain, on this model, replaces both the other sense organs and the hand as key instruments of human practice, as information processing replaces human practice and techne and poiesis alike.

In "The Ecstasy of Communication," Baudrillard (1983b) describes the media as instruments of obscenity, transparency, and ecstasy—in special sense of these terms. He claims that in the postmodern mediascape, the domestic scene—or the private sphere per se—with its rules, rituals, and privacy is exteriorized, or made explicit and transparent, "in a sort of *obscenity* where the most intimate processes of our life become the virtual feeding ground of the media (the Loud family in the United States, the innumerable slices of peasant or patriarchal life on French television). Inversely, the entire universe comes to unfold arbitrarily on your domestic screen (all the useless information that comes to you from the entire world, like a microscopic pornography of the universe, useless, excessive, just like the sexual close-up in a porno film): all this explodes the scene formerly preserved by the minimal separation of public and private, the scene that was played out in a restricted space" (p. 130).

One of Baudrillard's examples above, the Loud family, refers to an actual family's portrayal in a 1970s Public Broadcasting System (PBS) documentary series that anticipated reality TV; during the filming of the series, one of the sons came out as gay and the parents split up.

In addition, the spectacles of the consumer society and the dramas of the public sphere are also being replaced by media events that replace public life and scenes with a screen that shows us everything instantaneously and without scruple or hesitation: "Obscenity begins precisely when there is no more spectacle, no more scene, when all becomes transparence and immediate visibility, when everything is exposed to the harsh and inexorable light of information and communication" (p. 130). The ecstasy of communication: everything is explicit, ecstatic (out of or beyond itself), and obscene in its transparency, detail, and visibility: "It is no longer the traditional obscenity of what is hidden, repressed, forbidden or obscure; on the contrary, it is the obscenity of the visible, of the all-too-visible, of the more-visible-than-visible. It is the obscenity of what no longer has any secret, of what dissolves completely in information and communication" (p. 131). One thinks here of such 1980s US media obscenity concerning the trials and tribulations of Gary Hart and Donna Rice, of Jim Bakker and Jimmy Swaggart, of Ron and Nancy Reagans' cancer operations and astrology games, or the sleazy business deals of his associates, and the dirty transactions of Iran/Contra,—all of which have been exposed to the glaring scrutiny of the media in which what used to be private, hidden, and invisible suddenly becomes (almost) fully explicit and visible.

The 1990s saw an intensification of the ecstasy of communication with the Clinton sex scandals that displayed intimate details of his private life, the O.J. Simpson trial that depicted the minutiae of his tormented relation with his murdered wife Nicole, and countless other revelations of private affairs of the powerful and infamous in an increasingly tabloid infotainment culture (Kellner, 2003b). In the "ecstasy of communication," everything becomes transparent, and there are no more secrets, scenes, privacy, depth or hidden meaning. Instead a promiscuity of information and communication unfolds in which the media circulate and disseminate a teeming network of cool, seductive and fascinating sights and sounds to be played on one's own screen and terminal. With the disappearance of exciting scenes (in the home, in the public sphere), passion evaporates in personal and social relations, yet a new fascination emerges ("the scene excites us, the obscene fascinates us") with the very universe of media and communication. In this universe we enter a new form of subjectivity where we become saturated with information, images, events, and ecstasies. Without defense or distance, we become "a pure screen, a switching center for all the networks of influence" (p. 133). In the media society, the era of interiority, subjectivity, meaning, privacy, and the inner life is over; a new era of obscenity, fascination, vertigo, instantaneity, transparency and overexposure begins: Welcome to the postmodern world!

In his post-1980 writings, Baudrillard continues to call attention to McLuhan as the great media theorist of our epoch and continues to subscribe to the positions that I explicated above, though occasionally he goes even further in denying that the media are producers of meaning, or that the media content or apparatus is important. In Baudrillard's later writings, the "information society" produces noise and an acceleration of meaninglessness, implosion flips into a new realm of virtuality, and reality itself disappears in what Baudrillard calls the "perfect crime." Baudrillard continues to see the media, and especially television and computers, as producing a proliferation of information that erases meaning and further eroding distinctions between the media and the real (Kellner 1989b, 2004). What, then, does Baudrillard contribute to our understanding of the media in the contemporary moment and what problems are there with his perspectives?

Limitations of McLuhan's and Baudrillard's Media Theory

Undoubtedly, the media are playing an ever greater role in our personal and social lives, and have dramatically transformed the contemporary economy, polity, and society in ways that we are only now becoming aware of. Living within a great transformation, perhaps as significant as the transformation from feudalism to industrial capitalism, we are engaged in a process of dramatic mutation, which theorists are barely beginning to understand, as global societies enter the emergent world of media saturation, computerization, proliferating technologies, and novel discourses. Baudrillard's contribution lies in his calling attention to these novelties and transformations and providing original and innovative concepts and theories to understand them.

Yet in many ways Baudrillard follows McLuhan in envisioning the centrality of the media and technology in contemporary society and in some ways their theories share certain insight and blindness. While both brilliantly see the power and importance of new media and the impact of the very forms of media in terms of profoundly altering life, there are questions concerning whether their theories provide adequate concepts to analyze the complex interactions between media, culture, and society today. In this section, I suggest that Baudrillard's media theory is vitiated by *three subordinations* which undermine its theoretical and political usefulness and which raise questions as well about the status of his version of postmodern social theory. I argue that the limitations in Baudrillard's theory can be related to his uncritical assumption of certain positions within McLuhan's and that, therefore, earlier critiques of McLuhan can accurately and usefully be applied to Baudrillard. This critique will suggest that indeed Baudrillard is a "new McLuhan" who has repackaged McLuhan into new postmodern cultural capital.

My reading and critique of McLuhan and Baudrillard have been influenced by the work of Fekete (1973) and Kroker (1984). While Genosko (1999) is correct that the above authors have influenced my readings of Baudrillard and McLuhan, I am not claiming that "semiurgy" and "television" are "evil" (pp. 67f). Rather, I have always seen the media as a contested terrain, and unlike Baudrillard, who sees no good use of the media, I have been involved in the alternative media movement for decades and even had a public access TV show in Austin, Texas, for 18 years. In the passages discussed by Genosko, I am explicating Baudrillard's position, not indicating my own. Interestingly, in the light of the primacy of the concept of "evil" in the later Baudrillard, one could argue that Baudrillard himself does ascribe demonic force and power to the media that he puts on the side of "evil." I would myself avoid such moralistic concepts unless I was describing the Bush administration.

In the first of the three subordinations I have identified, which might be called a *formalist subordination*, Baudrillard, like McLuhan, privileges the form of media technology over what might be called the media apparatus, and thus subordinates content, meaning, and the use of media to its purely formal structure and effects. Baudrillard—much more so than McLuhan who at least gives some media history and analysis of the media environment—tends to abstract media form and effects from the media environment and thus erases political economy, media production, and media environment (i.e. society at large) from his theory. Against abstracting media form and effects from context, the use and effects of media should be carefully examined and evaluated in terms of specific contexts. Distinctions between context and use, form and content, media and reality, all dissolve, however, in Baudrillard's one-dimensional theory where global theses and glib pronouncements replace careful analysis and critique.

Baudrillard might retort that it is the media themselves which abstract from the concreteness of everyday, social, and political life and provide abstract simulacra of actual events which themselves become more real than "the real," that they supposedly represent. Yet even if this is so, media analysis should attempt to recontextualize media images and simulacra rather than merely focusing on the surface of media form. Furthermore, instead of operating with a model of (formal) media effects, it is preferable to operate with a dialectical perspective which posits multiple roles and functions to television and other media.

Another problem is that Baudrillard's formalism vitiates the project of ideology critique, and against his claims that media content are irrelevant and unimportant, one should see the importance of grasping the dialectic of form and content in media communication, seeing how media forms constitute content and how content is always formed or structured, while forms themselves can be ideological, as when the situation-comedy form of conflict/resolution projects an ideological vision which shows all problems easily capable of being resolved within the existing society, or when action-adventure series formats of violent conflict as the essence of reality project a conservative view of human life as a battleground where only the fittest survive and prosper (Kellner 1979, 1980). For a dialectical theory of the media, television would have multiple functions (and potential decodings) where sometimes the ideological effects may be predominant while at other times a medium like television functions as mere noise or through the merely formal effects which Baudrillard puts at the center of his analysis.

Consequently, there is no real theory or practice of cultural interpretation in Baudrillard's media (increasingly anti-)theory, which also emanates an anti-hermeneutical bias that denies the importance of content and is against interpretation (Best and Kellner 1987). This brings us to a second subordination in Baudrillard's theory in which a more dialectical position is subordinated to *media essentialism and technological determinism*. For—according to Baudrillard—it is the technology of, say, television that determines its effects (one-way transmission, semiurgy, implosion, extermination of meaning and the social) rather than any particular content or message (i.e., for both Baudrillard and McLuhan "the medium is the message"), or its construction or use within specific social systems. For Baudrillard, media technology and semiurgy are the demiurges of media practices and effects, separated from their uses by specific economic and political interests, individuals and groups, and the social systems within which they function. Baudrillard thus abstracts media from social systems and essentializes media technology as dominant social forces. Yet against Baudrillard, one could argue that capital continues to be a primary determinant of media form and content in neo-capitalist societies just as state socialism helps determine the form, nature, and effects of technologies in certain socialist societies.

Baudrillard, like McLuhan, often makes essentializing distinctions between media like television or film, ascribing a particular essence to one, and an opposed essence to the other. Yet it seems highly problematical to reduce apparatuses as complex, contradictory, and many-sided as television (or film or any mass medium) to its formal properties and effects, or to a technological essence. It is, therefore, preferable, for theories of media in the capitalist societies, to see the media as syntheses of technology and capital, as technologies which serve specific interests and which have specific political and economic effects (rather than merely technological ones). It is also preferable to see the dialectic between media and society in specific historical conjunctures, to see how social content, trends, and imperatives help constitute the media which in turn influence social developments and help constitute social reality.

For Baudrillard, by contrast, the media today simply constitute a simulated, hyperreal, and obscene (in his technical sense) world(view), and a dialectic of media and society is shortcircuited in a new version of technological determinism. The political implications of this analysis are that constituting alternative media, or alternative uses or forms of existing media, is useless or worse because media in their very essence militate against emancipatory politics or any project of social transforma-

tion. Such cynical views, however, primarily benefit conservative forces who presently control the media in their own interests—a point to which I shall soon return.

Thirdly, there is a subordination of cultural interpretation and politics in
Baudrillard to what might very loosely be called "theory"—thus constituting a *the-
oricist subordination* in Baudrillard. In other words, just as Louis Althusser subordinated concrete empirical and historical analysis to what he called "theoretical
practice"—and thus was criticized for "theoreticism,"—Baudrillard also rarely
engages in close analysis or readings of media texts, and instead simply engages in
abstract theoretical ruminations. Here, his arm-chair or TV screen theorizing might
be compared with Foucault's or Virilio's archival theorizing, or to more detailed and
systematic media theory and critique, much to, I'm afraid, Baudrillard's detriment.

Baudrillard also rigorously avoids the messy but important terrain of cultural
and media politics. There is nothing concerning alternative media practices, for
instance, in his theorizing, which he seems to rule out in advance because in his view
all media are mere producers of noise, non-communication, the extermination of
meaning, implosion, and so on. In "Requiem for the Media," Baudrillard explicitly argues that all mass media communication falls prey to "mass mediatization," that
is, "the imposition of models":

> In fact, the essential Medium is the Model. What is mediatized is not what comes off
> the daily press, out of the tube, or on the radio: it is what is reinterpreted by the sign
> form, articulated into models, and administered by the code (just as the commodity is
> not what is produced industrially, but what is mediatized by the exchange value system
> of abstraction) (1981, pp. 175–176).

All "subversive communication," then, for Baudrillard has to surpass the codes
and models of media communication—and thus of the mass media themselves
which invariably translate all contents and messages into their codes. Consequently,
not only general elections but general strikes have "become a schematic reducing
agent" (p. 176). In this (original) situation: "The real revolutionary media during
May (1968) were the walls and their speech, the silk-screen posters and the hand-
painted notices, the street where speech began and was exchanged—everything that
was an *immediate* inscription, given and returned, spoken and answered, mobile in
the same space and time, reciprocal and antagonistic. The street is, in this sense, the
alternative and subversive form of the mass media, since it isn't, like the latter, an
objectified support for answerless messages, a transmission system at a distance. It
is the frayed space of the symbolic exchange of speech—ephemeral, mortal: a
speech that is not reflected on the Platonic screen of the media. Institutionalized
by reproduction, reduced to a spectacle, this speech is expiring" (pp. 176–177).

In this text, Baudrillard conflates all previously revolutionary strategies and models of "subversive communication" to "schematic reducing agents" and manifests here once again a nostalgia for direct, unmediated, and reciprocal speech ("symbolic exchange") which is denied in the media society. Haunted by a disappearing metaphysics of presence, Baudrillard valorizes immediate communication over mediated communication thus forgetting that all communication is mediated (through language, through signs, through codes, etc.). Furthermore, he romanticizes a certain form of communication (speech in the streets) as the only genuinely subversive or revolutionary communication and media. Consistently with this theory, he thus calls for a (neo-Luddite) "deconstruction" of the media "as systems of non-communication," and thus for the "liquidation of the existing functional and technical structure of the media" (p. 177).

Against Baudrillard's utopia of immediate speech—which he himself abandons in his 1980s writings—, I would defend the project of structural and technical refunctioning of the media as suggested earlier by Brecht, Benjamin, and Enzensberger. Baudrillard, by contrast, not only attacks all forms of media communication as non-revolutionary, but eventually, by the late 1970s, he surrenders his commitment to revolutionary theory and drops the notion of revolutionary communication or subversive cultural practices altogether. Moreover, Baudrillard becomes a bit testy and even nasty in his later writing when considering alternative media. In a symptomatic passage in "The Ecstasy of Communication," Baudrillard writes:

> the promiscuity [note the moralizing coding here—D.K.] that reigns over the communication networks is one of superficial saturation, of an incessant solicitation, of an extermination of interstitial and protective spaces. I pick up my telephone receiver and it's all there; the whole marginal network catches and harasses me with the insupportable good faith of everything that wants and claims to communicate. Free radio: it speaks, it sings, it expresses itself. Very well, *it* is the sympathetic obscenity of its content. In terms a little different for each medium, this is the result: a space, that of the FM band, is found to be saturated ....Speech is free perhaps, but I am less free than before: I no longer succeed in knowing what I want, the space is so saturated, the pressure so great from all who want to make themselves heard. I fall into the negative ecstasy of the radio (1983c, pp. 131–132).

Against this snide and glib put-down of alternative media, I would argue that alternative television, radio, film, and now Internet movements provide possibilities of another type of media with different forms, content, goals, and effects from mainstream media (Kellner 1985, 1990, 2003a; Best and Kellner, 1988; Kahn and Kellner, 2004). A radical media project would thus attempt to transform both the form and the content of the media, as well as their organization and social functions. In a genuinely democratic society, mass media would be part of a communal public sphere and alternative media would be made accessible to all groups and individuals who wished to participate in media communication. This would presuppose dramatic expansion of media access and thus of media systems which would require more channels, technology, and a social commitment to democratic communication.

To preserve its autonomy, alternative television systems could be state funded but not controlled—much like television in several European countries, while public access television and community radio could provide more local programming. Eventually, all of this will be available on the Internet which proliferates the possibilities for alternative media tremendously. An alternative media system would provide the possibility for oppositional, counterhegemonic subcultures and groups to produce programs expressing their own views, oppositions, and struggles that resist the massification, homogenization, and passivity that Baudrillard and others attribute to the media. Alternative media allow marginal and oppositional voices to contest the view of the world, values, and life-styles of the mainstream, and make possible the circulation and growth of alternative subcultures and communities. Baudrillard's theoreticism, however, eschews cultural practice and becomes more and more divorced from the political struggles and issues of the day—though the question of Baudrillard's politics would take another long and very tortured paper to deal with. Reflecting briefly on Baudrillard's media theory leads me to conclude that his media theory is rather impoverished qua media theory and reproduces the limitations of McLuhan's media theory: formalism, technological determinism, and essentialism. John Fekete's critique of McLuhan might profitably be applied to Baudrillard, as might some of the other criticisms of McLuhan once in fashion which may need to be recycled a second time for the new McLuhan(acy). The theory of autonomous media also returns with Baudrillard; thus the critiques of autonomous technology can usefully and relevantly be applied to Baudrillard, and, more generally to certain forms of postmodern social theory (Fekete, 1973; Winner, 1977).

While both McLuhan and Baudrillard are important in calling attention to the power of the media in contemporary society, the question arises as to whether an implosive theory that collapses the boundaries of previous social theory is in a position to carefully and rigorously work out the complex relations and contradictions between the media, economy, state, culture and society. McLuhan and Baudrillard thus challenge us to develop critical theories of the media that build on their insights and overcome their limitations. McLuhan and Baudrillard are extremely valuable in calling attention to the centrality of the media in contemporary society and provide important insight and tools to further advance our understanding of media but more work remains to be done.

References

Baudrillard, J. (1967). Review of *Understanding media. L'Homme Et La Societe*, (5), 277.

Baudrillard, J. (1975). *The mirror of production*. St. Louis, MO: Telos Press.

Baudrillard, J. (1979). *De la seduction*. Paris: Galilee.

Baudrillard, J. (1981). *For a critique of the political economy of the sign*. St. Louis, MO: Telos Press.

Baudrillard, J. (1983a). *In the shadows of the silent majorities*. New York: Semiotext(e).

Baudrillard, J. (1983b). *Simulations* (P. Foss, P. Patton & P. Beitchman, Trans.). New York: Semiotext(e).

Baudrillard, J. (1983c). The ecstasy of communication. In H. Foster (Ed.), *The anti-aesthetic: Essays on postmodern culture* (pp. 126–134). Port Washington, NY: New Press.

Baudrillard, J. (1994). *Simulacra and simulation*. Ann Arbor, MI: University of Michigan Press.

Best, S., & Kellner, D. (1987). (Re)watching television: Notes toward a political criticism. *Diacritics*, , 97–113.

Best, S., & Kellner, D. (1988). Watching television: The limitations of post-modernism. *Science as Culture*, 4, 44–70.

Best, S., & Kellner, D. (1991). *Postmodern theory: Critical interrogations*. New York: Guilford Press.

Best, S., & Kellner, D. (1997). *The postmodern turn*. New York: Guilford Press.

Best, S., & Kellner, D. (2001). *The postmodern adventure*. New York: Guilford Press.

Enzensberger, H. M. (1974). *The consciousness industry*. New York: Seabury.

Fekete, J. (1973). McLuhanacy: Counterrevolution in cultural theory. *Telos*, 5, 75–123.

Genosko, G. (1999). *McLuhan and Baudrillard: The masters of implosion*. New York: Routledge.

Habermas, J. (1987). *The philosophical discourse of modernity*. Cambridge, MA: MIT Press.

Kahn, R., & Kellner, D. (2004). Virtually democratic: Online communities and Internet activism. In A. Feenberg & D. Barney (Eds.), *Community in the digital age: Philosophy and practice* (pp. 183–200). Lanham, MD: Rowman and Littlefield

Kellner, D. (1979). TV, ideology and emancipatory popular culture. *Socialist Review*, 42, 13–53.

Kellner, D. (1980). Television images, codes, and messages. *Televisions*, 7(4), 2–19.

Kellner, D. (1985). Public access television: Alternative views. *Radical Science Journal, 16, Making Waves*, 79–92.

Kellner, D. (1989a). *Critical theory, Marxism, and modernity*. Baltimore: Johns Hopkins University Press.

Kellner, D. (1989b). *Jean Baudrillard: From Marxism to postmodernism and beyond*. Stanford, CA: Stanford University Press.

Kellner, D. (1989c). Resurrecting McLuhan? Jean Baudrillard and the academy of postmodernism. In M. Raboy & P. A. Bruck (Eds.), *Communication for and against democracy* (pp. 131–146). Montreal: Black Rose Books.

Kellner, D. (1990). *Television and the crisis of democracy*. Boulder, CO: Westview Press.

Kellner, D. (2003a). Globalization, technopolitics, and revolution. In J. Foran (Ed.), *The future of revolutions: Rethinking radical change in the age of globalization* (pp. 180–194). London: Zed Books.

Kellner, D. (2003b). *Media spectacle.* New York: Routledge.

Kellner, D. (2004). *Jean Baudrillard.* Retrieved Jan. 16, 2010, from Stanford Encyclopedia of Philosophy, Stanford, CA. Web site: http://plato.stanford.edu/entries/baudrillard/.

Kroker, A. (1984). *Technology and the Canadian mind.* Montreal: New World Press.

Levinson, P. (1999). *Digital McLuhan: A guide to the information millennium.* New York: Routledge.

McLuhan, M. (1964). *Understanding media: The extensions of man.* New York: McGraw-Hill.

Poster, M. (1995). *The second media age.* Cambridge, UK: Polity Press.

Roderick, R. (1986). *Habermas and the foundations of critical theory.* New York: St. Martin's Press.

Turkle, S. (1995). *Life on screen.* New York: Simon and Schuster.

Winner, L. (1977). *Autonomous technology.* Cambridge, MA: MIT Press.

CHAPTER TEN

McLuhan, Virilio and Speed

Bob Hanke

Rewind to 1964. Marshall McLuhan pronounces:

> Today it is the instant speed of electric information that, for the first time, permits easy recognition of the patterns and the formal contours of change and development. The entire world, past and present, now reveals itself as a growing plant in an enormously accelerated movie. Electric speed is synonymous with light and with the understanding of causes (McLuhan 1964: 305).

Fast forward to 1979. In an article for *MacLean's Magazine* titled "Living at the Speed of Light," he begins: "In the '80s there is a general awareness that the technology game is out of control, and that perhaps man was not intended to live at the speed of light." "Excessive speed of change," he continues, "isolates already-fragmented individuals and the accelerated process of adaption takes too much vitality out of communities" (McLuhan 1980: 32). Amid runaway networked computer technology and real time data transmission, "speed of light man has neither goals, objectives nor private identity. He is an item in the data bank—software only, easily forgotten—and deeply resentful" (McLuhan 1980: 32). At the end of his life, McLuhan no longer believed that information flows at electric speed were synonymous with enlightenment; rather, he was more concerned about the social side effects of living the fast life.

The association of speed, modernization, and modernity has had a long, though until recently, little known or appreciated history. Jeremy Millar and Michiel Schwartz's *Speed–Visions of an Accelerated Age* is a major exploration of this uncharted area of our cultural history, highlighting some of the thinkers who have approached speed not only as a precept but as a concept, tool, or vehicle for cultural analysis. For speed is not merely a matter of overcoming distance or the rate of dissemination and retrieval of information; it is also a matter of mobility, the perception of the visual world, the construction of time, how we measure value, the synchronization of everyday life, and how people are disciplined within the political economic order. Ultimately, speed is also a question of desire and of how power is organized in society. "To possess speed," write Millar and Schwarz, "is to be modern; to control speed rather than to be controlled by it is perhaps the most important form of contemporary power" (1998: 17).

I want to argue that McLuhan offered a critique of media that probed, among other social and psychic consequences, the shift from the experience of time to the experience of speed. Simultaneity, instantaneity and the uncertainty and unpredictability of living in the "global present" were among his concerns from early on, and accelerating speed becomes a minor, yet significant, theme in his later works. But where simultaneity refers to experience itself, instantaneity is a "technological reduction of simultaneity to an immediate, nonverbal world of affect, action, and power" (Wilmott 1996: 132). The new "global times," McLuhan knew, could not be understood by resorting to "classical theories based on separation of past, present and future, linear causality and positivist methodology" (Adam 1995: 124). In these, and many other ways, McLuhan prefigures Paul Virilio's thoughts and Virilio may be more indebted to McLuhan than he recognizes. Virilio interprets immediacy at the absolute speed of light and electromagnetic waves in terms of the "information bomb." For both McLuhan and Virilio, the atomic bomb is a foreshortened representation of time and a symbol of the "necessity of being in existence" (Willmott 1996: 192). For McLuhan, "media fall-out" described the "totalizing, unconscious, and invisible penetration of a technological world. . .into human nature" (Wilmott 1996: 192). For Virilio, the "information bomb" means that media interactivity should be regarded in the same way as nuclear radioactivity. The annihilation of space and the increased effort to control the real-time environment of human relations and activities brings us to the brink of what Virilio calls a temporal accident–a mutation in the concept of time itself.

McLuhan's focus is on the message of the medium—"the change of scale or *pace* or pattern that it introduces into human affairs" (McLuhan 1964: 24, emphasis added). In the following pages, I also argue that Paul Virilio's writings on old and new media are extensions of and deviations from Marshall McLuhan's thesis on acceleration. While McLuhan was concerned with visual and acoustic space, and Virilio with territorial and vectorial space, they both have addressed the varying speeds of modernity and its effects, especially after the West's will-to-speed is finally able to annihilate space once and for all. Just as McLuhan revised Innis on the relationship of media to sensory perception, Virilio has upgraded Innis's (1951) "plea for time" by arguing that a real-time temporal bias has superceded the bias of space (Deibert 1999). Space is annihilated and "timeless time"—the negation of time—becomes the dominant social form of time in an informational economy and network society (Castells 1996). As Innis has shown, within early civilization, "the use of armed force in conquest and defence emphasized the spatial concept" and the religious institution was a temporal expression of power (Innis 1951: 106). Emphasizing the mobility of the military proletariat and the instruments of warfare that have made assault more convenient, as well as the new means of war at the speed of light, Virilio finds that the temporal expression of power resides in military institutions (Virilio 2002a).

At the "moment of Sputnik" (October 17, 1957), McLuhan observed that matrix of television, satellite, and computers succeeded in conquering space; being "'on the air'," he said, you are simultaneously here and in many other places in a manner that is discarnate and angelic. . . ." (McLuhan 1974: 56). At the moment of Pioneer 10 (March 2, 1972), Virilio noted that the "'real time' of the messages transmitted by Pioneer" became "practically the same as the time difference between Tokyo and Paris" (Virilio 1997b: 42). In 2000, two years after Switzerland's Swatch AG introduced Internet Time, various companies from cellphone makers to CNN.com to online game and chat enterprises were featuring Internet Time, whose central meridian runs through Swatch's headquarters in Biel, Switzerland. The same year, British Prime Minister Tony Blair launched Greenwich Electronic Time, a collaborative venture between the British government and an e-tailing industry group to network servers around the world to nuclear clocks based in London. As real-time communication technologies are coming to prevail over delayed-time communication technologies, a new digital age of speed, in which time is measured in nanoseconds, is upon us.

If, as McLuhan put it, the medium is the message, and the medium in question for us is the assemblage of real-time, network media and computer-mediated communication, then the message is that technology is now on the verge of conquering time, true velocity is being virtualized, and chronological local time is being superceded by universal world-time. Revising McLuhan, Virilio claims "the message is not exactly the medium . . . but above all the ultimate SPEED of its propagation" (Virilio 1997c: 6). In his later writings, McLuhan came to focus on discovering the "laws of media" that describe patterns of interlocking effects, where speed plays an ambiguous role and produces paradoxical effects, whereas Virilio concentrates his critical gaze upon the "coeval emergence of mass media an industrial army, where the capability to war without war manifests a parallel information market of propaganda, illusion, dissimulation (Der Derian in Virilio, 2002a: viii). Beginning with *Speed and Politics* (1986), Virilio's political economy of speed has traced the emergence of "dromocratic power—dromos comes from the Greek and means "race"—and every society is a "race society" (Virilio 1999: 14). In his subsequent writings, he examined the aesthetic, political and ethical implications of speed, and military, cinematic and televisual, and techno-scientific logistics of perception. For Virilio, speed effects are not at all ambiguous, nor are they merely paradoxical; contemporary "real time" interterritorial communication constructs a media ecology of social cybernetic control and a post-national state of emergency.

With the publication of various interviews (Wilson 1994; Oliveria 1996; Der Derian 1997; Virilio 1988, 1997a, 1998, 1999, 2001, 2002b), *The Virilio Reader* (Der Derian 1998a), a special issue of *Theory, Culture and Society* (Armitage 1999), *The Paul Virilio Reader* (Redhead 2004a) and *Paul Virilo: Theorist for an Accelerated Culture* (Redhead (2004b), there are a surplus of signs that Virilio's interest in speed as a dominant element of social life has captured the attention of various scholars. Der Derian believes that Virilio's critique "represents the most sustained and significant effort since Lewis Mumford, Marshall McLuhan, and . . . Martin Heidegger" (1998b: 12). Virilio has also been claimed as a worthy successor to Michel Foucault for his "radicalization of the politics of time" (Douglas 1997) and to Walter Benjamin for his inductive, montage approach to history (Manovich 1996). Redhead (2004b) concludes that Virilio is a resolute high modernist who does not fit any poststructuralist, postmodernist, sociological, or critical social theory mold.

Virilio's reception in Canada has been limited and mixed. Burnett (1995) narrows the scope of Virilio's theses to technology, human perception, and the individual body. On the other hand, Kroker (1992) has discussed Virilio in relation to technology and the French postmodernism of Baudrillard, Barthes, Deleuze and Guattari, Lyotard, and Foucault. His influence is evident in the Krokers's discussion of the war in Kosovo (Kroker & Kroker 1999). Deibert mentions the affinity between an Innisian perspective on speed and power and Virilio, but he considers Virilio to be a "postmodern" theorist for whom speed is "purely a discursive construct"(1999: 288). However, this assessment neglects how Virilio reframes Innis's plea for time as a critique of the tyranny of real-time. Going beyond Innis's concern for "present-mindedness," Virilio writes:

Power and speed are inseparable just as wealth and speed are inseparable. . . .
The role of speed differs according to the society in question. . . . Global society is
currently in a gestation period and cannot be understood without the speed of light

or the automatic quotations of the stock markets in Wall Street, Tokyo, or London (Virilio 1999:15).

Deibert himself aptly puts it, in the "Empire of Speed," "[c]ontrol of tempo and pace rather than territory and space . . . increasingly determines who gets what, when, and how" (Deibert 1999). Rather than applying economic or rhetorical principles to media study, as Innis and McLuhan did, Virilio applies military principles to the new hypermedia environment. His is a total war model, rather than a transmission or ritual view, of communication. A war model of the techno and infosphere is arguably more relevant for understanding the post-9/11, militarized present and events like the US-Iraq wars because the "information blitz" of the second U.S-Iraq war continued unabated even after a ground victory was declared.

Before we can claim that Virilio has succeeded McLuhan as a media ecologist, we must grasp their affinities and divergences in greater detail. To clarify their respective theory and method of speed, I turn to a closer—slower—reading of how the concept of speed has been defined, utilized and worked out in their various writings.

McLuhan on Electric Speed

McLuhan was already aware, at the time of the publication of his first book *The Mechanical Bride* in 1951, that mid-twentieth century media culture was a "whirling phantasmagoria that can be grasped only when arrested for contemplation (1951: v). However, McLuhan did not make Poe's notion of "relative velocities" a part of his method of media study until he undertook his examination of the cultural effects of print and electric media in *The Gutenberg Galaxy* (1962). By the time of *Understanding Media* (1964), McLuhan had added the concept of "electric speed." By examining some key passages in these two well-known, much discussed works, as well as the lesser-known *Take Today: The Executive as Dropout* (1972) and *The Global Village: Transformations in World Life and Media in the 21ª Century* (1992), we can observe more than a shift from amusement to anxiety; we can trace how McLuhan developed speed as a tool for media and cultural analysis.

In the opening pages of *The Gutenberg Galaxy*, McLuhan adopts the anthropological insight that all technologies are extensions of our senses. McLuhan compares the relative velocity of some old extensions of man with our new electric ones: "As long as our technologies were slow as the wheel or the alphabet or money, the fact that they were separate, closed systems was socially and psychically supportable. This is not true now when sight and sound and movement are simultaneous and global in extent" (McLuhan 1962: 14). To grasp the crisis means to grasp simultaneity and the fact of planetary being together at the same time.

McLuhan's "mosaic or field approach" to the Gutenberg "galaxy" and the new electronic media "galaxy" contrasts the "relative velocities" of media and their impact on thought and experience. Print represents, among other things, a speeding up of scribal culture (and of arts and sciences), and electric media represent a speeding up of typographic culture. Moos (1997), summarizing McLuhan, writes: "At preelectric speeds, our extended senses, tools, technologies remain separate, closed systems because they are always linked to "mechanism" and enclosure of the body, reliant in their articulation upon extensions of this or that physical organ, and functioning in this respect as "fixed charges" on the psychic life of individual and community alike" (159). But, he continues, "at electric speeds . . . the hybrid mechanoelectric forms of mass media begin to extend elements of our sensorium at speeds commensurate with those of dynamic interplay, clamouring as it were for collective consciousness, for a (public) consensus or conscience that makes *rational* co-existence possible" (1997: 160).

By the time of *Understanding Media*, McLuhan believed the electronic age was reprocessing the mechanical age, with young people growing up in an "electrically-configured world," a "world not of wheels but of circuits" (1964:viii). He thought that the increased range and rapidity of information flow requires a new approach to media study, one that would not rely on the classification, analysis, or criticism of media content. In his approach to media ecology, "electric speed" is a key concept.

We can follow the contours of McLuhan's thoughts on "electric speed" more closely by beginning with his notion that without "increases of power and speed," technologies as extensions of ourselves, "would not occur or would be discarded" (McLuhan 1964: 91). This implies that differences in speed are the key to understanding the social utility or political consequences of technological change. On the positive side, new perspectives may be enabled by speed: "Electric speed in bringing all social and political functions together in a sudden implosion has heightened human awareness of responsibility to an intense degree" (McLuhan 1964: 20).

For McLuhan, the dynamism unleashed by electric speed "tends to abolish time and space in human awareness" (McLuhan, n.d.). In this formulation, technology is abstracted as agency; "electric speed" is the "agent of spatial transformation" where "acceleration beyond a certain point . . . creates decentralism in the midst of the older centralism" (Berland 1997: 75). On the one hand, speed-up creates center-margin structure, while "electric speed" "dissolves this structure by "creating centers everywhere" (McLuhan 1964: 92). While acceleration always causes disruption within existing social forms, "total acceleration" supercedes space as the main factor in social arrangements. But speed-up also accentuates problems of form and structure. The older arrangements had not been made with a view to such speeds, and people begin to sense a draining away of life values as they try to make the old physical forms adjust to the new speedier movement. (McLuhan 1964: 95)

Besides draining away of "life values," electric speed mixes the past and the present, "the cultures of prehistory with the dregs of the industrial marketers" (McLuhan 1964: 31). Being inundated with new information and a surfeit of culture results in "mental breakdown." With this claim, McLuhan joins the long-standing vogue for deploring the hurried life. As Gitlin (2001) notes, the theme of speed-up and resistance is part of the literary record of the last two centuries; in *The Gay Science* (1882), Nietzsche writes: "One thinks with a watch in one's hand . . . one lives as if one might miss out on something" (Nietzsche quoted in Gitlin 2001: 73). Popular historian James Truslow Adams wrote in 1931 that "[A]s the number of sensations increase, the time we have for reacting to and digesting them becomes less" (Adams quoted in Gitlin 2001: 75). McLuhan updates this formulation for the TV and computer age: with every electronic extension or "outering" of the central nervous system, we have "acceleration and intensification of the general environment until the central nervous system did a flip" (McLuhan 1969: 32). At this point, "there is a great stepping up of physical awareness and a big drop in mental awareness" (McLuhan 1969: 32). Once again, the overuse of mind is at issue because "the velocity of human thought" is believed to be "more or less fixed" (Gleick 1999: 107).

A key principle of McLuhan's media analysis is that: "Before the electric speed and the total field, it was not obvious that the medium was the message" (McLuhan 1964:28). Acceleration makes the cultural historian's task of recognizing patterns, as well as the shape of change and development, easier, because the globalized future is already realized in the present. In the new world of the "global village," our "specialist and fragmented civilization of centre-margin structure is suddenly experiencing an instantaneous reassembling of all its mechanized bits into an organic whole (McLuhan 1964: 93). Speed-up before electrification produced "division of functions, and of social classes, and of knowledge. At electric speed, however, all of that is reversed. Implosion and contraction then replaces mechanistic explosion and expansion" (McLuhan 1964: 102). Rather than an exponential or parabolic curve of fast change, we have a sudden "reversal" effect which "involves dual action simultaneously, as figure and ground reverse position and take on complementary configuration" (McLuhan & McLuhan 1988: 228).

Increased tempo and pace also finds its complementary configuration in selective slowness and slow-down movements. McLuhan's response to late modern electric speed, a fusion of rhetoric, grammar and dialectics, argues that electric speed metamorphosizes the mechanical into the organic as the new basis for a knowledge-based civilization. "Our new electric technology now extends instant processing of knowledge by interrelation that has long occurred within our central nervous system. It is that same speed that constitutes "organic unity" and ends the mechanical age that had gone into high gear with Gutenberg. Automation brings in real "mass production," not in terms of size, but of instant inclusive embrace" (McLuhan

1964:303). In these terms, McLuhan's diagnosis of "mental breakdown" combines an organic model of society with his Roman Catholic humanist project of recovering the new universal community within technological culture (Kroker 1984: 63)

While his fascination with utopian possibilities of new technology is well known, McLuhan also addressed, even if he did not systematically and critically examine, the relationship between electric speed and the globalizing capitalist economy. Like writing, money "speeds up social exchange and tightens the bonds of interdependence in any community" (McLuhan 1964: 127). Not only does it enhance the spatial extension and control of political organization, "time is money." Under conditions of "instant electric interdependence," money acts less as a storage device and more as a transmitter and translator. Older forms of currency, like paper money, are in jeopardy when the "instantaneous creates an interplay among time and space and human occupations, for which the older forms of currency exchange become increasingly inadequate" (McLuhan 1964: 129). Wealth becomes related to information; acceleration of the translating power of money creates opportunities for enrichment not only by facilitating the exchange of goods but "by means of advance information in stocks and bonds and real estate (McLuhan 1964: 132). In sum, "Electric speed requires organic structuring of the global economy quite as much as early mechanization by print and road led to acceptance of national unity"(McLuhan 1964: 306). Beyond these dynamics, McLuhan had very little to say about speed and the global economy, and in comparison to Innis, McLuhan's analysis of money as a medium and message was trivial (Babe 2003).

For McLuhan, the shift from sequentiality to simultaneity also had implications for the organization and nature of work. "In general," he concludes,

> electric speed-up requires knowledge of ultimate effects. Mechanical speed-ups, how-ever radical in their reshaping of personal and social life, still were allowed to happen sequentially. Men could, for the most part, get through a normal life span on the basis of a single set of skills. This is not at all the case with electric speed-up. . . . The result of electric speed-up in industry at large is the creation of intense sensitivity to the inter-relation and interprocess of the whole, so as to call for ever-new types of organization and talent. (McLuhan 1964: 308)

"Electric speed" is an ambiguous agent then with paradoxical effects. McLuhan describes historical shift from "millennia of slow explosion, of 'expansion'" followed by "the all of a sudden "implosion" of electronic media in the second half of the twentieth century (Lash 2002: 186). In this reading of history, speed-up by wheel, road and paper were slow compared to "electric speed." Before "electric speed," communication is synonymous with transportation, and the "medium" is not even visible to us. While sceptical of the notion of technological "improvement," McLuhan combined utopian thinking about the dissolution of center-margin structures, at the same time he was aware that electric speed "accentuates problems of form and struc-ture" and induces "mental breakdown."

In the late 1960s, McLuhan became a celebrity for his "medium theory" of oral, print and electronic media. On the new hybrid medium of computing, he took a technotopian stance. Considering what the computer means in education, he assumed that as "information movement speeds up, information levels rise in all areas of mind and society. . . . (McLuhan in McLuhan & Zingrone 1995: 187). In an interview with *Playboy* magazine in 1969, he remarked:

> The computer thus holds the promise of a technologically engenderd state of univer-sal understanding and unity, a state of absorption in the logos that could knit mankind into one family and create a perpetuity of collective harmony and peace. This is the real use of the computer, not to expedite marketing or solve technical problems but to speed the process of discovery and orchestrate terrestrial—and eventually galactic—environ-ments and energies. (McLuhan in McLuhan & Zingrone 1995: 262).

In the 1970s, McLuhan begins to observe the clash between the "electric" and the emergent "digital" galaxy, visual and acoustic space slamming into each other at the speed of light. *Take Today: The Executive as Drop Out*—co-authored with Barrington Nevitt, a consultant in international engineering, marketing and man-agement—develops McLuhan's thesis of technological acceleration in the context of living and working with real-time computers. In this book, the authors make explicit that the "message" of the steam engine was not the product that could be produced, but the acceleration of all the functions in the social surround, i.e., the new "rim spin" (McLuhan & Nevitt 1972: 63). *Take Today* analyzes the paradoxi-cal effects of acceleration as a chiasmus pattern where "every process pushed far enough tends to reverse or flip suddenly (McLuhan & Nevitt 1972: 6). *Take Today* thus aims to offer an inventory of the effects of "electric speed" upon organizations operating within a post-industrial context.

In addressing the consequences of the new software upon managerial practices and organizational culture, McLuhan and Nevitt trace how "the old hardware" is *'etherealized'* by means of "design" or "software" (1972: 4, italics in original). In the shift from the production line to online, from slower to higher speeds of informa-tion, they argue, the social role of managers, workers and consumers changes. Managers who wish to avoid remaining "diehards" engaged in hardware thinking should become "dropouts"—that is, they should avoid specialism and adopt com-prehensivism. Workers in the new information can overcome old divisions of work, play and leisure. Beyond this workplace utopia, consumers become producers and the public becomes a "participant role player." When the real-time information envi-ronment becomes the new ground for social organization and action, they say "class," "history" and "economics" are meaningless (McLuhan & Nevitt 1972: 68).

Of course, this critique of a Marxist perspective cannot be sustained; new office technologies and multiple-user software, by enabling workers to get the job done no matter where they are, or what time it is, are extensions of Taylorism. Hyperproductivity becomes the main objective of a post-industrial firm integrated into real-time financial flows and stock exchanges. As Ross (2003) has documented, "no collar" knowledge workers in the internet industry had "good jobs" but faced a loss of stable work/life boundaries, excessive responsibility, and little job security.

But they are nonetheless on to something when they note that production entails image and information-making, and money becomes information only. In this way, they began to describe how informationalization drives commodification (Lash 2002: 3). Their description of how accountants have hijacked large corporations by misleading investors and rendering old measures of profit and performance meaningless anticipates the Enron and Worldcom accounting scandals. However, their analysis of this fundamental shift in wealth-making has a political economic blindspot when it comes to transnational corporate power and private property relations. In pursuing their theme of transformation and innovation, McLuhan and Nevitt offer no historical account or critique of power attached to media ownership, personal income, or the new source of corporate wealth—intellectual property (Lash 2002).

Another area of transformation and innovation that they cover is urban form and city planning. Drawing on Jane Jacobs's *The Economy of Cities* as well as Wyndham Lewis's "magnetic city of the 'wired' planet" (McLuhan & Nevitt 1972: 144), McLuhan and Nevitt posit a shift from "tribal community to Magnetic City," from the modern city to the instant, mobile, disposable city. They criticize Toronto city planners for being locked into suburban thinking and high-rise development, for failing to understand the decentralising effects of the automobile, and for not pursuing programs of "extreme decentralism," which would favor low-rise horizontal rather than high-rise vertical development (McLuhan & Nevitt 1972: 29). They claim that in the "information age of the "magnetic city" all 'hardware' city forms are obsolescent. . . ." (McLuhan & Nevitt 1972: 5). This "magnetic city" corresponds to Virilio's "*world-city*, the city to end all cities, a virtual city of which every real city will ultimately be a suburb, a sort of **omnipolitian** periphery *whose centre will be nowhwere and circumference everywhere* (Virilio 1997b: 74, italics in original).

What they call the new "rim spin"allows for creativity and discovery, but when accelerated too much, it produces other undesirable consequences. "Whenever the social speed exceeds the power of social and psychic assimilation, there is a sudden decline of satisfaction, which is the formula for DEPRESSION (McLuhan & Nevitt 1972: 59). The new information-as-service environment, when speeded up too much, flips into a disservice environment. "As speed-up in the environmental services occurs," they write, "there is a slowdown in the old system. Inefficiency is the natural accompaniment of all speed-up, simply because it shakes the old system apart" (McLuhan & Nevitt 1972: 221). With more complex, tightly-coupled technology, the effects of errors are much more damaging: "In the computer world mistakes become 'impossible' in all senses. *Whereas mechanical 'dehumanization' wrecked the person, electric super-'humanization' wrecks the entire system*" (McLuhan & Nevitt 1972: 221, italics in original). These misgivings are the closest they came to thinking about the effects of system failures, computer bugs and viruses, or technological accidents.

During the last years of his life, McLuhan collaborated with Bruce Powers to write *The Global Village: Transformations in World Life and Media in the 21st Century*. This posthumous book develops a framework of analysis that would go beyond rearview mirrorism and understanding the present in order to anticipate mankind's rapidly arriving robotic future. *The Global Village* is McLuhan's response to the speeded-up situation and its aim is two fold; first, it offers an analysis that attempts to pick up speed and make the contradictory effects of technology comprehensible. Second, it applies the "tetrad" to speed of light technologies to explore their contradictory satisfactions and dissatisfactions.

The tetrad is the intuitive and empirical probe for revealing the hidden ground of the new information and communication technology revolution, and for predicting the "cultural life of an artifact in advance (whether it be computer, data-base device, satellite, or global media network" (McLuhan & Powers 1992: vii). Rejecting sequential time and either/or explanation in favor of simultaneous experience and the recognition of pattern within continual, potential transformation, the tetrad harnesses the power of simultaneity to compress past, present, and future in order to understand both positive and negative aspects of any artifact. While technologies are still considered extensions of the body, and technology is synonymous with language, the tetrad is also a "diagram of the bifurcated mind." The balance Innis sought between time and space-biased civilizations is here transcoded into a balance between the left and right hemispheres of the brain. In this way, McLuhan hoped to legitimate his descriptions of visual and acoustic culture slamming into each other at the speed of light by grounding his observations in the science of asymmetrical brain development. With this new scientific method, he believed that struggle between left-hemisphere modes of thought and right hemisphere modes, between western and eastern values, would reveal itself instantly.

But the conflict or balance between left and right, east and west, that McLuhan sees or hopes for is complicated by a greater imbalance between man and nature. As "technological man races" into the "age of implosion after 3000 years of explosion," he will "lose nature as direct experience" (McLuhan & Powers 1992: 95).

What may emerge as the most important insight of the twenty-first century is that man was not designed to live at the speed of light. Without the countervailing balance of natural and physical laws, the new video-related media will make man implode upon himself. As he sits in the informational control room, whether at home or at work, receiving data at enormous speeds—imagistic, sound, or tactile—from all areas of the world, the results could be dangerously inflating and schizophrenic. His body will remain in one place but his mind will float out into the electronic void, being everywhere at once in the data bank. (McLuhan & Powers, 1992: 97)

Here, we return to the dualisms of culture and nature, mind and body, where nature stands for timeless laws and the body for natural rhythms. In a fast world, "constant change, for its own sake, everybody" (McLuhan & Powers 1992: 98); only those involved in "information monopolies" will not be threatened, presumably since they will be advantaged by belonging to the fast class.

Their tetradic examination of computer, satellite, data base, and the horizontally-organized, multi-carrier corporation shows their "nonexpansive, implosive character leading to total involvement" (McLuhan & Powers 1992: 103). Whereas media study, they argue, typically covers only enhancement and obsolescence, their analysis of tetrads also examines what is retrieved by a new form and what is reversed when a new form is pushed to its limits. This method describes how the computer both speeds up calculations and erodes mechanical sequences while at the same time retrieving the quantitative power of numbers and reversing into simultaneous pattern-recognition. Applied to satellites, it describes how global information exchange is enlarged and how it obsolesces language, how it retrieves world-view and reverses into iconic fantasies. It is difficult to determine whether their descriptions emphasize the positive potentialities of speed or whether they tend toward a catastrophic view. Sometimes they see change within a model of homeostatic structure; at other moments, they see people becoming anxious and violent, and planetary disequilibrium ensues.

What McLuhan's last book does clearly suggest is that we are at the end of a long modern, national cycle that began with the advent of the first "wave surfers" Marconi and Edison, and we are at the beginning of a "speed of light society." Accelerating computer calculations, data transaction rates, satellite image-based dialogues, and real-time global home/commercial high-speed information services "completes the process of disengaging man physically and psychically from the earth's surface" (McLuhan & Powers 1992: 114). In this approach to technology and culture, as Carey points out, there is one long secular trend that cuts across the shorter cycles of effects—"the progressively deeper penetration of technology into the body of society and the human body as well" (1998: 122). But rather than the much quoted "global village," a "robotic future" is rapidly arriving. Old private identity based on specialized knowledge will be out, while "robotic role-playing" will be in. "Robotism" is based on the aesthetic of the ear rather than the eye, whereas "angelism" emphasizes the eye: consequently, "robotic man is capable of instant adjustment" (McLuhan & Powers 1992: 70). On the other hand, everyone will lose their private identities—"everybody will be a nobody" (McLuhan & Powers 1992: 129)—just a data body that leaves the flesh behind.

After the Dromocratic Revolution

Genosko argues that the differences between McLuhan and Virilio are profound and that they "read contraction to dissimilar ends":

> While Virilio emphasizes the "fearful friction" of implosion, McLuhan reads it as a kind of embrace carried to mystical heights. The war machine of Virilio and the love machine of McLuhan create quite different worlds: contest or contact (1999: 97).

No doubt these differences are apparent; where McLuhan finds grounds for optimism, Virilio finds grounds for skepticism. But an appreciation of Virilio's debt to McLuhan requires us to reconsider their styles of writing as well as their mutual interest in the impact of technology in general, and speed, in particular. Virilio has noted that few writers have touched on speed: "for a more political vision of speed, there's Marinetti and the Italian futurists, and then Marshall McLuhan who took a step in that direction" (Virilio 1997a: 45). Virilio's writing and his contribution to the debate about media and postmodernity also exhibits the same rhetorical flair and hectic vivacity as McLuhan's. As Der Derian (1998b) remarks, there is also an ethical, spiritual, even Catholic pull to Virilio's writings that is comparable to McLuhan's Roman Catholic influences. Zurbrugg (1999) suggests that McLuhan and Virilio both addressed similar historical transitions and difficulties with identical values.

Virilio's writings on old and new media, owing to his particular architectural, philosophical, and scientific influences and his interest in military history, may be understood as both an extension of and deviation from McLuhan's thesis of technological acceleration. In 1984, Arthur Kroker observed that, "[t]he relentless speed-up of the pace of technological change which McLuhan could only prophecy has now taken place" (1984: 128). Whereas McLuhan tried to invent a "new science" of laws of media, Virilio is more concerned to critique technoscience as mass technoculture and as an agent for the acceleration of reality.

While McLuhan and Virilio were not the first to discern the impact of media on space and time, Virilio is unique in theorizing the technocultural shift from "the confines of space to the exigencies of time," our astrophysical leap from space-time to "speed-time." He is the inventor of "dromology"—the political economy of speed—which aims to supplement the political economy of wealth in order to map the impact that fast transportation, faster information transmission, and super-fast cybernetic means of telecommunication have had on warfare, the city, politics, and everyday life.

In *Speed and Politics: An Essay on Dromology*, originally published in 1977, Virilio's point of departure was the history of movement and the brakes or accel-erators which determine the circulation of people. For Virilio, this history progress-es at the speed of weapons systems (Virilio 1986: 68). Taking his cue from Sun Tzu—"speed is the art of war"—Virilio describes how the dromoscopic revolution ushered in empires of speed and dromocratic society. For Virilio, changes in wealth are inseparable from changes in speed; the industrial revolution, which resulted from faster machines, is to be understood as a dromological revolution and as a war against time itself (Virilio 1986). For the modern war machine, the speed of penetration and assault is everything and stasis is death. Since *Speed and Politics*, Virilio's writ-ings have continued to explore the military strategies of the military-industrial com-plex, since this is where new weapons, as well as new information and communication technologies, often first make their appearance (Virilio 2000). Beginning with *War and Cinema: The Logistics of Perception*, Virilio turned his attention to understanding media in order to advance the thesis that the war of "pic-tures and sounds is replacing the war of objects" (Virilio 1989: 4). The "watching machine" that develops along with the "war machine," within a model of total war, looms very large in Virilio's thought over the years.

The Art of the Motor (1995) represents Virilio's response to television, comput-ers, virtual reality and biotechnology. From the perspective of mobilization and motorization, it describes the role of the media in the shift from democracy to dromocracy. "Mediatization", he argues, has replaced communication. Without feedback or feedforward, we are deprived of the right of reply and the freedom to react, to make decisions on a rational basis. This thesis is related to a second thesis connecting speed and vision: real-time electronic media abolish geopolitical limits to our field of vision. For Virilio, real-time vision machines are a deviation from "nat-ural communication," which "demands audiovisual proximity and fairly restricted intervals or territory"(Virilio 1995: 8). Television is no "cool"medium bringing forth participation and the interplay of senses as McLuhan claimed, for it is the cam-era, and not only the screen, that comes between the viewer and reality. The tele-vision screen, whose electron-scanning beam traces the lines of the image at more than twice a second, brings us only the "false proximity of the world without any density or shadow" (Virilio 1995: 10).

Historically, the media have orchestrated a "perceptual shift of appearances" (Virilo 1995: 23) with increasing acceleration. Beginning with the steam press, the history of subsequent developments (rotary press, rotary image press, etc.) is the history of changing media vectors. Within 20th century screen culture, Virilio contends we have gone beyond the management of information into a new regime of representation—the "virtual theatricalization of the real world" (Virilio 1995: 33). This new regime of representation is made possible by the "fusion/confusion of information and data processing" in real time. In the contemporary media environment:

> *Speed* guarantees the *secret* and thus the *value* of all information. Liberating the media therefore means not only annihilating the duration of information—of the image and its path—but with these all that endures or persists (Virilio 1995: 53). (italics in original)

With the coming of computer-generated cyberspace, not only has a new fractional dimension been added to our environment, but calculating at absolute speed eliminates the "relative speed of the circulation of products, goods, and people"(Virilio 1995: 139). Thus, in cybernetic space-time, "information is of value only if it is delivered fast; better still, that *speed is information itself*"(Virilio 1995: 140). For Virilio, when information becomes the "last dimension of space-time-matter", and computer-generated virtuality is possible, the "far horizon" (beyond which the human eye could not see) becomes a "trans-apparent horizon" and the "mental image of far distances" yields to "instrumental imagery of a computer that can generate a virtual otherworld, thanks to the computing speed of its integrated circuits" (Virilio 1995: 143). With increases in processing power and graphic frame rates, and the advent of portable, personal virtual-environment systems, Virilio observes a change in the speed of history: from long-term to short-term to "real-term."

Thus, the technologies of transmission, which have conquered the extension of space, now aim to dynamize space, to eradicate duration itself. But once duration is eliminated, *real-space perspective* . . . then gives way to the *real-time perspective* of the computer cognoscenti . . . ." (Virilio 1995: 151, italics in original). Teleaction in virtual space brings about the already mentioned "delocalization," and thus confusion as to the physical location of virtual objects. Instead of a global-local dynamic, where the World Wide Web represents the localization of the global, Virilio sees a globalization of location in which "'WHERE' loses its priority to WHEN and HOW" (Virilio 1995: 155).

To read *The Art of the Motor* is to be drawn into a discourse on technological experience and a crisis of democracy, of history, and of the human(ist) subject (body). Virilio's theses on the industrial media complex is a lament upon the fate of vision, and thus, of consciousness in the new visual and temporal order. The accelerated simultaneity produced by our shared televisual experience produces the experience of confusion, of mediatized "dependence," of "televisual pathology", and "dyslexic versions of reality." With computer-mediated communication in digitized cyberspace, virtual thought supplants visual thinking. With the advent of digital reproduction, reality becomes a synthetic object, tied to synthetic vision. Just as "illusionism" was the center of the cinema, digital technologies are part of the coming "vision machine." Paradoxically, "the production of sightless vision is itself merely the reproduction of an intense blindness that will become the latest form of industrialization: the industrialization of the non-gaze" (1995: 65). For Virilio, this blindness is due to the accelerated movement of images: the speed of representation leaves us no time to see. Static vision in Cartesian space enables dissimulation, the ability to differentiate image (virtual reality) and (actual) reality, but the dynamics of live, "real-time" tele-vision leaves us blind.

Like McLuhan, Virilio is concerned with sensory perception but advances his critique of globalizing media and late modernity by situating the logistics of perception within military and scientific history. Our new vision machines provide ways of seeing that reinforce the historical tendency toward the dispossession of sight. All the faculties of the body, including the brain, are being transferred to machines. Rejecting the computer-as-brain metaphor, Virilio foresees an accident of the body—decorporation—and a "transfer accident in substantial reality" (Virilio 1997b: 131) as higher speed interconnectivity outpaces slower speed intersubjectivity. In this way, Virilio emphasizes the perils of our technological over-extensions and describes how the human body is being "pushed aside or obsolesced" by our media prostheses and biotechnology.

Like McLuhan, Virilio's understanding of the perils of technology proceeds from the body. Starting from Husserl rather than sense-ratios, Virilio adopts the notion that the corporal body at rest is the center of our living present; he assumes that the earth is the foundation for all sense, most especially our sense of being in motion or at rest. But "the more speed grows, the more "control" tends to supersede even the environment, the real time of interactivity definitely replacing the real space of activity . . . . *Speed is therefore the antiquation of the real environment of man.* . . . (Virilio quoted in Der Derian 1998a: 121, italics in original). Virilio is concerned that living at the speed of light means the "progressive disappearance of the space of anthropo-geographical reference" (Virilio quoted in Der Derian 1998a: 121). We will lose our being in the world in favour of inhabiting the non-place of the "space-speed" of technology. The danger is that the new media environment of real-time interactivity will usher in an omnipresent control that will supercede situated being in the here and now.

Running through Virilio's writings is the image of a shrinking globe and a series of binary oppositions, marking a radical break or discontinuity between earlier phases of speed-up and the cyberspace-time of the digital galaxy. Virilio's initial concern with the speed of moving bodies becomes a concern for the velocity of information under conditions of the second dromoscopic revolution brought about by global multimedia. Summing up the "global present," Virilio states:

> Our image of time is an image of instaneity and ubiquity. And there's a stunning general lack of speed, a lack of awareness of the essence of speed . . . .And this passage from an extensive to an intensive time will have considerable impact on all the various aspects of the conditions of our society; it leads to a radical reorganization both of our social mores and or our image of the world. This is the source of the feeling that we're faced with an epoch in many ways comparable to the Renaissance: it's an epoch in which the real world and our image of the world no longer coincide . . . .(Virilio quoted in Der Derian 1998b: 8).

In this way, he announces that the dromoscropic revolution is being televised and that a new temporal regime has begun. The resulting technocultural shift to living in real-time is always regressive; speeding along in our audiovisual last vehicles, we pass from the history of mobility to a new stage of ultimate polar inertia, where the only movements are those of teleactors in a global theater—where movement depends on the transmission speed of vision and teleaction rather than movement in space.

In this analysis, we are coming to live more and more in a time where time does not pass. While many contemporary theorists have discussed the role of communication technology in the restructuring of space (e.g., Wise 1997), Virilio's work is centrally concerned with the total compression and socialization of time (Van Dijk 1999). For Virilio, "Standardization and synchronization are the two sides of modern architecture's space-time" (Virilio 2002b: 74). Temporal compression modifies our cognitive map, real-time synchronization gives impetus to military command and control, and real-time media interactivity enhances technocapitalism's control of the pace and the tempo of human activities. With the emergence of a new world order of timeless temporality, Virilio calls for a new kind of politics—a grey ecology—less concerned with first or second nature, but technology as our third nature, and electronic proximity's role in the "degradation of the physical proximity of beings, of different communities" (1997b: 58).

Against the pollution of distances and the contamination of the "real life geospheric proportions of the planet," this ecology aims to retain distances and temporal differentiation (2002b: 80).

Bringing Media Studies up to Speed

As we have seen, McLuhan's later work attempted to move beyond observing a dialectic of speed and slowness to an analysis of speed effects. Perhaps as McLuhan's own life became more hurried, it was more obvious to him that new "rim spin" was the message. In the 1970s and 80s, he understood that changing technology gave impetus to social acceleration whose paradoxical effects could be described in terms of a chiasmus pattern.

The McLuhans's tetradic analysis has, however, been criticized as a manifestation of their will to a "new science." Stamps (1995) argues this method of media study has little critical value because the four laws of media are not verifiable or falsifiable; therefore, without an analysis of context, the "laws of media will neither reveal the hidden ground nor predict the effects (reversals) of human artifacts"(Stamps 1995: 149). Here the explanatory value of the McLuhans's approach to speed effects is limited to that of a heuristic device. Their examination of particular technologies are tautologies, or, at best only first approximations.

However, it must be remembered that for McLuhan, as for Virilio, media study is the study of hidden grounds or dimensions of media. What matters most in an ecological approach is the environment of instant information, changing technologies which alter space and time, and the perception of their social consequences. For McLuhan, it is "nature" and the "unconscious", rather than capitalism, that form the final ground (Willmott 1996). In McLuhan's prognosis, the new "speed of light society" will deprive us of our relationship to our body, and to natural and physical laws: "it is this deprival, not the technology of postmodernity, that is for McLuhan apocalyptically catastrophic" (Wilmott 1995: 193). In this sense, McLuhan was a proto-dromologist; where his last work leaves off, Virilio's work begins. In Virilio's work, war is the paradigm for the fabrication of speed; it is the runaway technologies of transmission—the descendants of early modern fast machines—plus the development of simulators and virtual technologies, that form our contemporary environment, our situated body's horizon, steering us toward the derealization of reality, the decentering of the human observer, and a mutation of the time concept itself. For Virilio, this is the hidden ground of the present communication revolution. Parallelling McLuhan, it is ecology, rather than economics or epistemology, that forms the ontological ground that is becoming concealed by cyberspace-time.

McLuhan considered the "electric galaxy" to be a break from the preceding mechanical age; for Virilio, digital technology is a continuation of the mechanization of perception that begins with early vision machines. Whereas McLuhan compared and contrasted oral, print and electronic eras, Virilio discusses three major epochs of real war, three types of weapons, and three modes of deterrence (Virilio 2002a: 6–7). Any such periodization calls for caution as do the binaries he deploys as rapidly as McLuhan deploys juxtapositions. Any particular binary, such as synchronicity and asynchronicity, may, upon further analysis, be far removed from computer users's synchronous or asynchronous practices (Slack & Wise 2002). From the perspective of technology as cultural practice, Virilio's mapping of technology and society may be too overdetermined by the medium and his mapping of speed- effects too one-dimensional and mechanically determinisitic. On the other hand, in moving from military space to cyberspace, Virilio's work foregrounds the articulation of military and media that other accounts of the technology and culture have ignored. While the military may not be the whole message, "US Pentagon capitalism" is the center of the neoimperialist American empire today.

While the new physics influenced McLuhan's approach to the "total field," the new physics becomes, for Virilio, a source of metaphors like the "information bomb" while scientific research drawing on such disciplines becomes part of a competitive race toward the future. Virilio is much more critical of "post-scientific" technoscientific knowledge and practice, especially as it is used for military or biogenetic purposes. By "going to the extremes" he writes as if acceleration is crashing all time barriers and scales. In the language of McLuhan's tetradic analysis of media artifacts, Virilio concentrates on transportation and transmission technologies, what they accelerate, and what they erode or obsolesce. Accidents are no longer contingent and locally specific, but probable and "integral." What is more, Virilio's emphasis on the development of vision machines, on the omnipresent and the omnivoyant electronic panopticon, and his total neglect of other senses and media, is nondialectical in comparison to McLuhan's dialectic of visual and acoustic space (Grosswiler 1998). But what Virilio's catastrophic triptych—information bomb, cyber bomb, genetic bomb—may suffer in complexity compared to the heuristic value of McLuhan's tetrads, he more than makes up for in political value.

McLuhan's modernist critical ideology attempted to respond to speed by arresting them in a four-part metaphorical structure that was simultaneous, rather than sequential, in time. Virilio's response to the acceleration of cyberculture indicates a shift from modern/postmodern theories to "hypermodern theories" (Armitage 1999). Virilio's approach to the global multimedia's "de-localization"of being updates Williams's (1975) concept of "mobile privatisation," extends McLuhan's notion of "discarnate man," resonates with Meyrowitz's analyses of the media's impact on our sense of place (Meyrowitz 1985) and "generalized elsewhere" (Meyrowitz 1989), and shares affinities with Sloterdijk's post-Marxist political economy of kinetics, where (im)mobilization, rather than the concept of labour, is the basic category of historical analysis (Sloterdijk 1998).

However, Virilio's conceptualization of media deserves scrutiny. On the one hand, it is grounded in a transmission model of communication, where communication means detection, guidance and deception. In this respect, Virilio's approach completely ignores and bypasses media studies's work on representation and signifying practices. Our conventional understanding that media construct reality is challenged when Virilio pushes us to consider how media create a split or 'stereo' reality that de-realizes reality as we have known it. So it is not the "image of war" but the war of images that should concern us, and their confusion of near and far. It is not the Stealth bomber's appearance that should interest us; rather; "the electronic representation on the screen, the radar console, modifies the aerodynamic silhouette of the weapon, the virtual image dominating in fact "the thing" of which it was, until now, only the 'image'" (Virilio 2002a: 111).

On the other hand, commercial, transnational television news networks are not a cultural form, or an audiovisual space of representation, but a medium with a real-time bias. As part of the military industrial media complex, CNN has won the commercial race for ubiquity and instantaneity. With their capacity to contract space and reduce duration or delay, CNN and spy satellites are parallel vectors for the real-time exchange of video signals that blur distinctions between advertising and information, news and propaganda, and any boundary between military combatants, civilians, citizens and shoppers. Thus, the problem of interpretation is no longer a matter of distinguishing true and false but actual and virtual; what is false about live TV news is not only its framing of "facts" but its temporality. Real-time exchanges of video signals and military orders do not allow time for the sharing of facts, and thus for the formation of public opinion. The military's longstanding war against time has now been extended into the public sphere.

How then are we to understand the present as we live more and more in the "empire of immediacy, " with its US-based tendency toward technological fundamentalism? Warning us of the "behaviorism inherent in the technologies of instantaneous broadcasting" will not suffice (Virilio 2002a: 100). Nor will a return to an autonomous view of technology with its master-slave dialectic (Virilio 2002a: 132). What Virilio teaches us is that the relation between technology and culture is a geophilosophical, environmental, and urban issue. Media are agents of spatial decentralization and temporal implosion that (de)construct our environment. The more we live in a world-city existing in global time, the more real-time responsiveness and control will tend to replace the height, breadth and depth of our environment. Our recent technological upgrading from "electric speed" to optoelectronic and electroacoustic speed, along with an emerging interface culture in higher definition and fidelity, reduces the gap between thinking and doing, planning and executing, action and reaction. While many commentators have emphasized the advantages of speeding up, McLuhan noted as early as 1964 that "War is accelerated social change . . . .(McLuhan 1964: 306). The later McLuhan began to stand apart from electric crowd in order to observe both satisfactions and dissatisfactions of living in a "speed of light society." His probes of electric speed point us toward further research into our on-and off-line chrono-experience. Virilio observes that when "All is governed by lighting" (Heraclitus), the tyranny of distance yields to the tyranny of real time. His report on speed points us toward further research into which groups are advantaged, which groups disadvantaged, by speed-effects, and a politics of temporality that would supplement our well-developed politics of space. After the first "Persian Gulf" TV war between the US and Iraq in 1991, Virilio asked a fundamental question that has yet to be answered: "*can one democratize ubiquity, instantaneity, omniscience and omnipresence*, which are precisely the privileges of the divine, or in other words, of autocracy?" (Virilio 2002a:134, italics in original).

In 1960, McLuhan wrote: "To high speed change no adjustment is possible. We become spectators only and must escape into understanding" (McLuhan quoted in Gordon 1997). For those of us who are convinced that we have become "telespectators" and "teleactors," Virilio urges us to escape from technological fundamentalism and respond politically to the challenge of a real-time bias.

References

Adam, Barbara. 1995. *Timewatch: The social analysis of time.* Cambridge, MA: Polity.

Armitage, John, ed. 1999. Special Issue on: Paul Virilio. *Theory, Culture & Society.* 16(5–6).

Babe, Robert. 2003. Money and Culture. *Topia: Canadian Journal of Cultural Studies,* 9: 3–13.

Berland, Jody. 1997. Space at the margins: Colonial spatiality and critical theory after Innis. *Topia: A Canadian Journal of Cultural Studies,* 1, 55–82.

Burnett, Ron. 1995. *Cultures of vision: Images, media & the imaginary.* Bloomington and Indianapolis, IN: Indiana University Press.

Carey, James. 1998. Marshall McLuhan: Genealogy and legacy, *Canadian Journal of Communication,* 23, 293–306.

Castells, Manuel. 1996. *The rise of network society.* Malden, MA: Blackwell.

Der Derian, James 1997. Interview with Paul Virilio. Speed: Technology, Media, Society. http://proxy.arts.uci.edu/~nideffer/_SPEED_/1.4/articles/derderian.html, accessed on July 9, 2003.

Der Derian, James (Ed.) 1998a. *The Virilio reader.* Malden, MA: Blackwell.

Der Derian, James. 1998b. Introduction. In J. Der Derian (Ed.) *The Virilio reader* (pp 1–15). Malden, MA: Blackwell.

Douglas, Ian. 1997. The Calm Before the Storm: Virilio's Debt to Foucault, and Some Notes on Contemporary Global Capital. Speed: Technology, Media, Society. http://proxy.arts.uci.edu/~nideffer/_SPEED_/1.4/articles/douglas.html, accessed July 9, 2003

Deibert, Ronald. 1999. Harold Innis and the Empire of Speed. *Review of International Studies*, 25, 273–289.

Genosko, Gary. 1999. *McLuhan and Baudrillard: The masters of implosion*. New York: Routledge.

Gitlin, Todd. 2001. Speed and Sensibility. In T. Gitlin, *Media unlimited: How the torrent of images and sound overwhelms our lives* (pp. 71–117). New York: Metropolitan.

Gleick, James. 1999. *Faster: The acceleration of just about everything*. New York: Pantheon.

Gordon, W. Terrence. 1997. *Marshall McLuhan: Escape into understanding*. Toronto: Stoddart.

Grosswiler, Paul. 1998. *Method is the message: Rethinking McLuhan through critical theory*. Montreal: Black Rose.

Innis, Harold. 1951. A Plea for Time. In H.A. Innis, *The bias of communication* (pp. 61–91). Toronto: University of Toronto Press.

Kroker, Arthur. 1984. *Technology and the Canadian mind: Innis/McLuhan/Grant*. Montreal: New World Perspectives.

Kroker, Arthur. 1992. *The possessed individual: Technology and the French postmodern*. New York: St. Martin's.

Kroker, Arthur & Marilouise Kroker. 1999, March 29. Fast war/slow motion. *CTHEORY.NET*, http://www.ctheory.net/text_file.asp?pick=209

Lash, Scott. 2002. *Critique of information*. Thousand Oaks, CA: Sage.

Manovich, Lev. 1996. Film/Telecommunication–Benjamin/Virilio. http://www.manovich.net/text /Benjamin-Virilio.html, accessed August 22, 2003

McLuhan, Marshall. n.d. *The Dew Line*. Toronto: McLuhan Centre for Technology, University of Toronto, Occasional Papers.

McLuhan, Marshall. 1951. *The mechanical bride: Folklore of industrial man*. Boston: Beacon Press.

McLuhan, Marshall. 1962. *The Gutenberg galaxy: The making of typographic man*. New York: Mentor.

McLuhan, Marshall. 1964. *Understanding media: The extensions of man*. New York: McGraw-Hill.

McLuhan, Marshall. 1969. *Counterblast*. Toronto: McClelland and Stewart.

McLuhan, Marshall. 1974. At the moment of Sputnik the planet became a global theatre in which there are no spectators but only actors. *Journal of Communication*, 24(1):48–58.

McLuhan, Marshall. 1980. January 7. Living at the Speed of Light. *MacLean's Magazine*, 32–33.

McLuhan, Marshall & Eric McLuhan. 1988. *Laws of media: The new science*. Toronto: University of Toronto Press.

McLuhan, Marshall & Barrington Nevitt. 1972. *Take today: The executive as dropout*. Don Mills, Ontario: Longman.

McLuhan, Marshall & Bruce Powers. 1992. *The global village: Transformations in world life and media in the 21st century*. New York: Oxford University Press.

McLuhan, Eric & Frank Zingrone (Eds.) (1995). *Essential McLuhan*. New York: Routledge.

Meyrowitz, Joshua. 1985. *No sense of place: The impact of electronic media on social behavior*. New York. Oxford University Press.

Meyrowitz, Joshua. 1989. The Generalized Elsewhere. *Critical Studies in Mass Communication*, 6(3):326–334.

Millar, Jeremy & Michiel Schwarz (Eds.) 1998. *Speed-Visions of an accelerated age*. London: The Photographer's Gallery and the Trustees of the Whitechapel Art Gallery, association with the MacDonald Stewart Art Centre, Guelph and the Netherlands Design Institute, Amsterdam.

Moos, Michael. 1997. McLuhan's Language for Awareness Under Electronic Conditions. In M. Moos (Ed.) *Marshall McLuhan essays—Media research: Technology, art, communication* (pp. 140–166). Amsterdam: G+B International.

Oliveria, Carlos. 1996, June 12. The silence of the lambs: Paul Virilio in conversation. *CTHE-ORY.NET*, http://www.ctheory.net/text_file.asp?pick=38

Redhead, S. (2004a). *The Paul Virilio reader*. New York: Columbia University Press.

Redhead, S. (2004b). *Paul Virilio: Theorist for an accelerated culture*. Toronto: University of Toronto Press.

Ross, Andrew. 2003. *No-collar: the humane workplace and its hidden costs*. New York: Basic.

Slack, Jennifer & Greg Wise. 2002. Cultural Studies and Technology. In L. Lievrouw & S. Livingstone (Eds.), *Handbook of new media: Social shaping and consequences of ICTs* (pp. 485–501). Thousand Oaks, CA: Sage.

Sloterdijk, Peter. 1998. Modernity as Mobilisation. In J. Millar & M. Schwarz (Eds.), *Speed-Visions of an accelerated age* (pp. 43–52). London: The Photographer's Gallery and the Trustees of the Whitechapel Art Gallery, association with the MacDonald Stewart Art Centre, Guelph and the Netherlands Design Institute, Amsterdam.

Stamps, Judith. 1995. *Unthinking modernity: Innis, McLuhan and the Frankfurt School*. Montreal & Kingston: McGill-Queen's University Press.

Van Dijk, Jan. 1999. *The network society*. Thousand Oaks, CA: Sage.

Virilio, Paul. 1986. *Speed and politics: An essay on dromology*. New York: Semiotext(e).

Virilio, Paul. 1988. The Third Window: An Interview with Paul Virilio. In C. Schneider & B. Wallis (Eds), *Global television* (pp. 185–197). New York and Cambridge: Wedge Press and MIT Press.

Virilio, Paul. 1989. *War and cinema: The logistics of perception* (P. Camiller, Trans.) London and New York: Verso.

Virilio, Paul. 1995. *The art of the motor*. Minneapolis, MN: University of Minnesota Press.

Virilio, Paul. 1997a. *Pure war*. New York: Semiotext(e)

Virilio, Paul. 1997b. *Open sky*. London: Verso.

Virilio, Paul. 1997c. Cybernetics and society, *Any*, 1–13.

Virilio, Paul. 1998. Cybermonde: The politics of degradation. *Alphabet City*, 6, 192–203.

Virilio, Paul. 1999. *Politics of the very worst*. New York: Semiotext(e)

Virilio, Paul. 2000. *The information bomb*. New York: Verso.

Virilio, Paul. 2001. My Kingdom for a Horse: The Revolutions of Speed. *Queen's Quarterly*, 108(3):329–338.

Virilio, Paul. 2002a. *Desert screen: War at the speed of light*. New York: Continuum.

Virilio, Paul. 2002b. *Crepuscular dawn*. New York: Semiotext(e).

Williams, Raymond. 1975. *Television: Technology and cultural form*. New York: Schocken.

Wilmott, Glen. 1996. *McLuhan, or modernism in reverse*. Toronto: University of Toronto Press.

Wilson, Louise. 1994, December 1. Cyberwar, god and television: Interview with Paul Virilio. *CTHEORY.NET*, http://www.ctheory.net/text_file.asp?pick=62

Wise, Greg. 1997. *Exploring technology and social space*. Thousand Oaks, CA: Sage.

Zurbrugg, Nicholas. 1999. Getting "The Real Facts": Contemporary Cultural Theory and Avant-Garde Technocultural Practices. *Angelaki: Journal of Theoretical Humanities*, 4(2):183–191.

Patrick Brantlinger is professor emeritus of English at Indiana University in Bloomington. He has written seven books, including *The Spirit of Reform: British Literature and Politics, 1830–1900* (1977); *Bread and Circuses: Theories of Mass Culture as Social Decay* (1983); *Rule of Darkness: British Literature and Imperialism, 1830–1914* (1988); *Crusoe's Footprints: Cultural Studies in Britain and America* (1990); *Fictions of State: Culture and Credit in Britain, 1694–1994* (1996); *The Reading Lesson: The Threat of Mass Literacy in Nineteenth-Century British Fiction* (1998); and *Who Killed Shakespeare? What's Happened to English since the Radical Sixties* (2001). He is also the editor of several volumes, including the forthcoming, co-edited *Blackwell Companion to the Victorian Novel*.

Richard Cavell is professor of English and director of the International Canadian Studies Center at the University of British Columbia. He is the author of *McLuhan in Space: A Cultural Geography* (2002; 2003; UTP "Classic" 2005; digital publication 2007) and creator of the website *spectersofmcluhan.net*. He has edited or co-edited three other books and has published more than 70 chapters, articles and reviews.

Donna Flayhan is associate professor of communication and media at the State University of New York at New Paltz. She also is director of the Lower Manhattan Public Health Project. Flayhan has published media ecological articles in *Explorations in Media Ecology* and *The Atlantic Journal of Communication* and has published public health work in *Annals of Behvioral Medicine* and *Archives of Environmental Health.*

Gary Genosko is Canada Research Chair in Technoculture and director of the Technoculture Lab at Lakehead University in Ontario. He has recently published his newest book, *Félix Guattari: A Critical Introduction.* His 15 books include *Marshall McLuhan: Critical Evaluation in Cultural Theory,* 3 vols. (Routledge, 2005) *Felix Guattari: An Aberrant Introduction* (Continuum, 2002); *The Uncollected Baudrillard* (Sage, 2001); *Deleuze and Guattari: Critical Assessments,* 3 vols. (Routledge, 2001); *McLuhan and Baudrillard: The Masters of Implosion* (Routledge, 1999); *Undisciplined Theory* (Sage, 1998); *The Guattari Reader* (Blackwell, 1996); and *Baudrillard and Signs: Signification Ablaze* (Routledge, 1994). He is the general editor of the *Semiotic Review of Books.*

Paul Grosswiler is chair and associate professor of communication and journalism at the University of Maine, where he teaches history of mass communication, international mass communication, media ethics, and media ecology. He is the author of *The Method is the Message: Rethinking McLuhan Through Critical Theory* (1998), as well as 30 articles, chapters, and essays in publications including the *Canadian Journal of Communication, Explorations in Media Ecology, Harvard International Journal of Press/Politics, Journal of Communication Inquiry, Journal of International Communication,* and the *Journal of Human Subjectivity.* He has conducted media research in Tanzania and China, where he was a Fulbright scholar at Wuhan University in 2000, and he is currently on the Fulbright Senior Specialist roster.

Bob Hanke teaches media studies at York University and OCAD University in Toronto. His most recent work has been published in the *International Journal of Communication and Cultural Politics.* He is co-editing a special issue of the *Canadian Journal of Media Studies* on Media, Knowledge and the Network University and working on a book titled The Network University in Formation. He also serves on the advisory board of *TOPIA: Canadian Journal of Cultural Studies.*

Douglas Kellner is George Kneller Chair in the Philosophy of Education at UCLA and is author of many books on social theory, politics, history, and culture, including *Camera Politica: The Politics and Ideology of Contemporary Hollywood Film,* co-authored with Michael Ryan; *Critical Theory, Marxism, and Modernity; Jean Baudrillard: From Marxism to Postmodernism and Beyond;* works in cultural studies such as *Media Culture and Media Spectacle;* a trilogy of books on postmodern theory with Steve Best; and a trilogy of books on the media and the

Bush administration, encompassing *Grand Theft 2000, From 9/11 to Terror War,* and *Media Spectacle and the Crisis of Democracy.* Author of *Herbert Marcuse and the Crisis of Marxism,* Kellner is editing collected papers of Herbert Marcuse, four volumes of which have appeared with Routledge. Kellner's *Guys and Guns Amok: Domestic Terrorism and School Shootings from the Oklahoma City Bombings to the Virginia Tech Massacre* won the 2008 AESA award as the best book on education. Kellner's latest book *Cinema Wars: Hollywood Film and Politics in the Bush/Cheney Era* has just been published. His website is http://www.gseis.ucla.edu/faculty/kellner/kellner.html

Nick Stevenson is currently a reader in Cultural Sociology at the University of Nottingham. He is currently writing a book called *Education and Cultural Citizenship.* More recently, he has published a book on David Bowie in 2006 for Polity Press. His books include *Culture, Ideology and Socialism* (Avebury, 1995); *Understanding Media Cultures; Social Theory and Mass Communication with Sage* (Sage, 1995, 2002); *Making Sense of Men's Life Style Magazines* (Polity Press, 2001); *The Transformation of the Media; Globalisation, Morality and Ethics* (Longman, 1999); *Culture and Citizenship* (Sage, 2002); and *Cultural Citizenship: Cosmopolitan Questions* (Open University, 2003.)

Lance Strate is professor of communication and media at Fordham University in New York City, and executive director of the Institute of General Semantics. He is the author of *Echoes and Reflections: On Media Ecology as a Field of Study*(Hampton, 2006), and co-editor of several anthologies, including *The Legacy of McLuhan,* with Edward Wachtel (Hampton, 2005). He is a founder and past president of the Media Ecology Association, founder and former editor of the journal *Explorations in Media Ecology,* and has served as the super-visory editor of the Media Ecology book series for Hampton Press, in addition to being one of the partners in NeoPoiesis Press.

Glenn Willmott is professor of English at Queen's University in Canada. He has published widely on modernity, modernism, and Canadian, American, British and Irish writers. Recent publications include, "The Birth of Tragedy in Digital Aesthetics" in Fluid Screens, Expanded Cinema, ed. Marchessault and Lord (2007), and two books, *Modernist Goods: Primitivism, the Market, and the Gift* (2006) and the just-completed *Living Like an Animal: Literature, Comics, and the Limits to Growth.* His other books include *Unreal Country: Modernity in the Canadian Novel in English* (2002); *McLuhan, or Modernism in Reverse* (1996); and a scholarly edition of Bertram Brooker's 1936 *Think of the Earth* (2000). He has published articles in *New Literary History, University of Toronto Quarterly, Essays on Canadian Writing,* and *Canadian Poetry.*

Index

C

Carey, James W., xii, xvi, 28, 70, 84–87, 100–101, 105, 214.

Certeau, Michel de, 4, 13, 14, 16.

Communication technology, 23, 69, 84–86, 100, 104–106, 100, 172, 184, 187, 205, 213, 216, 219.

Communication theory, xiii, xvi, xvii, xv, 3, 87, 119.
    Biology of perception, 72.
    Cognitive science, 72.
    Engineering communication theory, 6.
    Ethnographic research, 72.
    Information theory, 12, 70, 150.
    Mass communication theory, 25.
    Mathematical model, 3–5, 14–15, 16, 72.
    Media and communication theory, 72.
    Reader response theory, 72.
    Ritual view of, xvi, 74, 207.
    Shannon and Weaver model, 3, 4, 7, 8, 11, 70, 150.
    Transformative, xvi, 9, 12, 18, 21, 25, 26, 28, 30, 32, 54, 74, 85, 114, 119, 122, 124, 140, 150, 153, 155, 163, 171, 184, 191, 193, 195, 208, 212.
    Transmission communication theory, xvi, 4, 5, 11, 15, 207, 222.
    Uses and gratifications, 72.

Computer, xii, xviii, 25, 37, 40, 69–70, 72, 76, 78, 111, 157, 164–165, 167–168, 171–176, 180, 181, 183–184, 188–189, 193, 195, 203, 205, 209, 211, 213–214, 216–218, 221.

Consumer society, 19, 186, 193.

Counter-environments, 13, 192.
    See also anti-environments.

Crash theory, xviii, 164–165, 167–172, 175–177.

Critical theory, xii, xv, xvi, xvii, xv, 39, 73–74, 83, 85–89, 106, 137–138, 166, 183, 185, 200.

Cultural studies, xiii, xiv, xv, xvi, 3–4, 11–12, 15–16, 18, 34, 35, 93, 97, 109, 146, 166.
    See also British cultural studies.

Cultural technologies, xiii, 26, 28, 57.

Cultural theory, xi, xv, xvi, xvii, 25–26, 37, 39, 141, 164, 183.

Cybernetics, xvi, 3, 4, 63, 70, 156, 165, 167, 169, 172, 188, 189, 206, 216, 217.

Cyberspace, 145, 181, 183, 217–221.

D

Deleuze, Gilles, 164, 170, 206.

Derrida, Jacques, xviii, 39, 49, 135–138, 140, 143, 145–146–158, 164.
    Teletechnology, xviii, 135–136, 151, 155–158.
    Materiality, 137–138, 142, 144–148, 151.
    Spectral, 135, 145, 151–154 158.
    Writing, 136, 147–151, 153–158.

Dialectics, 69, 73–74, 76, 85, 86, 91, 93, 95, 96, 97, 99, 127, 190, 196.
    And class, 93–94, 97.
    Dialectical materialism, xvii, 83–86, 95, 97, 100, 106.
    Dialectical method, xvi, 83, 84, 85, 86, 95, 99, 165, 196.
    Dialectical theory, xviii, 109, 196.
    Global village as, 77.
    Hegelian, 99, 154.
    In Adorno, Theodor, and Horkheimer, Max, 88.
    In Baudrillard, Jean, 190, 196–197.
    In British cultural studies, 87.
    In Ellul, Jacques,109, 126–128.
    In Luxemburg, Rosa, 96.
    In Marx, Karl, 86, 165.
    In McLuhan, Marshall, 73, 85, 209, 220, 221.
    In media ecology, 73.
    In nature, 95.
    In Virilio, Paul 222.
    Negative dialectics, 84.

Alphabet, 20, 42, 63, 69, 73, 120, 124,
  136, 164, 207.
Gutenberg Bible, 19.
Printing press, 20, 69, 73, 85, 166,
  180–181, 184.
Typography, 20, 70, 73, 77, 119, 122,
  124, 182, 208.

R

Radio, 19, 22, 29, 41, 45, 50, 53, 69, 72, 84,
  114, 117, 125, 155, 184, 198–200.
Reflexivity, 30, 33–34, 60, 105, 140.

S

Saussure, Ferdinand de, 27, 141–142.
Semiotics, 8–9, 11, 12, 15, 18, 70.
  Ethnosemiotics, 8, 11.
Service environment, 6, 7, 113, 212.
Shannon, Claude, 4, 6, 7.
Sontag, Susan, 58.
Space, 20, 26, 32, 122, 138, 193, 199, 219,
  223.
  Acoustic space, 12, 141–142, 145, 147,
    152, 154, 157.
  And cyberspace, 245, 181, 183,
    217–221.
  Annihilation of space and time, xix,
    22–23, 204, 208.
  Bias of space, 22, 99–100, 205.
  Bias of space and time, 73, 213.
  Cartesian space, 218.
  Euclidian space, 63, 141.
  Postmodern world space, 49.
  Premodern space and time, 31.
  Real-space, 217.
  Space and print culture, 19.
  Space and time, xi, 17–18, 20, 22–26,
    28–33, 73, 100, 153, 156, 170–171,
    181–182, 198, 208, 210, 215, 216,
    218, 220.

Space speed, 218.
Space, time and perception, xvi, 17.
Space-time, 141, 216–217, 219.
Time-space distanciation, 31, 32.
Transformational TimeSpace, 124.
Virtual space, 151–152, 154, 217.
Visual and acoustic space, xiii, xix, 142,
  205, 211, 221.
Visual space, 141–142, 152.
Stamps, Judith, xii, xiii, 73–74, 83–85, 166,
  220.
Star Trek, 11, 29.

T

Technical media, xvi, 17, 18, 25, 27–29,
  31–34, 144, 155, 185, 166, 199.
Technological humanism, 110, 130, 147.
Teilhard de Chardin, Pierre, 173.
Telegraph, 5–7, 14–15, 28, 32, 69, 85,
  100–101, 117, 120, 122–123, 168, 185.
Telephone, 7, 14–15, 21, 28–29, 45, 72, 129,
  142, 155, 199.
Teletechnologies, xvii, 135–136, 155–158.
Television, 8–9, 11, 17–18, 21–25, 27–29,
  31, 33–34, 37, 41–42, 45–47, 59, 70, 72,
  101–103, 111, 117, 119–120, 125, 136,
  138–139, 143–144, 155, 158, 167–168,
  170, 180, 183–184, 186–188, 191–193,
  195–200, 205, 209, 216, 222–223.
Theall, Donald, xiii, 3, 73, 164, 168.
Thompson, J.B., xiv, 28, 30, 140.
Thoreau, Henry David, 71.
Time, xvi, 17, 18–20, 22–26, 28–33, 73–74,
  85, 100, 119, 153, 171, 182, 198,
  204–206, 208, 210, 213, 215–223.
Transformation
  And electric light, 18.
  And quest for profits, 111.
  As mental breakdown, 122.
  By telegraph, 32.
  In modern world, 31.
  Of McLuhan into "McLuhan," 46.